A Place of Her Own

A Place of Her Own

The Legacy of Oregon Pioneer
Martha Poindexter Maupin

Janet Fisher

TWODOT®

GUILFORD, CONNECTICUT
HELENA, MONTANA
AN IMPRINT OF GLOBE PEQUOT PRESS

A · T W O D O T® · B O O K

Note: All photos from author's collection were digitized by Anvil Northwest, a graphic design company in Roseburg, Oregon.

Project Editor: Lauren Brancato
Layout: Melissa Evarts
Map: Melissa Baker © Morris Book Publishing, LLC

Library of Congress Cataloging-in-Publication data is available on file.

ISBN 978-0-7627-9601-4

Printed in the United States of America

10 9 8 7 6 5 4 3 2 1

To my earliest family on Martha's farm,

Martha, Mary, and Cap

To my parents who kept it,

Gene and Marian

To my family who came with me to keep it longer,

Carisa, Robin, Alex, Christiane, and Calliope

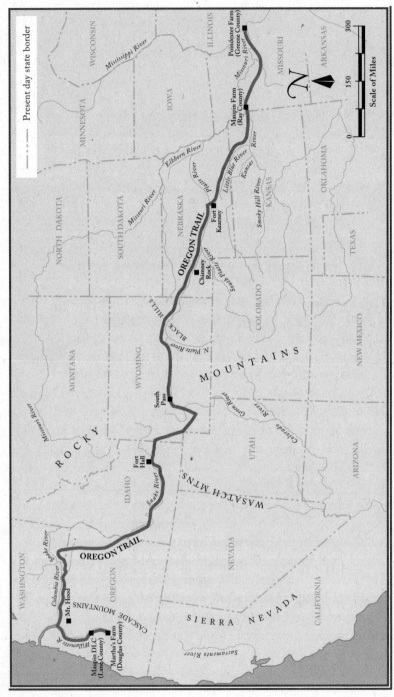

Martha's journey from Green County, Illinois, to Western Missouri, across the Oregon Trail to Lane County, Oregon, and to her own farm in Douglas County, Oregon.

CONTENTS

In the world's broad field of battle
She has nobly done her part. she
Was always kind and loving, for she
Had a noble heart. a tender loving
Mother, a true and faithful wife, she
Is gone, but not forgotten: twas
A grand and noble life.

—EPITAPH, MARTHA ANN MAUPIN

ACKNOWLEDGMENTS

So many people helped make this book happen, whether helping me dig out information or advising on language or opening the right doors for me. I want each of you to know how much I appreciate everything you did. My newfound cousin Linda Maupin Noel generously shared the fruits of her genealogical searches into the Maupin family, while another newfound cousin Gloria Atwater shared her discoveries on the Poindexter side. These two helped provide a framework for Martha's life story, leading me into shadows of a past I never knew. Thank you so much, both of you.

In my continued search I found helpful people everywhere I went. A special thanks to Jenne Sue Layman, Carol Proffitt, and Lisa Smalley from the Ray County Missouri Historical and Genealogical Society in Richmond, Missouri, for providing material and camaraderie, Jenne even going to the old Maupin place with me. And special thanks to Glen Hill Jr., who provided information about Carroll County, Missouri, and drove me around that county where Martha first lived after trekking to Missouri with a couple of her brothers.

Many thanks to my first readers, who gave their time and talents to help turn a rough draft into a more polished work: Leslie Budewitz from one of my former Montana critique groups; my daughter Carisa Cegavske, who is a reporter for the local Roseburg newspaper, *The News-Review*; and longtime friend Judy Emmett, who'd read for me when I last lived in Douglas County, Oregon.

The right doors began to open after I met New York agent Rita Rosenkranz at the 2012 Pacific Northwest Writers Conference in Seattle and she agreed to represent me. With keen focus she helped me ready the work (which meant cutting a lot of words) and got the manuscript into the hands of Erin Turner, editor at Globe Pequot Press. Thank you so much, Rita, for making this happen, and thank you, Erin, for your clear editorial direction that made it work.

On the long road to publication I had many other helpers. I must thank members of my writing group from my days in Montana when I really began to hone my writing skills, especially my two critique groups there. Besides Leslie, already mentioned, I want to thank Debbie Burke, Sami Rorvik, Deborah Epperson, and Rena Desmond from one critique group and from the other, Olivia Diamond, Rod Rogers, David Myerowitz, and Todd Cardin. Great writers. Wonderful friends. And they never hesitated to tell me what was wrong with my stuff—in a nice way.

Thanks to others who encouraged me along my journey, writers Stephanie Bartlett and Darlene Roth, readers Judy Ammerman and Patricia Kellam.

And I'd like to mention another longtime friend and reader who didn't live to see this happen, though she never lost faith, and I wonder if she isn't smiling down on me now, Lorraine Walker. Thank you, Lorraine.

Others who helped specifically with Martha's book include James Phillips, Circuit Court Clerk of Clay County, Kentucky, where Garrett Maupin was born; Charles House from the Clay County Genealogical and Historical Society in Kentucky; Carole Mann, Deputy County Clerk in Greene County, Illinois, Martha's girlhood home; Peggy Camden at Greene County Historical and Genealogical Society in Illinois; Karl Moore at Illinois State Archives; Linda Kmiecik, genealogical researcher in Macoupin County, Illinois, next door to Greene, who helped search for Martha's family there.

Thanks also to Sandi Carter, a distant cousin and Maupin researcher I met online; George Engelmann, professor of geology and biology at the University of Nebraska at Omaha for information on the Platte River basin; historian John Hinz of Waverly, Missouri, for information on Missouri River ferry crossings. I wish I could thank Maupin researcher William Albertson again for the wealth of information he gave me before he died.

I also wish I could thank my late cousin Florence Maupin McNabb, one of Martha's granddaughters, for her research and writing that provided so many colorful details.

Closer to home, my thanks go to Karen Bratton, research librarian at my local Douglas County Museum of History and Natural History; Linda VanOrden at the Oregon Genealogical Society in Eugene; Cheryl Roffe at the Lane County Historical Museum; Kay Livermore from the

Douglas County Genealogical Society; Sharon Leighty, program coordinator for the Oregon Century Farm and Ranch program.

These, and many others in courthouses and archive research departments and genealogical and historical societies across the country, all helped pull out hidden threads to create the tapestry representing Martha's life.

I also want to thank everyone at the Pacific Northwest Writers Conference in Seattle who helped create such a positive environment and all the attendees who encouraged me and helped me improve my pitch so I could better express the excitement I felt about Martha's story.

On the production side, thanks to videographer Geno Edwards at Anvil Northwest for his excellent work digitizing the old photos, especially the challenge of the damaged print of the old house. And thanks to project editor Lauren Brancato for making the birthing of this book such a delightful experience.

Of course thanks to all my immediate family who shared this journey with me. Thanks to my son-in-law Robin Loznak for his amazing photography, to my daughter Christiane for saying, "Why don't you write about Martha?" Carisa I mentioned before. And thanks to the grandchildren, Alex and Calliope, for their enthusiasm and sometimes advice. Even when Calliope was only five she told me I could not refer to the tree outside my window as *the oak* because there were two trees bound together. She accepted *the double oak,* and I revised accordingly.

Thank you, thank you, thank you, all, whether named or not. I do appreciate you very much.

POINDEXTER-MAUPIN FAMILY TREES

JANET'S DIRECT LINE WITH SIBLINGS OF MARTHA, GARRETT, AND MARY

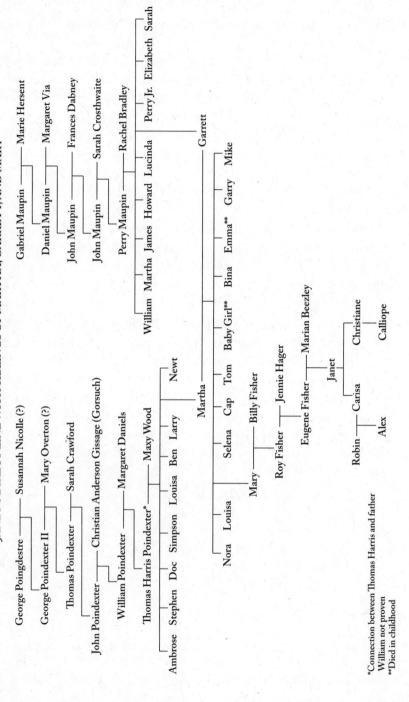

*Connection between Thomas Harris and father
William not proven
**Died in childhood

PROLOGUE
UNDER THE OAK, MAY 2010

A gentle breeze whispered through the new leaves of the scattered oaks crowning the ridge by my house. Echoes stirred in me. I moved into the dappled shade of a double oak overlooking the field below, where lush spring grass shimmered across the land like waves of green silk. The old tree leaned toward the long downward slope as if keeping watch over the stepped pasture to the river valley at the bottom. Its second trunk, a late offshoot, smaller, younger, stood in its shadow.

I ran a hand over the rough bark and looked into the intertwined branches. A subtle sweetness of emerging growth scented the air. Again a whisper rustled the leaves, and I wondered what the oak was trying to say to me. It felt like a sentient presence.

Or was it her presence I felt? Martha. My great-great-grandmother.

The breeze riffled the hair on my neck and sent a chill down my back despite the warmth of the late afternoon. Did she stand here on this same spot on the hill, marveling that this land was hers? Not the land of her husband. Not the land of a landlord. Hers. As now it was mine. Her husband died less than two years before she came here. My marriage ended twenty years ago, and my father had been gone three years. I bent forward to glance at the far side of the old tree and imagined her there, sharing this wonder across time.

A torrent of feelings must have flooded Martha when her husband died, leaving her alone with their many children on the Oregon frontier. Lone mothers had few options in her day, but after harrowing experiences of crossing the plains, facing death, bitter regret, even shame, she bought this place herself to make a home for her family. This was the Martha A. Maupin Century Farm, one of the few Century Farms in Oregon named for a woman. Now, more than 140 years later, another woman in the family owned it.

How did Martha dare make such a choice? It was more daunting for me than I had anticipated. When she took over operation of the farm in 1868, women had so few rights they couldn't even vote. The farm had barely been carved out of the wilderness by the previous short-term owners. By the time I acquired it, the place had resources, an antiquated commercial prune dryer, a prune orchard, timber. But the price had dropped out of the timber market. Prune crops were scanty and the old dryer ran on oil with its soaring costs.

I took a sudden ragged breath and gazed at the long view. From where I stood I could see across the river to a tree-covered range of mountains on the western horizon, and in the middle distance a long sweeping plain. The river made a loop, extending along the far side of that plain before curving in a wide crescent to cut below it on this side. Pioneers called it Pleasant Plain. My grandfather once owned part of it, and my father grew up there. My property ran as far as the river below and continued up the hill behind me in a broad oak-dotted savannah surrounded by swaths of fir forest.

What would Martha have seen from here? The plain certainly. Perhaps a distant cabin or two. Was this double oak alive then? If not this one, perhaps the one that dropped the acorn from which this grew?

Whether this part of the land was always open savannah with these widespread oaks, I didn't know. But it was likely similar in Martha's day. Some of the oaks could have been as much as two hundred years old, each open and free of form with no sign of ever being crowded in a forest.

Did she walk this place, as I loved to do, just to know every ridge and canyon, every open field and enclosing woods? Family legend described her as a walker. She walked all the way from Missouri to Oregon, but less perhaps for the love of it than because she couldn't bear the jolt of the wagon in her condition. Still, she must have come up here, gazed at this view, or whatever view lay before her then.

I watched as the afternoon sun slipped low in the sky, turning the distant hills a deep misty blue. The long expanse of Pleasant Plain gleamed vivid green, the fields broken by clumps of glistening oaks and other hardwoods, a few bold lines of tall firs almost blue-black against the muted blues of the farther hills. I could see the bend of the river off to my right, and the wide teal band coursing between tree-rimmed banks below. The sun backlit the new leaves of gnarled oaks nearby, a tracery of their dark branches outlined within the delicate young foliage.

The beauty evoked a tug of warmth, like the face of a loving friend. I'd explored nearly every part of the farm's 641 acres, from rushing creeks and waterfalls, into the hush of towering trees standing like nature's own cathedral, to the high ridge where you could see the snaking river on both sides and look into the top of a scraggy fir to exchange glances with a bald eagle. I'd grown up on this rich land bordering the Umpqua River in southern Oregon, and I felt linked to it, rooted as the old oak.

Of the three generations between Martha and me, two had owned it. Her son Cap held ownership for a long time, and my dad bought it from Cap, his great-uncle. Although my line ran through Cap's sister Mary, my dad's purchase kept the farm in the family. Now that he had died after tending this place for many years, my kids and I were determined to continue keeping it. They had moved to the farm with me to help out.

Martha had a large brood of children—nine, ranging in age from two to twenty-one when she settled here, the final one born in 1865. Her husband, my great-great-grandfather Garrett, died the year after that child's birth. Would the babies have continued had he lived? Did she breathe a sigh of relief? And feel guilty about it? I wondered, given hints of trouble along the way.

I glanced again at the far side of the tree's double trunks, wishing she could answer my growing questions. As a woman I was drawn to Martha's story, especially now that I owned her farm, but I would need to search for answers through the remnants of recorded memories, and the echoes, left behind. I hoped to do more than write a family narrative. I wanted to know her.

"What brought you here, Martha?" I whispered. "How did it all begin?"

Murmurs stirred in the leaves overhead, and I tilted my head to listen.

Chapter 1

The Missouri Edge

Greene County, Illinois, Early Spring 1844

Sweet, crisp air wafted into the little cabin through the wide-open door and windows. Birds twittered. A jay screeched. Sap was rising in every branch in the surrounding woods. Martha held the broom upright with both hands and took a twirl in the middle of the floor.

Two long steps brought her to the wall, where she reached up and swept the bristles across the dingy logs, wanting to make the place gleam with welcome. Her brother Doc was coming home, and her brother Stephen and his family were visiting from Macoupin County. How she'd missed them, especially Doc.

She gazed about the small log structure with its sideboard for cooking and its fireplace, all cleaned and ready for a cozy fire. She loved this cabin. Nestled in the woods behind her parents' big log house, it had been a place of joy for her from her earliest memory. Pa built it for Grandpa and Grandma Wood, Ma's folks, soon after the family settled this farm on the western Illinois frontier, back in 1830 when Martha was only a year old.

She'd spent many happy hours here with her beloved grandparents. Grandpa always had time to laugh and play with her, and to show her the wonders surrounding them—plants and how they grew, tiny insects and frogs, the delight of a tugging magnet, the mystery of a sundial he built out in the clearing. He taught her the pleasure of reading and writing, and clever tricks with numbers. She remembered him so well, though she was only six when he died.

Grandma died soon after, but Ma would not let Pa turn this cabin into a corn crib or work shack. She kept it for visitors, like Stephen and his family, and maybe for the memory of her parents. Martha and her younger brothers used to play here and make believe all sorts of exciting stories. Smiling, she lifted the broom again to whisk out a dusty corner, feeling feather light as she thought of those free and happy days.

A familiar voice drifted across the wooded yard. "Where's my little sister?"

"Doc!" She dropped the broom and ran out the door. He strode toward her, a wide smile on his bearded face, and she bounded to him, giving him a fierce hug. "You're here."

He lowered his voice in mock seriousness. "Yep, the Doc is back."

She giggled at his usual greeting. He wasn't a doctor. Ma and Pa only named him Doctor Harvey after some medical doctor they admired. Now her brother liked calling himself Doc. Martha leaned back to study his face. "When did you grow a beard?"

His grin lifted the trimmed brown mustache as he ran a finger over the close-cropped hair on his jaw. "Does it make me look older?"

"Is that what you want?"

He tugged gently at one of her dark-brown pigtails. "Why not? And you. Did you turn fifteen while I was gone?"

She put on a smug face. "I did."

Ma called from the other house. "Martha Ann Poindexter! You done with that sweeping? I need your help in here."

Martha gave Doc a quick smile and ran for the house, pigtails flying. "Coming, Ma!"

Stephen stood in the doorway. She hugged him, and Jane and little Peter.

"Martha!"

"Yes, Ma."

Bustling from table to sideboard, Ma wiped her hands on her outer apron, voice tense with excitement. "Put bread and milk on the table and set out plates and cups. We can't all fit around the table but fit what you can, and the rest of us will find places as we're able."

Martha picked up a loaf of Ma's warm bread, relishing the delicious aroma, and set it on the cutting board to slice. Family members poured into the house, talking and laughing. Ambrose, Martha's oldest brother, gave Martha a wave and smile across the room, as his wife Polly ushered in their two boys. It had been a long time since the whole family was together.

"Where's Louisa?" Ma asked. "Looks like everybody's here but Louisa."

Martha shook her head, breathless with all the rush. She'd be glad for Louisa's help.

"Missouri?" Pa's voice, rising above the murmur in the room.

Martha glanced his way. Doc and some of the other boys had gathered near Pa, their hands animated as they spoke. Pa leaned forward, intent on the conversation. The room vibrated with excitement. What was going on?

They all went silent and turned as one to face the door. Martha's sister, Louisa, stood in the doorway in a fine blue-flowered dress, ruffled apron over full skirts, dark hair topped by a trim bonnet of the same fabric as her dress, the bonnet's solid blue bow looped like an elegant flower—as only Louisa could tie a bow. Her face glowed. "Hello, everyone. Sorry we're late."

Her tall, handsome husband stepped up behind her carrying little Perry. John Bronough looked every bit the gentleman with his tailored suit. Even a vest. He took off his tall hat, hung it on a peg on the log wall, and gave a passing smile to everyone, proceeding to greet each one.

After quick hugs for the long-absent relatives, Louisa grabbed an old apron and went right to work helping Ma. She always seemed to know what to do without Ma having to tell her. Martha would never forget how her own life changed when her sister left. There were only two girls, and since Louisa was older than Martha by seven years, Louisa was usually the one Ma called on to help her. Oh, Martha had her chores, but being so much younger, she always had time to run and play with her brothers. Then Louisa married her handsome John Bronough, and Martha's freedom ended.

She heaved a sigh, remembering. Eight years old and a drudge already.

Something in the men's conversation caught her attention, something about new land, and she slipped closer to hear what they were talking about. Doc had become the center. He turned to John, as if to catch him up on the discussion. "Well, according to our cousin William, there's fine land to be had in Missouri."

John nodded. "So when are you thinking of leaving?"

Martha snapped her head around to give Doc a straight look. Leaving? Doc? Missouri? He'd just gotten home from Stephen's place in Macoupin County. But that was right next door to Greene County, here in Illinois. Now he was going to Missouri? She bit her lower lip. Well, Missouri wasn't so far. Greene County was near the western border of Illinois, her home maybe a day's ride from the Mississippi River and the state of Missouri just the other side of the Mississippi.

Deep in thought she missed Doc's answer, but John was quizzing him further. "So where is Carroll County?"

"In western Missouri," Doc said. "Not the farthest edge, but close."

Martha's mouth dropped open. Close to the edge? The western edge? She'd never see Doc again.

Doc went on. "It's fine rolling prairie and rich bottomland along the Missouri River, land virtually for the taking." He swung around to face Ambrose. "Are you sure you don't want to go with us?"

Ambrose shook his head. "Sounds mighty interesting, but I don't think I could be ready this spring. You and Simpson look into it and let me know what you think."

Martha turned to Simpson. He stood behind Doc, thumbs in the slash pockets of his linsey-woolsey pants, shoulders high so he seemed somehow taller. Simpson was going too?

Looking from brother to brother, she studied them as she always saw them—in layers. First, the older ones, Ambrose and Stephen, who seemed more like uncles than brothers. They'd been gone from the house, married, for years. Next came Doc and Simpson, now in their early twenties. Then the three younger boys, all in their teens, Ben and Larry, who were older than Martha, and little brother Newt.

"How will you go?" Pa asked. He bent toward Doc, eyes gleaming. "Will you take a wagon? Or just packhorses?"

John leaned back in his chair. "You can take a steamboat all the way there, can't you? That way you could check it out, see if you like it, buy supplies there. I'm sure they have everything we do, with all the transportation on the Missouri River."

Pa gave a soft grunt. "Pretty expensive."

Martha glanced at John. Maybe not for him. But the rest of the family didn't have John Bronough's resources. A good man, John. He just didn't always understand folks who had less.

Doc leaned on the table. "Well, I think we'll need a wagon of some kind."

"You could fix up that old cart," Pa said.

Doc grinned. "Are you sure you don't want to go, Pa?"

Pa let out a huff. "I'm too old to move again."

"No, you're not. I'm surprised you stayed in this spot as long as you did. How many times did you move in the early years? And you'd be with us boys. Isn't that right, Simpson?"

Pa lifted one side of his mouth in a lopsided grin. "But I'm too *young* to be tagging along after my boys."

A chorus of laughter rose from the table. Ben put a hand on Doc's arm. "I'd like to go. Can I go with you?"

Pa reached for Ben and yanked at his shirt. "I'll need you here, Ben. With my big boys gone, I'll need your help. Besides, you aren't even twenty yet."

"Almost. I'm nineteen."

Pa shook his head, and Ben's shoulders sagged. Martha knew how Ben felt. Now he'd be Pa's main help and be confined.

A sudden overwhelming desire engulfed Martha. She couldn't bear the idea of losing Doc. But underlying that intolerable prospect arose an even more powerful feeling, a compelling need to escape the confinement she'd felt since Louisa left and Martha lost her freedom. She blurted out her wish without considering the sheer audacity. "Can I go? Please?"

The entire gathering quieted as faces turned to stare at her. She tried to think, grasping for reasons, any reason that could make this preposterous desire a reality. Everything in the room stopped, as if frozen like a pond in winter.

Pa thawed first, his single word as brittle as a dropping icicle on that same winter day. "No."

Martha ducked the icicle and barreled ahead. "I can cook for them. You know neither Doc or Simpson can cook to save themselves. They could faint dead away from hunger out there all alone."

Ma spoke up. "Missouri is no place for a girl, especially the west. It's a wild country."

Martha faced her mother, hands spread wide. "Didn't you travel to the frontier in Kentucky and Illinois?"

Ma's tone didn't yield. "With my parents, and then with your father."

"But Doc and Simpson will look out for me, won't you?" Martha looked at Doc first, then Simpson. The boys glanced at each other, brows raised.

Pa had his jaw set, but a tenderness touched his voice. "Give yourself some time. Find a nice young man here in Greene County, and then if he wants to take you west you can go. You're only fifteen."

Doc cleared his throat a few times, as if searching for words. "A lot of people are going that way, people on their way to Oregon even. Last year, I understand almost nine hundred people went west over the Oregon Trail. Families. Children. Clear to Oregon."

Martha couldn't contemplate Oregon. But was Doc leaning her way? She tried for a gentle nudge further. "But Missouri isn't so far. Is it?"

Ben barged in. "How can Ma manage without Martha?"

Doc laughed. "Well, Louisa lives close, and with most of us boys out from under foot, Ma will wonder what to do with her time."

Ma huffed at that.

Simpson stood straighter. "Missouri isn't far. Martha's right. And she *can* cook." He gave her a quick smile that set her head spinning, and directed his words to Ma. "Doc and I—we'll both come home to visit pretty often. I'll come home next year after the first harvest and can bring her back with me. Maybe Doc will find a woman by then who can put up with him." A chuckle circled the table, and Simpson went on. "Doc can come the year after. You'll see. It's not far at all for a visit now and then."

Doc grinned and looked at Pa. "Or maybe you'll decide to follow."

Pa shook his head. "If I was a younger man . . ."

May 1844. Martha stood gripping the lead rope of their horse Red as they all awaited the ferry at the Illinois River. Heart racing, she motioned across the river toward a ridge cloaked in spring's bright greens. "Look at the mountains." She'd never seen such mountains.

Doc shrugged, one hand on the massive neck of their one ox, Kip. "Those aren't mountains. Just hills."

Martha lifted her brows. "They look like mountains to me. I never saw hills so high." Whatever folks called them, she thought they were fine to see.

The flat open ferry slipped this way across the broad stretch of water and thumped against the near shore. The three Poindexters led their animals onto the wooden planks, and Doc pulled out cash for their passage. They had two horses, each saddled with a pack behind the saddle, one ox pulling their refurbished cart covered with a pale canvas top, and a milk cow tied on behind the cart. The ferryman tallied people, animals, and property, calculated the fare, and Doc paid it.

Martha held tight to the horse as the ferry rocked forward. Rails on the sides offered protection, but the ends were wide open. She'd never been on a ferry before. Any streams she'd crossed—at least since she was old enough to remember—were small enough to ford. The Illinois River was huge. The horse snorted and stepped back and forth, as unaccustomed to this as Martha. She tried to soothe him. "Easy, Red."

"Wait till you see the Mississippi," Simpson said. "I hear it's even bigger."

Martha could scarcely contain her joy at this fantastic adventure. She felt buoyant as a log floating on that water. They'd stayed at a farmhouse last night with some pleasant people, the first night out, and got back on the road early this morning. The sun shone on them now as if to shine favor on their journey.

When the ferry bumped to a stop, the travelers led their animals onto solid ground, maintaining a firm grasp on the horses to keep them from plunging forward. A narrow road led into the ridge ahead, but as they trudged up the slope, it soon became clear the ridge was little more than a rounded height. The road cut through the lowest part, a broad gap that allowed easy passage.

After a gradual decline they came out on flat ground, as level as any table Martha had ever seen. Doc made a sweeping gesture with one hand. "This would be the Mississippi Bottoms."

Martha pointed to another ridge in the distance. "Look there."

Doc smiled at her. "I believe that's Missouri."

"Really? It doesn't look far."

"Farther than you think, but we should get there before dark."

As if the hills of Missouri tugged at her, Martha walked a little faster, smiling at one brother, then the other. She felt so thankful to them for bringing her along, allowing a young woman like her to enjoy such rare freedom.

The day grew long, and her legs began to feel heavy. Not being very tall, she had to take more steps than the boys. The flat table of land never seemed to change. The ridge never got any closer. The sun moved across the sky and they could not keep up with it.

When she'd begun to wonder if she and her brothers were progressing at all, she noticed the line of trees ahead growing larger. She imagined a race with the sun and stepped faster. Her horse was ready, but the ox had one speed. Slow. She soon outpaced the others and had to wait.

Fidgeting with Red's lead rope until the fibers dug into her palm, she took a long breath. "Hurry, Kip," she whispered. She wanted to see those wild lands of western Missouri. They were becoming part of her dreams—the day kind, and the night.

Simpson's voice carried on the breeze that played across the flat. "Look at the land right here. It's rich ground, Doc. Why are we going so far west?"

"Because somebody owns every last piece of this, and the Missouri River has good bottomland like it." Doc pinched his brow. "I don't think I want a place in the bottoms, though. You know what makes this land so rich?"

"What?"

"Floods."

Martha frowned. *Floods?*

Doc bent toward his brother, using his hands to illustrate. "How'd you like to have your crops in the ground and a nice cabin built and the river just rolls through and washes it all away?"

Martha scanned the broad landscape and tried to envision a river so big it filled the entire flat. She was good at seeing things in her mind, but she couldn't quite picture that much water.

"When do these floods happen?" Simpson asked.

Doc jutted his lower lip out and looked overhead. He sounded like an old farmer making lazy talk about the weather, but his tone had an edge to it. "Oh, about this time of year."

Martha slowly raised her eyes. The sky was as clear as Mama's blue china pitcher, but she studied it anyway. The boys caught up with her, and she turned to march on, though she still gave the sky an occasional glance.

Reaching the trees at last, they followed well-worn tracks into the woods. Their footsteps softened, muffled by the enclosing greenery. Birds flitted in the branches. The scent of rank weeds mingled with the sweetness of new growth. They heard the rushing water before they saw it. Walking next to Simpson, Martha passed a curtain of trees and the mighty river came into view. She opened her mouth to speak but said nothing, just stood there gaping while currents stirred up and down her like the roiling river.

Doc stepped up beside her and put a hand on her shoulder. "Now, that's a river."

A couple of big boats skimmed across the water in the distance. On the near shore a large covered wagon waited at the ferry landing. The Poindexters started to move on again, when a man from the wagon ambled back toward them. He took off his hat and tilted his head forward. "Howdy."

Doc answered for the family, putting on his deep voice. "Hello. Where you headed?"

"Oregon."

Martha let out a sigh. *Oregon.* That name again of unimaginable wonder.

The man nodded. "Yep. I figure to get me some free land out there. Where you folks headed?"

"Missouri," Doc said. "*Western* Missouri."

The other man clamped his lips tight and nodded again.

A hallo sounded on the water, and Martha saw that one of those boats was a ferry, coming quickly this way. It looked more like a ship than the crude plank ferry back on the Illinois River. Paddle wheels churned on the sides, while black smoke poured out of a tall smokestack above a wide cabin, a deep well below for passengers, hemmed in by white slatted rails.

By the time the Oregon-bound folks got their large wagon with four oxen, three horses, ten cows, and other miscellaneous animals on board, the ferry barely had room for the small Poindexter party. But with careful nudging, the ferryman got them on.

The boat shuddered and plowed forward against the strong current. Martha edged her way to the side and grasped the sturdy top rail so she could see the broad expanse of brown water surging beneath. Her stomach churned like the powerful water, but a slow grin spread across her face, and she didn't try to hide it.

When they reached the Missouri shore, the people from the covered wagon bid the Poindexters good-bye and took a northerly route toward those towns on the western edge of Missouri that were jumping-off places to the Oregon Trail. The Poindexters headed for Montgomery County, a little to the south. That would be their first stopover with family. William's uncle Richard lived there and would welcome his kin on this trip west.

"Do you actually know any of these relatives?" Martha asked Doc.

"William and his family stopped to visit us when they came through on their way from Kentucky to Missouri. Back in the early thirties, I believe." Doc lifted a brow at her. "You were pretty little. I don't know if you remember."

"No. So how are we related?"

"William's a second cousin, I think, something like that. Pa never was too clear on the family connections."

Martha thought a minute. "Poindexters, anyway."

Doc nodded, smiling.

As the trio hurried down the road, trying to make a little more headway before night fell, Martha noticed something strange about the farms they passed. "Look. All the people working in the fields have dark skin." In Illinois they'd seen many farmers in their fields, but none dark. "Why is that?"

Doc gave her a quick glance. "Negro slaves."

"Slaves?"

"Yeah. Missouri's a slave state. Illinois is a free state—what you're used to."

Martha frowned and stared at a worker with near-black skin. She'd heard about slavery, but had never given it much thought. "Don't the farmers here work?"

Doc shrugged, and a little shiver skimmed across Martha.

The sun was about to dip below the horizon. Doc stopped Kip and looked around. "We'd better find a place to spend the night." Kip rubbed his broad face against Doc's arm as if agreeing.

Simpson pointed off to the right. "There's a farmhouse back in those trees."

The thought of rest made Martha realize how exhausted she was. Her whole body felt weighted down. This had been a much longer day than their first. They found the lane to the large two-story house and made their way between tall trees bordering the narrow track.

"Whoa, Kip," Doc said, and left the ox standing as he marched to the front door to knock.

A dark-skinned woman answered. She asked him to wait a moment and disappeared into the interior. A portly man with pallid complexion and elegant whiskers soon came to the door. His deep voice resounded. "You looking for a place to stay?"

Doc stood taller. "Just for the night. My brother and sister and myself."

"Where you younguns from?"

"Illinois. Greene County."

The man let out a huff and talked over his shoulder to a blonde-haired woman behind him. "Folks from Illinois want to stay the night. Don't know if we have room. Do we?"

Doc kneaded the back of his neck. "Maybe we could just set up camp by the barn, or in a field, or—"

The man's face reddened. "We don't much cotton to Northerners around these parts."

Martha's heart pounded an odd rhythm. Tightness gripped her temples. *Northerners?*

Simpson spoke up. "Let's go, Doc."

"Look," Doc said. "My sister is tired and we need to rest."

Martha began to protest. "I'm not—"

Doc ignored her. "Besides, my pa's from Virginia by way of Kentucky." He waved a hand toward his brother and sister. "Every one of us three was born in Kentucky."

The woman leaned close to the man and spoke with animated gestures, her voice too low for Martha to hear. Finally he nodded, stroking his whiskers. "You can use a room upstairs. And your livestock can go in the barn." He turned and called out. "Jimmy, you take care of these animals, now." A dark man came running, and the man of the house smiled at Martha. "Heddy will take care of you folks."

Martha hesitated, still trying to take in the odd situation, but by the time she managed to utter a soft thank you, the couple had disappeared inside the house.

The young dark woman who'd first answered the door came outside. A soft luster rose on her velvety brown skin. She smiled but dipped her head, her eyes, though bright, not quite meeting Martha's. "You can come on upstairs, miss, and you, sirs."

———

Great sheets of rain drenched the travelers and their animals and all their goods. The window of good spring weather had closed on them. Martha wondered if they would ever be dry again. She watched the sky and the dark threads streaking down from heavy clouds like a frayed hem. How much would it take to fill those giant rivers to overflowing?

The rain had started shortly before they reached Richard's place in Montgomery County. "Never saw the like," he'd said. He and his wife, Mournin, were friendly and insisted the cousins needn't rush off. But the travelers were anxious to get on their way. After several days of rain, a little blue sky showed, luring them into thinking they'd have an opening.

They left Richard's and traveled about half a day when it started again. By the time they got to their next stop with kin, the deluge was back. They had a pleasant stay with William's brother Waddy and his family in Callaway County, but finally decided they'd better go on, rain or no.

Land was uneven here, soft rolling hills. The water ran in rivulets, cutting small gullies, and the cart's wheels kept slipping on the road's slimy surface and sinking into the ruts. Martha led both horses so Simpson could help Doc guide the wagon and pull it out when it got stuck.

The wheels mired to a stop, and Doc stood frowning, hands on his hips. "I wonder if we made a mistake crossing the Missouri at Boonville. This route's shorter, but we have to cross again to get to William's on the north side."

They'd opted for the shortcut, bypassing a long bend of the river to save time and struggle, but they were hearing more talk about high water from folks along the way. Martha kept thinking about what Waddy had said. "William's smack down in the Missouri Bottoms, and with all this rain right on top of the June rise from the snowmelt, I do worry about him."

Martha drew her arms close to her body and clutched the lead ropes against the wet fabric of her skirt. William's land might be flooded already.

Simpson blew out a heavy breath. "Well, if we can't get this cart moving, we won't get back to the river anytime soon."

Together they pushed as Doc gave the ox a sharp command. "Get up, Kip." And the little cart slithered back up onto firmer ground. By keeping it on sod, away from the tracks where water ran like small creeks, they managed to make better time. Still, they were soaked and caked with mud by the time they saw a line of trees that marked the river.

Doc grinned. "Now, isn't that pretty."

Simpson glowered at him. "Pretty wet, I'd say."

"Well, one good thing," Doc said. "I don't see any river water this side of the trees."

Encouraged by the hope of cover on this rainy day, the travelers pushed the ox to hurry down the gentle slope. If they could get a ferry to take them across, they should get to William's before dark.

Near the tree line, a lone rider came toward them. Doc called out. "Hallo! Can you tell us where to get a ferry to cross over to Carroll County?"

The man pointed. "Right through there. But I don't know if he'll take you across. River's mighty high."

"Will the ferryman be down there?"

"Maybe. He's got a shed not far, if he ain't. You'll see it."

Thanking the man, they headed in the direction he'd pointed. Once into the trees they got a full view of the raging river. Martha's stomach tightened into a knot. The brown water churned as it raced downstream. Its roaring raged through her.

A twangy voice penetrated the din. "You wanting to go across?"

She looked up to see a small, wiry man limping down a trail to where she and her brothers stood, no doubt looking a bit forlorn.

Doc stepped toward him, reaching out to shake his hand. "Can you do it? Is it safe?"

The man gazed at the river, angular face scrunched tight. Finally he ran a hand over his thinning hair and gave a curt nod. "She's nigh on bank full. Water's fast, but she ain't flooding. I'll take you."

Martha swallowed hard, wishing he'd said they ought to stay in a nice cozy farmhouse somewhere around here until the river went down. She seemed stuck in place when her brothers started to lead their animals down the slope to the waiting ferry.

The man let out a yell, making Martha jump, but she soon saw a young man racing toward them, barefoot, arms pumping. Yellow hair stood straight up on the top of his head like wheat stubble that looked more chewed than mown, his twiggy limbs sticking out below slashed-off sleeves and pants.

Doc paid the ferryman and gave Martha a quick smile. She drew a deep breath and took a step forward, remembering how she'd begged to come on this trip. Each led an animal as they'd done before, the cow following behind the cart. What a good cow. Gentle. Never balked. But this time she hesitated. Martha patted the cow as she moved her horse ahead and stepped onto the rocking planks of the open flatboat ferry. The cow followed.

Both horses snorted and danced, until Martha had to put all her attention on keeping her horse still. The long, narrow craft had low rails on the sides, less than knee high, not much to hold a person in—or keep the river out. Martha kept Red to the center.

When they were settled in place, the ferryman untied the heavy rope that bound the boat to a large tree, and the river's current took them. Martha wondered if it wouldn't sweep them all the way down to the

Mississippi River and St. Louis. The man picked up a long pole, while at the rear the boy held a heavy oar set into a crude-cut wooden lock, nothing to hold it in place but his scrawny hand. The young man pointed the oar hard askew, as the ferryman strode toward the front on the downriver side and shoved the long pole into the murky water with hefty jabs. The ferry slowly turned to point upriver into the current and moved out onto the water, going slantwise toward the far shore.

For such a small man, the ferryman appeared rather mighty in his fight with the powerful river, using its flow even while the force of it ran against them. Thick mounds of muscle clenched on his slim arms below short sleeves. Water swirled and sloshed around the rough-hewn wooden pole at every thrust, creating small dissolving wakes. Meanwhile, the boy began to ply the rear oar back and forth like a fish whipping its tail, until Martha felt the forward motion.

The fierce rush of water grew louder the farther out they went. What had been eddies and slow-churning roils became the steady hammering of a determined current. The water reeked of disturbed soil and plant. Her mouth felt dry despite the cloying humidity and steady drizzle, an acrid taste rising from low in her throat. The ferryboat trembled. Or was it only her own trembling? She hugged Red's warm neck, her fingers twining into the coarse hairs of his mane. He stepped back and forth, feet wide to brace himself.

The bow of the ferry turned straighter toward the far shore, but that shore seemed to move, slipping right on by. The current had them, carrying them downstream. The ferryman yelled at the boy. "Turn 'er harder upriver less'n ye wanta end up in Saint Loo-ee!"

Martha stared at the brown froth dashing ahead toward a distant tree-lined bend, and she hunkered closer to Red. *Saint Louis.* Her own thought.

The man gouged the pole into the water again but didn't appear to touch bottom anymore. Pulling out the pole, he slammed it onto the floor of the boat.

Doc's voice rose above the water's roar. "Can I help?"

"Hold this pole here so it don't slide off. She's movin' a little faster'n I figgered on."

Doc leaped toward the pole, dropping onto his knees to grasp it.

The wiry little man lunged to the rear and snatched the oar out of the boy's hand. "What ye still scullin' fer?" He set the oar hard to one side and glared at the boy. The young man ducked his head low, face flushed into his hair, and grabbed the handle again, holding it in both hands so tight his knuckles whitened. The rough water shook the length of the oar and the boy struggled to hold it, his whole body quaking with the effort.

The ferryman bounded back to the downriver side, where he picked up another oar and began sweeping it through the water. The craft gradually turned slantwise again. The far shore slipped by slower, but it kept falling behind. Finally the man yelled out. "Ease her back, now. Scull her a little." He stood to his full height, scanning the river, and his face took on a sudden hard set. Martha tried to follow his gaze but saw only the heaving river coming at them as if ready to swallow them up.

He wheeled about and snatched the pole out of Doc's hands. "Watch out." As Doc leapt out of the way, the man carried the long pole across the narrow deck, circling in front of the animals. At the upstream side he jabbed the pole's tip toward the water and whacked a submerged log before Martha even saw the snag coming.

The impact of his thrust jarred the ferry. The log sheered aside and missed the boat but sent a wake against the corner. Water sloshed across the deck. Cold spray slapped Martha's cheek, and she sucked in a gulp of air. Her knees turned soft as the Missouri mud, holding her up only because they'd somehow locked.

Why did I ever come out to this wild country with the boys? Why?

Looking up, she was surprised to see the north shore, right ahead. But no landing. It was probably far upriver now. She gripped Red tighter. The ferry swerved toward the riverbank and ran against the ground. The jolt nearly threw her off her feet despite her firm grip on the horse.

The ferryman swung a rope around a nearby tree and brought the long craft about. The ferry bucked. He plunged the pole down, pressed back, jostled the craft to the tree again and tied it firm. There was no landing, only a clear spot on the bank, somewhat level. Maybe that would do. The man and his helper scooted a ramp over to bridge the gap. It swayed, but held. Martha's legs wobbled when she led the snorting Red toward land, his hooves resounding on the wet planks.

Once ashore, everyone thanked the ferryman. "Will you go back now?" Doc asked.

"No, we'll stay on this side until somebody wants to go across." The man took another long look at the river. "May wait until the water goes down."

Martha shivered.

The three travelers started across the flat, open ground. With every step they sank into the deep soil. The treeless landscape appeared endless, so they didn't seem to make any progress. Was the sky growing dim already? Or was it the heavy cloud cover? Would they be caught out here for the night with the Missouri River rising?

Rain poured harder. Martha's hair streamed down her back, all her pins having dropped somewhere along the way. Mud coated the lower half of her skirt and made it weigh heavily around her ankles. She couldn't take a step without more mud clinging to her shoes. How could she possibly go on?

Doc touched her shoulder. "Look. A rider."

She thought he was imagining it, until she saw through the streaks of rainwater, a man on a horse, a dog bounding beside him. Riding up to them, he waved. "Hello there. Would you be the Poindexters? My dog saw you coming."

They all nodded while Doc answered. "We're looking for William Poindexter."

The man smiled. "You've found him. And you're Doc?"

"I'm Doc. This is Simpson, and this is our sister Martha."

Doing her best to stand straight, she tried to tuck a little of the stringing hair off the back of her neck, but it was impossible. A glint of humor showed in William Poindexter's eyes. She began to laugh and cry at the same time, and laughter erupted around her.

Chapter 2

Garrett

Carroll County, Missouri, July 1844

Martha shifted in the soft leather sidesaddle as she rode with her brothers and William up another gentle hill in the northern part of Carroll County. She appreciated William's wife, Eliza, loaning her the saddle, along with the pretty little bay mare. Martha had never used a lady's sidesaddle before. It offered a level of comfort unfamiliar to her, but this had been a long day of riding after several long days. She rubbed the perspiration from her forehead. At least the worst of the heat was gone as the sun lowered in the sky.

They'd seen several nice properties. Doc had found a couple of forty-acre parcels he liked, but he wanted to check out the northern townships before he decided.

The ground felt spongy, even here. Martha hoped the hot days would dry it soon. A stench of rotting debris still clung to her nose, though they were far from the river now.

Martha and her brothers hadn't been with William's family more than a few days when the river surged and overran its banks. Racing the river, they all took refuge in Carrollton, Carroll County's foremost town and county seat, which stretched above a soft-edged bluff overlooking the bottoms. William set up a tent, part of a tent city laid out along that bluff top, and there they watched the spectacle of floating houses, chickens and pigs and other animals riding roofs downstream, the water spreading right to the bluff.

William and Eliza's house hadn't washed away, but it would need considerable work. Nothing could be done until things dried, so he'd gladly joined his cousins to look at land. Now at the top of the rise, William pulled his horse to a stop and tilted his wide-brimmed hat back. "Nice country."

Martha drew the mare alongside him. The land was all hills and hollows as far as she could see. Only one landmark interrupted the rolling pattern. Ahead, a tall mound rose above the surrounding countryside, crowned with trees, like a monstrous head with bushy hair poking out of the ground.

William smiled. "I do like the rich soil of the bottomland, though."

Doc raised a brow. "It's rich, all right, but I want higher land."

William pointed at the mound. "How about the top of that?"

"That's it," Doc said with a firm nod. "I'll just build my cabin right on the top there, and slide down a rope to do my chores. We'll let Martha pull me back up at dinnertime." He let out a chortle and the men laughed. Martha tried not to smile.

Simpson pointed to the left of the mound. "Is that a house?"

William squinted. "Looks like it. Shall we go see?"

Once they'd started down the gentle slope, Martha saw the log house nestled among trees. A barn and shed flanked the house on either side. Cattle and horses grazed in green fields, and a large square of flattened, yellow-brown vegetation steamed behind the buildings. Another drowned grain field. They'd seen many on their trip north.

The riders approached the house, and chickens scattered, squawking their protest. A horse nickered, and William's horse answered.

Doc swung to the ground first. "I'll see if anybody's home."

William dismounted and came to Martha's side, reaching up to help her down. She thought she could manage on her own, but realized as a lady she wasn't supposed to—at least, not in company. But when her feet touched the ground she was glad for William's strong hands. It took a minute to feel steady after all that riding.

Someone came to the door, a young woman probably about Martha's age. The girl said something to Doc, but he appeared unable to speak. What was wrong with him? Doc never lacked for words. He could outtalk anyone in the family. The girl offered him a sweet smile, and he mumbled something. What was the matter with him? Martha started to ask when she heard trotting behind them.

She turned to see a young man on a fine tall horse. For an instant horse and rider seemed made of a single piece, cast of some precious metal. The late afternoon sun gleamed on the animal's tawny hide, turning the color a shimmery bronze, and the man, dressed in tan, took on a similar sheen. He doffed his hat and his sandy hair glistened like a golden highlight on the bronze.

His gaze locked with hers, and his mustache, gilded as the top of him, tilted with a smile.

After a moment Martha became aware she wasn't breathing, but her heart was galloping like a wild horse. She took a breath.

With unusual grace and agility, the young man swung down off his horse and walked straight toward her, hat clutched to his chest. "Hello, I'm Garrett Maupin," he said in a soft drawl. He glanced at William, but only briefly before turning his eyes back to Martha.

She heard her cousin's response as if from far away. "I'm William Poindexter. This is Martha Poindexter, my cousin." He motioned toward the boys. "These are her brothers, Doc and Simpson."

Garrett reached out and took Martha's hand, holding it, and his mustache lifted again as he gave her a smile that set lights to dancing in his blue eyes. "Not *Mrs.* Poindexter?"

She let out a soft laugh, wondering if she shouldn't take her hand away, and shook her head. "No, I'm not married."

The young woman from the door came over to Martha with Doc trailing after her. Garrett finally released Martha's hand to shake William's before striding toward Doc. He pumped Doc's hand. "I see you've met my sister, Elizabeth—*Miss* Elizabeth Maupin." He grinned. "She's not married either." At that news Doc's face took on a glow, and Martha understood the reason for her brother's strange behavior.

"You a doctor?" Garrett asked.

Doc lifted his shoulders. "Naw. It's just my name, not my profession. I'm planning to be a farmer, like my pa."

Another man and woman came out the door with several children hovering close behind. Again Garrett spoke. "My aunt and uncle, Hannah and Jim Bunch. This is their place. Elizabeth and I are just visiting."

After introductions all around, William told the Bunches the boys were looking for land. "Do you know of anything around here?"

Mr. Bunch shook his head. "No, but we could ask the neighbors tomorrow."

Hannah smiled. Not an old woman, she had lines in her face and large rough hands that told of hard work. Still, her eyes reflected a bright warmth. "It's late. We'd be happy to have company if you folks would like to stay and look around."

Garrett beamed. "Good idea." He turned to Simpson. "So, where you folks from?"

"Illinois," Simpson said.

Garrett's mouth tightened. "Northerners?"

Simpson's response echoed the one Martha had heard Doc give on that earlier occasion. "Our family's from Kentucky. Pa's from Virginia before that. And then Ma—she was born in North Carolina."

Garrett spread his hands wide and shook his head. "Well, what do you know? Can you believe that? *Our* family's from Kentucky, and *our* pa came from Virginia, and *our* ma from North Carolina. That is something." He turned to face Martha. "I don't suppose you were born in Kentucky?"

She smiled. "That is a lot of coincidence. Yes, I was born in Kentucky."

He threw his head back and laughed, then looked straight at her. "I was born in Kentucky too. We are almost kin." He raised a finger to his lips. "But not too close. So, you have Southern roots." Crinkles formed at the corners of his eyes and lit them up once more.

❧

Martha sat next to Elizabeth on one of the logs circling the low fire outside the Bunch house. An occasional breeze stirred the muggy night air, giving slight respite from the hot day. The fire served for light, now that Hannah had finished cooking over it. The day too hot to light a fire indoors, she'd resorted to camp cooking to feed them all.

Now as the sky darkened, everyone gravitated to the circle around the fire, like moths to flame. Garrett set a small log on the glowing coals, making sparks fly in a snapping spray of lights. Then he eased his slim, wiry frame onto the log opposite the girls, every motion fluid with control and self-assurance.

He smiled up at Doc and Simpson when they sat beside him. "I was thinking. Elizabeth and I are heading home to Ray County day after tomorrow. Our pa has a farm there. Did I mention that? Nice land in Ray County. Why don't you folks come with us and look at property over there?"

Doc glanced across the soft-licking flames at Elizabeth, his expression changing rapidly, brow furrowed, lips pursed, flickering to a smile.

Elizabeth turned to Martha. "Ma and Pa will be glad to have you visit." She grabbed Martha's arm, voice bright. "And you can come to my birthday party. Oh, do. Please come."

Martha had to laugh. She had the warmest feeling she'd found a friend here in Missouri. She could see what had caught Doc's attention. Elizabeth had pretty features, and beautiful honey-gold hair, a shade darker than her brother's. But more than that, her face glowed with exuberance, sometimes barely contained, words spilling out like sugar in her subtle drawl. Martha put a hand on Elizabeth's. "When is your birthday?"

"It's the thirteenth of this month, and we always have a big party. Neighbors will come over, and there'll be lots of food and games and—please, we'd love to have you. You can stay in the house." Elizabeth reached out in a sweeping gesture to include the rest of the Poindexters. "All of you. We have so much extra room since most of our brothers and sisters have left home to get married—or chase after adventure of some kind or another." She laughed. "Why, we just rattle around in that big old house."

Garrett leaned forward, arms flexing, as if his stirring tension was about to burst out. "That's right. We have lots of room. You're sure welcome to stay awhile."

Martha smiled at his enthusiasm. "You live at home?"

He straightened, sobered. "My pa needs my help. He's not too well."

"Oh. Would our visit upset him?"

Garrett waved a dismissing hand and let out a short laugh. "No, not at all. In fact, you'll cheer him up. Nothing he likes better than company—especially the company of a charming young lady."

Garrett's eyes caught a glitter of firelight as he gave Martha a direct look, sending the warmth of that light right into her. She shifted on her log seat, wishing she could undo a button at the top of her dress. She was much too warm.

Elizabeth kept a hand on her. "What do you say?"

Martha looked at Doc and Simpson, then over at William standing away from the circle, visiting with Jim Bunch. "You'll have to ask my brothers—and William."

Doc stroked his beard. "Well, we did find a couple of nice forty-acre pieces south of here, but we want to keep looking—see if anything compares. We might think about it."

"Good," Garrett said, nodding as if the decision were made.

Elizabeth smiled at Martha. "How long have you lived in Illinois?"

"Most of my life." Martha shrugged. "We moved there from Kentucky when I was little—too young to remember. Pa came over the mountains from Virginia to Kentucky when he was a young man. Ma and her family were already there."

"Why Illinois?" Garrett asked.

"It was the frontier. Pa always looked to the frontier." She smoothed her skirt with one hand. "I'm surprised he stayed in one place so long. I could see it in his eyes when we planned this trip—how much he wanted to come. Maybe he will someday."

Garrett lifted his chin, a set to his jaw, his prominent cheekbones sharper. Without comment he got up to head for the log pile against a large tree.

Martha leaned toward Elizabeth and whispered, "Does your brother have some dislike of Illinois?"

"It's Northern. Garrett's a devout Southerner." A gleam lit Elizabeth's face. "But you're all right. You're from Kentucky. And your pa from Virginia, just like ours, and even your ma from North Carolina. You're all right." She let out a small bubble of laughter. "Besides, he likes you. He wants you to be all right."

Martha almost laughed with her but stopped when Garrett returned with a log. He looked at his sister, brows raised, but didn't speak.

Instead, Simpson spoke up. Martha wasn't sure her brothers had heard the hushed exchange between her and Elizabeth, but Simpson turned the conversation anyway. "How far is it to your place in Ray County?"

Garrett glanced at Simpson, then directed his gaze at Martha as he sat again, resting his arms on his legs. "It's a two-day ride." A quick smile tilted his mustache. "With the ladies."

Martha tried to look away but seemed unable to move as he continued to watch her. Firelight danced in his eyes, and her heart thundered once more, like that wild galloping horse.

— ◦ —

Martha rode beside Garrett over low rolling hills and into gentle hollows on their way to the Maupin farm. The clip-clop of the horses' hooves made a steady rhythm, while birds added a trill here and there. A warm July sun beat down on them, but her bonnet shaded her face and kept the worst of the heat off.

The road was little more than a double track cut through the grass by the passage of many wagons. A green swath ran down the center, and the riders proceeded two by two on either side of the green line. She'd never seen a man sit a horse the way Garrett did, moving with the animal's rhythm like a part of it. The reins lay in his slender fingers so lightly he didn't appear to be holding on. And the horse moved one way and another, stopping or starting, without his seeming to guide it at all.

She glanced back, such an easy thing on the sidesaddle. Doc still rode alongside Elizabeth, the two caught up in endless talk and laughter. Whatever stopped his tongue on first sight of Elizabeth had released him for sure. Still, he didn't seem quite the silly tease Martha so loved. Something new had come over her brother. Simpson and William followed behind, both quiet.

When she turned to face ahead once more, she saw Garrett watching her, brows lifted. He spoke under his breath. "I think my sister is smitten."

Martha laughed. "And my brother."

Garrett's gaze continued to rest on Martha. His mustache twitched with a subtle smile that crinkled the corners of his eyes and set those stars twinkling in the blue. She waited for him to speak, but he didn't say anything. Shifting in the saddle, she looked away but, feeling undefended against his intent focus, stared back at him. "What?" she said.

He smiled wider. "I just like looking at you, Miss Martha Ann Poindexter. Does it make you uncomfortable?"

"No—yes! I don't know."

"I'm sorry." He faced ahead, releasing her. "I never met anybody like you. You're smart." He gave her another quick look. "I like that. You're brave, coming out here to Missouri without your ma and pa, just you and your brothers. Why did you?"

"I—" She shrugged. "I needed to get away, do something exciting. It seems like ever since my sister got married and left home, it's been nothing but housework. When I was little I used to play with my brothers, but when Louisa left I had no freedom at all anymore. I wanted—"

Martha stopped herself. Why was she telling him this? What would he think of her? Freedom? She was about to tell him how much she wanted freedom. That wasn't a proper thing for a lady to say, especially to a man. She didn't want him thinking she was a *free woman*, whatever free women did, and it had to be something terrible, considering the way Ma and Louisa looked at her when she told them she wanted to be one and they told her she most certainly did not.

His voice when he answered resonated with tenderness. "I understand. I'm glad you came."

She dared a look in his direction. His face reflected all the tenderness she'd heard in his tone, and in that moment the warmth welled in her breast so full she thought she would burst with appreciation for Garrett Maupin. He understood her need for freedom—and not as a bad thing.

"This way," he said when they came to a small track that angled left off the main route. As they turned onto the new track, he pointed to their right. "That's my pa's field. Not looking good after the rain."

The field had the same yellowy flattened debris they'd seen on so many farms. Another wheat field destroyed by the deluge. "I'm sorry you were all hit so badly," Martha said.

"There won't be time for another wheat crop this year, but we'll put in some corn when it dries enough. That'll keep us for now." He smiled, the lights in his blue eyes like ripples glinting in the sunlight on a rushing stream. She felt the currents, reflecting, warm.

Then his back went straight, his head high as he focused ahead. She followed his gaze and saw the house. A large two-story log building stood on a rise in ground, the logs dark with age, the trim and shutters painted green. A canopy of large trees shaded the wide yard like massive umbrellas.

Hounds began to bugle, and soon Martha saw them loping around the house, long ears flying. A man's sharp voice silenced the animals, and they disappeared, only an occasional whimper reminding her of their presence.

The road approached from behind the house and came around one side before making a wide curve in front. When Martha rode nearer she saw why the house faced that way. A broad covered porch looked to the south over rolling fields that extended so far into the distance she couldn't see where they ended.

She drew her horse to a stop and sighed. "It looks like you can see forever."

Not realizing she'd spoken aloud, she was surprised by Garrett's answering voice. "Seems like it, all right."

Woodland skirted the fields on the left, a deep hollow on this side of the woods adding to the lofty feel of the house site. On the open fields cattle and horses grazed, their colors of brown and gold a vivid contrast against the bright-green pasture. A tall, sleek sorrel trotted up to the fence and nickered a greeting to the arriving party. The Maupins did have fine animals.

Garrett's mount moved forward, and Martha's mare followed. Martha turned her attention from the broad fields to the house itself, and her gaze riveted on a figure standing on the wide front porch. He seemed fixated on those fields below, as if he hadn't noticed the six approaching riders. A scowl carved deep lines in his face, and he squinted as if to see to the end of that endless distance. His silver-gray hair rose like a wind-blown ruff about his face, though the sultry summer air lay still as glass. His mustache, more of steel gray than silver, drooped like Garrett's.

He stood rigid as stone, a fierce energy emanating from him. Then he barked out a command. "Junior! Now!"

A young man burst out the door of the house. "Coming, Pa! I'll see to it." The younger one glanced over at the riders and raised an arm in greeting. "Hallo, everybody." He charged across the yard and driveway, leaped the fence into the pasture, and ran down through the field.

The older man slowly turned his head to look straight at Garrett. Martha watched the older one, waiting for a smile of recognition that didn't come, then tore her gaze from him to witness Garrett's reaction. She'd never seen Garrett's face so tight. A steady pulse throbbed in his temple, sending underlying waves beneath his taut skin. He spoke in a tone barely audible above a rising sound of the dogs inside. "Hello, Pa."

His father gave a curt nod, and Garrett went on. "We brought company. The Poindexters." A bit of warmth crept into his voice. "This is Miss Martha Poindexter. These are her brothers Doc and Simpson, and her cousin William." Garrett gave Martha a quick smile. "My pa, Perry Maupin."

Mr. Maupin finally spoke. "Nice to meet you all." His gaze scanned the lot of them, without lighting for a second on anyone.

Martha wanted to answer, but feeling not the least warmth in Perry Maupin's expression, she doubted if he thought it was nice at all to meet them, and she wasn't feeling terribly nice about meeting him. Instead, she felt an overall impression of an imposing house on its rise in ground above the wide rolling fields, like an extension of the imposing man on its front porch.

Elizabeth's bright voice lifted above the tension. "Good to see you, Pa. Aunt Hannah and Uncle Jim send their love."

As if allowed to move now, Doc leaped from his saddle and hurried to Elizabeth's side to help her off her horse. The others dismounted quickly, and Martha looked down to see Garrett reaching for her. He smiled, but she didn't see the usual crinkles at the corners of his eyes, or the little lights she'd come to look for in the blue.

When her feet touched the ground, she glanced up at him. He appeared to be stretching to his full height. He was a bit taller than average, she thought, or seemed so anyway, maybe because of his stance, or his lean build—or because he had such a big personality. Of course, almost everyone seemed tall to Martha, who'd always been on the small side.

Elizabeth went straight to her, hand outstretched, face beaming with her ready smile. "Come on in and meet Ma and the others, and I'll show you our room."

Taking Martha's hand, Elizabeth whisked her past the intimidating man of the house and led her inside. The size of the main room surprised Martha. Their own two-story log house had always seemed large, but this was enormous, a huge fireplace at one end, another on the opposite wall, apparently for cooking, although a freestanding cookstove stood near it. A gray-haired woman bent over a long table at the kitchen end, kneading bread, while a young woman with sunny gold hair stirred something in a pot on the cookstove.

Both women looked up when Martha and Elizabeth entered. The elder one's expression softened but didn't quite make a smile. The girl's face glowed with delight. Elizabeth quickly introduced Martha to her mother and Sarah Catherine, her sister. "I'm going to show Martha our room," Elizabeth said, hurrying Martha to the open log steps leading upstairs.

The second story, narrower than below due to the pitch of the roof, was still spacious. A fireplace, smaller than below, graced the end where beds and trunks lined either wall, glass windows flanking the chimney.

Elizabeth drew Martha in the other direction, toward a wall that partitioned off that end. "We girls have our own room." The girls' room took up the other half of the upstairs with another fireplace for their warmth, and similar windows.

Martha smiled. "Very nice."

Elizabeth patted one of the beds. "You can sleep here in Lucinda's old bed. She's one of my married sisters. And that's Martha's bed." Elizabeth pointed to another narrow bed across the room. "My *sister* Martha."

"Oh yes. The other Martha. You told me about her. So there are four of you girls."

"That's right. Two married and two still at home." Elizabeth motioned toward Lucinda's bed and sat on the one next to it. "And the five boys."

Martha sat across from her. "Five?"

Elizabeth nodded. "There's just Garrett and Perry Jr. left. James and Howard are on their own. Howard's been married a few years, and James probably will be soon. But my brother William never came out to Missouri with us. He stayed in Kentucky, so I don't even remember him. I was only two when we came."

"When was that?"

"In 1829."

Martha made the quick calculation. "So you're going to be seventeen on your birthday."

"That's right. Didn't I tell you? I don't think you ever told me how old you are, but you must be about the same."

Martha looked down at the pattern of the quilt on her bed, and back at her new friend. She wasn't sure she wanted to answer. "I'm fifteen."

Elizabeth's mouth widened. "Really? I thought you were older. You do seem older. Sarah Catherine's fourteen, and she's a child."

A soft laugh escaped Martha's lips. "I guess there's a big difference between fourteen and fifteen. I think I grew up pretty fast all of a sudden. Maybe from this trip."

Bending toward Martha, Elizabeth reached out and put a hand on hers, as if to assure her of their bond. "I've never had a friend I felt closer to than you."

Martha appreciated the gesture, but she didn't feel nearly the composure in herself that she saw in Elizabeth. And while she loved Elizabeth and thoroughly enjoyed her company, Martha couldn't help feeling the difference in their circumstances. The Poindexters were a fine family, highly thought of in their community, as well as her mother's family, the Woods. But they were far from wealthy. Only Louisa had come anywhere near that when she married John Bronough. And Martha knew her own parents would greet company with warmth.

She didn't understand the tension she sensed here, or the change she'd observed in Garrett. She was ready to ask Elizabeth about that when Sarah Catherine burst into the room and plopped onto one of the beds on the far wall. No dark clouds dimmed this ray of sunshine. She leaned forward on the bed, hands on her knees, oblivious to grace, and began to talk. "It's so nice to have company. Garrett said your family's from Kentucky, like ours, but he didn't say where you came from. Are you traveling just with your brothers? They seem like a lot of fun. I'd like to travel with just my brothers, especially Garrett and Junior."

Martha glanced at Elizabeth and saw the glint of humor in her eyes, as Sarah rattled on.

Sarah stood then, as abruptly as she'd sat. "Well, I have to get back to help Ma. She wants you too, Elizabeth." She smiled at Martha. "I can't wait to hear about your trip."

Martha wondered how she would ever wedge that into the conversation as she followed the two sisters downstairs.

Interlude I

Who were these Maupins?

Early in my research I was sitting at my desk trying to figure out how to put Martha's story together, assessing what I knew and what I would need to find out. At the time I knew a little about the Maupins but not enough. And Martha, a Poindexter? I knew nothing of them.

"How will I find you, Martha?" I asked, glancing up from my notes to the window above my desk overlooking the broad expanse of valley and mountains.

My focus sharpened. An unusual white bird flitted across the field below, the white form sweeping over the green grass, nearly stopping in flight to do an aerial dance, plunging low, then up again, never lifting high in the sky. What was it? I'd never seen such a bird. It turned around and flew right past the window so close I could look into its eye. I leaned toward the glass, heart pounding.

The head feathers, not quite pure white, looked more the color of pale ashes. Dark stripes trimmed the wings and tail feathers, but the breast and underbelly gleamed white. From its configuration—the sharp curved beak, flattish head, front-facing predator eyes—I guessed it was some kind of hawk.

When it disappeared around the front of the house, I called my little granddaughter, Calliope, and we dashed out the front door. The bird was flying up the hill toward the upper barn, hovering low to the ground above the hill road, and we followed as fast as we could along the steep grade. The creature seemed unaware of us as it skimmed over the narrow track, but it soon veered to the left and dropped out of sight where the land curved away. We ran to the spot we'd lost sight of it, but it had vanished. Still, the image lingered, along with a sense of awe.

Calliope and I stood catching our breaths. Five years old at the time, she looked up at me, dark eyes aglitter. I was glad she'd shared this enchanting moment with me. We would have to tell Alex about the bird. My grandson, then thirteen. He loved the creatures on this place, and liked to take pictures of them to post on his blog. He and his folks—my daughter Carisa and her husband, Robin—lived in my father's old house in the valley. Calliope and her mother, my daughter Christiane, lived with me on the hill.

When I returned to my research, I kept wondering. Was the white bird some kind of sign? I couldn't shake the feeling this one held some meaning for me, and, whatever that might be, it seemed positive. In so many ways I needed good fortune right now—in the farm venture, in the search for Martha, in my project of writing a book about her. I would later identify the bird as a northern harrier, commonly known as a marsh hawk, and I felt it leading me to something.

My kids and I had been drawn here by some deep tug the place had on us. Beyond the unseen forces that bound us to this land, the family legacy held us. For many years I'd known we had something special here. Members of our extended family talked about it. This was Grandma Martha's farm and we could not give it up lightly.

Others in Oregon's Century Farm and Ranch program recognized the terrible odds generations had to overcome to keep these working farms or ranches in their families for one hundred years. By the spring of 2010 just over eleven hundred had received Oregon's Century designation. Only twenty-two had received the Sesquicentennial Award. If my family could hang on until 2018, we would join those few.

I couldn't remember when I first knew about Martha buying this farm, but a plaque had stood on the buffet of my parents' dining room since the 1960s or 1970s with the finely scrolled words, "The Martha A. Maupin Farm, Founded 1868, With the Award of this Certificate is duly enrolled by the Oregon Historical Society as a Century Farm." I took pride in the farm being named for a woman, and I knew she'd bought it after her husband was killed. I didn't know much more about it.

Long before, as a child, I knew the Maupins were tough. When I hurt myself or got into trouble and began to whine, my father would prompt me to keep the stiff upper lip, with a twist. "You're a Maupin," he'd say, "and the Maupins are tough." Then he'd launch into the story of Uncle Howard Maupin, the great Indian fighter. "Yessir, he was in a fierce battle one day and they sliced him right across the belly and his innards started coming out. And you know what he did? He poked 'em back in and went on fighting."

Wow! What a story for a little kid. What a legend to cling to.

Now I wondered how much truth was in that tale of Uncle Howard. He was Garrett's older brother, and he and Garrett were in the Mexican War. After Howard moved to Oregon, eventually settling east of the Cascades, he did get into some Indian fighting. He went after Chief Paulina, a chief in eastern Oregon who evidently took exception to white folks taking over the land of his people. Paulina had been threatening settlers and killing their livestock. Howard hunted Paulina down and killed him, then scalped the chief and kept the scalp over his cabin door. I didn't know that part of the story as a kid. Howard became something of a folk hero and had a town named after him in eastern Oregon.

To what extent tales of Howard's toughness altered my life, I couldn't say. But whenever things got rough for me, I did have a tendency to keep on keeping on. Poke them back in and go on fighting.

One of my favorite people as a child was Edith Maupin Edwards, one of Martha's granddaughters, the eldest daughter of Martha's son Cap. Edith was for me the essence of a Maupin. She had also grown up on this farm, and visited us often. She had a wonderful touch with horses, a quality I came to believe typical of the Maupins, and she helped me with my horse in my pre-teen and early teen years.

I loved to hear her tell stories. The words spilled out of her in a deep, honey-toned voice that always captivated me. Edith was twelve when Martha died, so some of those tales of the old days might have come from Grandma Martha herself. Of course when I heard them I couldn't have realized how significant Martha's viewpoint might be to me one day. But some small bits might have settled in my memory to emerge when inspiration flowed into this work.

Later I learned stories about the earlier ancestors, marvelous legends about Gabriel Maupin, the first Maupin in America—how he escaped religious persecution in France and fled to England, how he associated with French royalty, how he married a daughter of the English Earl of Spencer and received land in Virginia from his father-in-law in colonial days. The Spencer connection held a certain intrigue for us at a time when Princess Diana, a Spencer, gained such popularity in Britain and the world. We could call her Cousin Diana.

Unfortunately, not true.

But a leading Maupin researcher, Dorothy Maupin Shaffett, sought the truth and found truth exciting too.

Part of Gabriel's myth checked out. Gabriel Maupin did in fact flee France as a Huguenot during the Catholic persecution of the late 1600s. Dorothy described her intriguing quest in her 1993 book, The Story of Gabriel and Marie Maupin, Huguenot Refugees to Virginia in 1700. I hadn't seen that book before starting my story of Martha, but when I got a chance to read it, the account of Dorothy's search gripped me.

She looked for Gabriel and Marie in France and England, and in the Netherlands, where many French Huguenots fled. To answer the question of the Spencers, she went to sources in England. While many of us struggled to build our family trees with scant records and too many missing files, the Spencers of England had no such problem. They were well documented. And they had no Gabriel Maupin married to a Marie Spencer.

Setting that aside, Dorothy searched for Gabriel in Salt Lake City through the Mormon records. He didn't show up in France. But after scrolling through microfiche listings for the Netherlands until her eyes and arm grew tired, she saw the name. Maupain, Gabriel. She nearly shouted in the strict quiet of the library. She had earlier found his name spelled that way on the passenger list of the ship Le Nasseau, which carried Huguenots from England to Virginia in 1700.

She found marriage banns posted for Gabriel and Marie in September of 1691 but couldn't make out Marie's last name. At the suggestion of the attendant in Salt Lake, she wrote to the archives in Amsterdam. The director of the archives responded, confirming Dorothy's findings on Gabriel, giving her Marie's last name as Erssen, or more properly Hersent in the French spelling. The couple was married in Walloon Church in Amsterdam. The man had names of witnesses, which led to further connections, including the identification of Marie's parents in the Dieppe region in northern France, so she could be traced back two generations more.

Gabriel listed his home as Gargau, but no one could find the place. With the help of other researchers, Dorothy learned of Maupins in northern France near Abbeville, and of Gabriel's town Jargeau, which had changed from the Old French spelling.

Were there ties to royalty? On some level, perhaps. Some were apparently landed gentry. A branch of Maupins owned the estate of La Bouvacque near Abbeville for hundreds of years. They probably held this land by virtue of swearing to fight for their overlord, and their overlord may have been the king.

They apparently intermarried with other leading French families. Gabriel's ancestry remained uncertain.

Gabriel and Marie came to America with three children, according to a headright document giving a family head count to establish how much land could be acquired in Virginia. Son Daniel, next in my own line, was born in 1700 in England before the ship Le Nasseau sailed for America.

Once in this country Gabriel and Marie settled with their small family in Williamsburg, Virginia, and had one more son. Dorothy followed the generations forward, as the family tree continued from branch to branch, down to the many twigs we've become today.

According to legend the first Maupin was given his name by a King Louis, one of the many, this first Maupin being a keeper of the king's pine forest. The name meant "head of, or keeper of, the pines," Mau meaning "head of" and pin meaning "pine tree." A fitting heritage for our own family farm, where we were keepers of the forest—if not pines, at least conifers.

The Maupin shield displayed three golden pine cones on a field of red, a unicorn rising on the crest. Dorothy came up with a different definition of the name's first syllable. Because shields were meant to be menacing to increase their force in battle, shield names tended to sound brutal, like a war cry. The Mau she described as an Old French word meaning "baneful." The pin by her definition still meant "pine tree."

Whether we were fierce or merely keepers, the tall conifers were important to us. My early impression of the Maupins, from the Howard story, implied ferocity. At the least, they were tough, unconventional, rugged individualists, even a little wild and reckless. I wasn't always sure why I held that view. Perhaps the tone when they were mentioned? The unsaid elements in stories about them, as if a lot more could be said but not in my company? Story gaps made good fodder for vivid imaginations. Thus the Maupins gained a mystique greater than their own reality.

Or maybe not. As I proceeded to seek information about them, I found I was still capable of shock.

Having a start on the Maupin research, I turned to the Poindexters, who were so unknown to me. On a whim I sat down with my computer to search Martha Poindexter Maupin. And I got something. I let out a squeal of delight. "She's on here. Martha." I called out to my daughter. "Martha's on the Internet!"

I found more than I ever dreamed I would, thanks to a fourth cousin I came to know via cyberspace, Gloria Atwater. I clutched the edge of my laptop and read.

A descendant of Martha's younger brother Newt, Gloria had searched diligently for our Poindexter ancestors and had come up with volumes of material, which she had put together on a delightful website entitled Thomas H. Poindexter, A Brief History of the Thomas Poindexter Family of Kentucky, Illinois, Missouri and Oregon. *Reading her accounts of Martha's parents and siblings, I developed a richer sense of the family than I'd ever experienced.*

Next I found a website for the Poindexters. Like the Maupins, they went back a ways in this country, back to George Poingdestre, who immigrated to Virginia in 1657 from the Isle of Jersey, one of the English Channel islands, a land not quite English, not quite French. Gloria found a tenuous connection between George's line and Martha's father, Thomas. She discovered a will for Thomas's probable father, William Poindexter of Louisa County, Virginia, which provided an inheritance for Thomas similar to the amount the man left to his named sons, but Thomas wasn't named as a son. Was he estranged? Illegitimate? A foster child? One of the unanswered questions.

Continuing my web search, I found on a message board the name of someone well acquainted with stories of Howard Maupin, Garrett's brother. Clues led to a phone number, and I called. It was Linda Noel, a third cousin, one of Martha's descendants through Martha's oldest son, Cap. Linda had done extensive research on the Maupin family. She'd been a chief source of information for Gloria on Martha's branch of the Poindexters, and for another Maupin researcher, Florence McNabb, one of Cap's younger daughters.

I had some idea of Florence's work beforehand and had shared a delightful conversation with her prior to a trip I took to France in 2000. Although I'd long thought I might write something about Martha, I was working on a different book then and didn't think to ask what I wished I could ask Florence now. But she died in 2002. Linda sent me a copy of Florence's seventy-five-page manuscript, The Maupin Family—*a treasure of family lore and colorful tidbits—along with reams of other material. Providing both information and encouragement, Linda became a great help to me in this project.*

So with the excellent start given me by these family members, I launched into my own search. I looked through census records, property records. I called and e-mailed courthouses and genealogical societies. I read histories and diaries of women on the Oregon Trail. In the archives deep in the local courthouse, I even discovered a note Martha had written to the county clerk giving permission for a daughter to marry. I recognized Martha's graceful signature, and my fingers shook touching this scrap of browned paper I knew she'd put her hands on.

One morning early in my search, I was surprised to get a phone call from a gentleman with a soft Southern drawl. He introduced himself as James Phillips, Circuit Court Clerk of Clay County, Kentucky, where Garrett Maupin was born and where his father and grandfather had lived before him. I had e-mailed asking for information but hadn't given my postal address.

Mr. Phillips kindly called to tell me he had material for me and needed to know where to send it. We had a pleasant visit about the hillbillies of Clay County in the Kentucky hills, and he described the area for me. He said he was happy to find someone out West with hillbilly connections. This was the first time I'd heard the hillbilly reference.

I found many people willing to help in my searches. Like Gloria, I wanted to learn not only about the mainstream of the many tributaries, in my case Martha and Garrett, but also about their brothers and sisters and parents and grandparents. Where did these people go? What happened to them? I searched the offshoots in the census records, compiling huge files.

"Are all these people important to the story?" my daughter Christiane asked. "Or are you just obsessed to find out about them?"

I had to concede sometimes it was the latter. But since I intended to tell Martha's story in fictional form, scene by scene, I did want to know who might actually be in any given scene. Small details could be significant, say, place of birth, which showed on the census records. Family legend might put a person one place, but if census records consistently showed a birth somewhere else, that could open possibilities for a whole new chapter.

Many times I thought I'd found something new, then looked at Gloria's findings to see she'd discovered it already. In a few instances I found information that turned the story in a different direction. Like me, Gloria used conjecture to put her story together. When the history was scanty, that was all you could do.

Gloria assumed Martha went to Missouri with her brothers Ambrose and Doc because those two were on the 1850 census for Carroll County, Missouri. When I asked researcher Glen Hill Jr. in Carroll County to check land records to see when Ambrose and Doc first bought land, which might tell me when they arrived there, he found no Ambrose listed. He did find Doc and T. S. acquiring land in September 1844. T. S. was Thomas Simpson, who often went by Simpson in the records. Further study showed Ambrose still fathering children back in Greene County, Illinois, in 1846. His daughter was born there in April 1847. Ambrose didn't go with them.

I checked with Gloria to be sure she hadn't found other information that put Ambrose in Missouri earlier. She hadn't. I wrote Ambrose out of those scenes. And wrote Simpson in.

One thing stumped both Gloria and me. What happened to Martha's parents, Thomas and Maxy Poindexter? They were on the 1840 census for Greene County, Illinois. No one to my knowledge, or Gloria's, had ever found any record of them after that. What kept compelling me on this search for Martha's parents was a family legend suggesting they were still alive much later, alive and unhappy about her connection with Garrett Maupin. I kept looking for them.

During this phase of the research, I trekked to the upper ridge above my house on my daily walk, thinking of Martha on this place. Though my dad had doubled the farm's size over time, adding land slightly higher, this ridge was the highest point of Martha's property. I stepped into the tall Douglas firs lining the crest and looked up the straight trunks into the graceful draping boughs. They were the dominant conifer in Oregon and our primary timber tree.

Where they bordered open pasture I could see through to the wide overlook from this lofty site. The distant mountains spread across the horizon, ridge after ridge, in ever-paler ranks. Below, a long, narrow drift of fog looped around Pleasant Plain, marking the river's course. Within the woods I felt enclosed in quiet, bird calls soft. A gentle breeze carried the rich scent of the firs, a trace of honey or sweet flowers. I tried to be still, to absorb the hush.

Was she here? Martha? Did she move among these trees or those that stood before? An odd tightness gripped my chest. Did I sense her wonder? Her pain?

I'd been learning more about Martha through lists and files and cryptic notes on long-cold paper. But I kept wanting to know the life within her story. Here on this land we'd shared could I find her echoing spirit and connect?

The breeze riffled my hair, murmuring through the needled boughs and skimming across the grass like an invisible shadow of the white hawk.

Chapter 3

The Maupins

Ray County, Missouri, July 1844

A confusion of voices stirred through the great room of the Maupin house, punctuated by Sarah Catherine's higher pitched chatter, while everyone found places at the long table in the center. Martha had counted them all with Elizabeth's help when she set the table. Six Maupins and four Poindexters.

Mrs. Maupin invited William and Simpson to sit on either side of her, with Doc beside William, across from Elizabeth. Martha began to sit next to Elizabeth when Mr. Maupin spoke to her. "Miss Poindexter?"

She started at the sound of her name in his gruff voice, and wheeled about to look toward him. A smile creased his face like the rumpling of tanned leather. Light from the low candle on the table reflected in his gray-blue eyes, and familiar crinkles formed at the eye corners.

His tone softened when he extended his hand toward the chair on his left. "Please, my dear, won't you sit next to me?"

Martha couldn't stop the gulp in her throat. She forced a smile and nodded. Stepping forward, she found her legs had turned to wood, but somehow she made them move, and they took her to the high-backed chair. With surprising grace, he came around behind the chair and pulled it out for her, easing it carefully forward when she sat.

She managed a quick thank you, but the words came out in a raspy whisper.

Garrett took the place across from her and gave her a smile, brows raised. The sparkle had returned to his eyes, or maybe it was only the candle reflecting. The tautness still pulled at the skin of his face and throat.

Mr. Maupin picked up the platter of dark-brown meat in front of him and smiled again at Martha. "Do you like venison, my dear?"

Taking a quick breath, she managed an even tone. "Yes, very much, thank you."

"Do you have a lot of game where you're from?"

"We do, yes. My pa and brothers hunt and keep us in good supply."

He started to hand her the platter, but apparently thought better of it. "Here, I'll serve you. This is heavy." He stuck the large serving fork in several pieces, then tapped a nice chunk, coated in gravy. "How about this piece? I think it's tender."

"Yes, thank you—very much."

He continued to serve her with solicitous attention, taking his focus from her only occasionally to speak to the others. His fondness for his daughters was obvious, and whatever had been bothering the Perrys before supper seemed forgotten now. The younger Perry sat beside Martha, and while not as talkative as his little sister, he was quite the charmer.

"So your brothers were telling us about the flood. You actually outran the river?" he asked. "That must have been pretty exciting."

Martha laughed. "Well, the scariest was the ferry."

"I'll bet. You're a brave lady."

Surprised to be called a lady, she glanced at young Perry and saw a resemblance. He was a younger version of Garrett—but without the mustache—his round ruddy cheeks and unserious manner making him seem more boy than man.

Garrett leaned forward, drawing her attention. "She sure is a brave lady to come all the way out here." He grinned, his gaze direct. "I think she had to talk hard to get permission. She's not only brave but very persuasive."

Young Perry laughed. "I can see that, brother."

Garrett reared back in the chair, as if he'd taken a friendly jab. If he was about to offer a rejoinder, his father's voice silenced it.

"Well, my dear, I appreciate a young lady of spirit, and I see you have that in good measure. I hope we'll see a lot of you here." Mr. Maupin nodded toward her brothers before facing her again. "You can certainly stay at our house as long as you like. I hope you find property in Ray County so we'll have the pleasure of your company for a long time to come."

Martha glanced at Mrs. Maupin, who smiled and gave a slight nod in agreement. The woman seemed unusually quiet, but she spoke finally, directing her words to Garrett. "I'm glad you're home, Garrett. I hope you can ride over to Mansur's store in the next day or two and pick up some supplies for Elizabeth's party."

Garrett's voice softened. "I'll do that for you, Ma, first thing tomorrow."

Martha saw real warmth in the woman when she responded to him. "Thank you, son. I appreciate that."

Young Perry turned toward Martha. "It's going to be a good time. The Maupins put on a party like nobody else. You'll see."

———

July 13, 1844. Garrett stayed close to Martha's side as they mingled among the guests gathered on the Maupins' wide front lawn for Elizabeth's birthday party. He'd introduced her to so many people she couldn't begin to remember them all. "Are you hungry?" he asked.

She shook her head. "Not really." The sweltering heat of the day took away whatever appetite she might have had.

Two long tables were set up under the big trees on the east side of the lawn, covered with heaping plates of food on gleaming white tablecloths. Lots of food. Lots of whiskey. A couple of dark-skinned women tended the tables, while another kept washing dishes inside. Martha hadn't seen them before.

She leaned closer to Garrett, voice low. "Do you have slaves?"

He glanced at the women and shrugged. "We hire them from a neighbor when we need help—like today. We don't own them."

Martha thought about that. "But your neighbor does?"

"What?"

"Own them."

"Sure. Of course." He raised his right elbow toward her. "Here, would you like to take my arm? The ground's a little rough." She glanced at the arm, then up to his face. She'd never taken a gentleman's arm before. A smile flickered on his lips, and not wanting him to feel uncertain, she wrapped her fingers around his arm and let him lead her forward.

He looked quite fine today in a gleaming white cambric shirt, open at the neck with long blousy sleeves, pants of jeans fabric in a sky blue, trim fit on his long legs. Hoping she looked as fine, she fingered the delicate material of her skirt, her coolest calico dress with its pale-blue flowers, puffy sleeves, buttons all down the front, white collar and cuffs.

Elizabeth had done Martha's hair in a roll and curls on top of her head that made her look rather grown up, she thought. At least seventeen.

With every step on the uneven grass, she was aware of her good black slippers, a gift from Louisa, carried all the way from Illinois in that little cart. Martha was glad William's wife had encouraged her to bring the good clothes on this ride north. "You never know when you might need to dress up," Eliza had said.

Garrett stopped and touched Martha's hand on his arm, the brief contact setting up gentle currents. "My brother James just got here. Come meet him."

Martha saw a sandy-haired man resembling the other Maupin men, still holding his horse. He gave the reins to a man black as night, evidently another slave hired for the occasion. Garrett started forward with long strides, forcing Martha to step quickly lest she lose her footing, but he soon slowed, ducking his head and giving her a sideways look. "Sorry. I didn't mean to hurry you."

James covered the distance himself and grasped his brother's free arm. "Garrett! How are you? And who do we have here?"

"James! Glad you're here. I want you to meet Miss Martha Poindexter. Miss Poindexter, my big brother James."

Martha liked him right away. He seemed gentler, more soft-spoken than the others, with the calm self-assurance of an elder brother. Like Garrett and his pa, James had the sloping mustache and strong cheekbones, but he also had a tuft of beard that distinguished him.

"Can I get you a drink?" Garrett asked.

"I'd better find the folks and say hello first." He took Martha's hand. "I'll look forward to talking more with you later."

Martha clung to Garrett's arm as they watched James work his way through the crowd. "Ma expects he'll be getting married soon," Garrett said. "A young lady named Anna."

"Will she come to the party?"

"I don't think so or Ma would have said."

Martha gave Garrett a quick smile and leaned a bit closer. The Maupin boys were all charming, but she had her own favorite and didn't want him to doubt that for a minute, even if she didn't want to say so outright. The brightness glittered in his eyes when he smiled back at her, almost taking away her breath on this hot airless day.

They continued to meander through the crowd, seeing little but each other. They nearly bumped into Doc and Elizabeth, who seemed lost in their own private sphere. Simpson and William stood close by, talking with James.

Raucous laughter erupted on the far side of the lawn. Several men had gathered there to play games. They were tossing soft buckskin-covered balls at bottles on a rail, seeing who could hit the most. A handy keg of whiskey sat against the nearest tree. Most of the players had glasses in their hands. Simpson turned and headed that direction. He loved games. Ordinarily, Doc did too, but Martha doubted he'd leave Elizabeth's side today.

Garrett patted Martha's hand and slipped his arm away. "Excuse me, but I think they need somebody to show them how this is done."

Martha watched as he strode toward the players. First he filled a glass at the keg and took a long drink. Men around him began calling out bets. Then he picked up a ball and threw. One after another, every one hit its mark. A cheer rose from the group.

Not to be outdone, Simpson had to try. He missed the first, took a long moment to recalculate the distance, and hit one, two, then missed. A word spat from his mouth, and Martha was glad she couldn't hear it. He threw another. A hit. He missed one more and pounded a fist into his palm. "Let me try that again."

Garrett handed him a glass of whiskey. "Here, try this first."

Martha felt a twinge in her stomach. Simpson didn't like to lose. He lifted the glass and drank it down in one draft. The whiskey didn't help his aim. This time he hit two out of the six and went to the keg to fill his glass again.

Young Perry darted away but soon returned with a leather riding whip in his hand. "How about this, Garrett? How many can you take down with the whip?" A knowing grin spread across the boyish face.

Martha bit her lip. Garrett let out a jovial laugh and took the whip from his brother's hand. Men placed more bets. When all the bottles were replaced on the rail, he raised the whip and with nimble speed whisked the end of it around the neck of the first bottle, lifting that one off the rail. Then the next and the next, on down the line, until every one lay on the ground, not a one broken. The crowd cheered again.

"Here," Garrett said, setting a bottle in his brother's hand. "Hold it steady."

Perry held his arm straight out in front of himself, the bottle balanced on his palm. A murmur rose from the crowd. Garrett took a few steps backward, leaned one way and the other, gauging the distance. Like the strike of a snake, he lashed the whip out and lifted the bottle off his brother's hand, clean. Perry extended the flat of his hand to show his unmarked palm. The crowd loved it. More whiskey flowed. Simpson stood back by the keg, scowling.

"How about this?" someone shouted.

Martha located the speaker when he approached Garrett, holding a pistol. She drew her collar away from her neck. The day felt warmer yet.

Simpson bolted toward Garrett. "You're not going to shoot that bottle out of your brother's hand." It wasn't a question.

Garrett laughed. "I won't shoot him straight on."

Martha couldn't hear Simpson's answer, but her shoulders clenched. Her brother could be pretty touchy sometimes, and he didn't like being laughed at—not that Garrett was laughing *at* him, but he might take it that way.

Garrett's little brother grabbed another bottle and smiled as he held it on his outstretched hand, his side to Garrett now. Garrett raised the gun, took slow aim. The gunshot exploded so loud, Martha jumped and let out a soft cry. The bottle shattered and Perry Jr. raised his hand in a broad sweep, palm toward the crowd again to show he hadn't suffered a scratch.

One of the men at the keg grabbed another bottle. "I heard a story once about a man putting an apple on his friend's head and shooting the thing off. How about it, Garrett?"

Silence settled over the gathering. Garrett tilted his head as if considering the possibility. Martha uttered a soft, "No."

With a lopsided grin, Garrett held the gun toward its owner. "I believe this is yours. I think it's time for another game."

The crowd let out a long breath, as one. Gradually the babble of conversation rose, along with the laughter of the game players. Martha moved away from the mass of people, looking for better air, but the sultry heat lay across the yard like a smothering blanket.

Another lone figure emerged from the cluster. Garrett's father. He stumbled, then caught himself, and swiping a hand over his forehead, he headed straight for the large tree near the far corner of the front porch. Martha frowned, watching him. He walked with a wooden stride, weaving a little. What was wrong? Too much to drink? She recalled Garrett mentioning his father's poor health. Maybe he wasn't well.

Despite the intimidating aura of the man, she hurried after him. She caught up just as he reached the tree. "Are you all right, Mr. Maupin?"

He stood with one hand on the tree trunk, the other on his forehead. "I . . . I need to sit down for a little bit."

Filled with a growing sense of urgency, she looked around for something he could sit on and noticed a couple of chairs on the porch. "I'll get you a chair." She ran for the porch steps with little thought to ladylike dignity. Bounding up the stairs she grabbed a wooden high-backed chair and carried it down to where he remained standing, as if stunned. "Here." She set it close to him, and he heaved a ragged sigh as he plopped onto the seat.

"Thank you, my dear. That's what I needed. Good of you."

Martha stayed close, studying his face. The color looked wrong, cheeks too red, but the rest of his face ashen white. "Do you need something to drink?"

For a moment she thought he hadn't heard her, and she began to ask again when he nodded slightly. "Yes. That would be nice, yes."

She put a hand to her throat. Where would she find the nearest water? The tables were on the far side of the wide yard. The well in back. Would there be a cup for him there? The house. They must have water in the house. Again she acted without thought to dignity. Mr. Maupin needed water now. Back up the porch steps, she ran into the house, heart pounding. Two dark-skinned women bustled about the kitchen area, one washing dishes, the other piling plates.

Martha hurried toward the nearest one. "Do you have drinking water in the house? And a cup?"

The woman motioned toward a pitcher behind her. "Yes'm."

Without waiting to be served, Martha rushed to grab the pitcher, accepted the cup the woman offered her, and filled the cup. She gave the woman a quick smile. "Thank you." Careful not to spill, she turned and hurried out to where Mr. Maupin sat leaning back in the chair, chin on his chest, eyes closed.

"Mr. Maupin?" She held the cup out to him, her voice rising with concern. "Mr. Maupin?"

His eyelids fluttered, and he looked up at her, then down at the cup in her outstretched hand. "Oh. Thank you, my dear. Thank you."

He clutched the cup in shaking hands and lifted it to his lips. Taking a sip, he stopped and stared into the vessel, shivering a little. "What is this?"

"It's—it's water, sir."

A grimace twisted his face. He drank a little more and handed the cup back to her, still half full. "That's—that'll be plenty, thank you." Again he sank back in the chair, eyelids drooping.

Martha held the cup against her chest, brow pinched in worry. "Would you like for me to fetch a doctor? Or someone who could—?"

"No! No doctor." He gave her a wavering smile. "Just—maybe you can sit with me a short spell."

Putting the cup on the ground, she sat on the grass near him, a little to the front where she could keep an eye on his face in case she needed to run for help.

He appeared to be falling asleep, but he spoke. "I guess the boy thought better of it."

"What, sir?"

"Garrett." The man breathed out a soft sound, like a low growl. "I told him if he ever did that again I'd shoot one off of *his* head. He used an apple that time. I guess he doesn't trust my aim as much as his own, or he doesn't think much of his brother."

A shudder rippled through Martha. The marksmanship game. Garrett actually performed the trick once? But she'd seen the fondness between brothers. "I'm sure he cares for his brother."

Mr. Maupin nodded. "Oh, Garrett's a sharpshooter, all right, best I ever saw. Doesn't think he can miss, but . . . we don't need any more shootings. No . . . no more." Mr. Maupin drifted off, then spoke again. "I didn't mean to do it. He . . . he gave me no choice. I didn't . . ."

Martha stared at the man. Was he dreaming? He wasn't making a lot of sense, but the gravity of his words tore at her. The heat rose inside her, the lovely dress damp and clinging. She couldn't seem to draw enough air.

A sheen beaded on Mr. Maupin's forehead and dripped into his half-closed eyes. He continued in the same dreamy tone. "Hot days can touch a man's mind. Make you do things. But what else could I do?" He sat up, opened his eyes wide and looked at Martha as if surprised she was there. "Sorry to . . . to ramble. I . . . I shouldn't . . ." He slumped again. "Sometimes a man has to do things against his will. Do you understand what I'm saying?"

"I suppose so." She noticed a wrinkle in her skirt and tried to press it out with her fingers. She had no idea what he was talking about.

Then she became aware of Garrett right next to them. She hadn't seen him approaching. His gaze focused on his father, brows raised, head tilted to one side. "What you telling this young lady, Pa?"

"Garrett, why don't you give me a drink?"

Martha started to reach for the cup beside her. "Here's water."

Garrett extended a staying hand toward her and gave his father the glass of golden liquid he'd been holding. Mr. Maupin took a long swig and let out a heavy sigh, smacking his lips. He smiled at Martha. "Now, that's a drink, my dear."

"More?" Garrett asked, taking the empty glass his father handed him.

"No, I think I'll go in now."

The older man began to raise himself off the chair, but sat back hard.

"Here, Pa." Garrett took his father's arm and lifted.

Mr. Maupin made a snarling noise. "I'm fine. I don't need any help."

"I know you don't, Pa." But Garrett didn't let go, and his father leaned heavily when he stood beside his son.

Martha scrambled to her feet. "Can I help?"

Mr. Maupin turned toward her and smiled. "Thank you, my dear. It was nice talking with you. I'll be all right now."

She watched them go, Garrett keeping a firm grip as his father took slow, labored steps toward the front porch, and her heart tightened.

———

Lanterns hanging from low tree branches cast spots of light on the revelry that continued even as the dark of night closed in. Fireflies twinkled in and out of the tremulous glow, like low golden stars fallen from the steadier stream of white stars overhead.

The elder Mr. Maupin had gone to bed, and some folks had left. But many remained. The games grew rowdier, as if to defeat the encroaching darkness, whiskey adding succor to that cause. The heat had dropped a little without the sun's fire, but nothing relieved the airless humidity that made Martha's dress cling and a cloying warmth swell inside her.

She sat on the porch steps next to Elizabeth, her brother Doc at Elizabeth's other side. A roar of laughter rose from the men playing games on the edge of the broad lawn. She glanced back toward the house, concerned about Mr. Maupin. "Will they disturb your father?"

Elizabeth shrugged. "He's used to it. He likes having parties here, likes to see people have a good time."

Martha wished she dared unbutton one or two buttons. She thought about Mr. Maupin and the tension she'd seen between him and Garrett. "Does Garrett—?" How could she ask this? "Do he and his pa get along, or—?"

Elizabeth's soft laugh eased Martha's own tension. "They've had their problems. I guess you can see it. Garrett's pretty headstrong, and Pa likes to have things his way. Men like them—they're bound to collide sometimes."

"I suppose." Martha had seen a little of that with her own brothers and her pa, but not to the extent she saw here.

Elizabeth went on. "They had a real falling out a few years ago. Garrett had one of Pa's best horses out." She glanced at Martha. "You can see Garrett's good with horses, but he was young, maybe fifteen or so. He liked to race, and he ran the horse pretty hard, I guess. Came home and didn't take care of it like Pa thought he should. Didn't hang up the bridle. Well, Pa took that bridle and whipped Garrett with it."

Martha winced. "What did Garrett do?"

47

Elizabeth blew out a soft huff. "Left home. He went down to Texas and helped fight Santa Anna after the Alamo. Stayed a few years." She grinned. "He grew a beard and when he came home he knocked on the front door. Ma came to the door and she didn't even know him. I did, though. You can't miss Garrett."

Martha watched him standing in the orb of light from a lantern where the men were tossing a ball into a ring. "How old is Garrett?"

Elizabeth paused. "Let's see. Twenty-two. He'll be twenty-three in September."

Martha did the calculation. Twenty-two. Seven years older. That wasn't too much, was it?

He pumped his hands up and shouted for joy, the sound of his pleasure rippling out to evoke a smile on Martha's face. Her smile faded when Simpson stood up, knuckles pressed to his hips, and leaned his head directly toward Garrett's. He said something to Garrett. She heard the angry tone, but couldn't make out the words. Garrett shook his head, hands spread, as if trying to smooth it over, but Simpson wheeled about and stomped off.

Their cousin William hurried after Simpson. "Wait a minute, Simpson. Wait."

Simpson stopped and stood with his back to William and all the other players, head hunkered down. William stepped around to face Simpson and they carried on a heated discussion, all too low for Martha to hear.

Doc rose slowly on the other side of Elizabeth and headed toward the pair. Hesitating only a moment, Martha sprang to her feet and followed. The conversation between Simpson and William came to an abrupt stop when Doc and Martha reached them. Doc tilted his head and spoke to his brother. "What's wrong, Simpson?"

Stabbing a finger toward the players, Simpson let out a soft snarl. "He's cheating."

"Who?"

Simpson slurred a response. "Garrett Maupin, that's who."

Martha looked up to see Garrett walking toward them, weaving a little. Clearly, he'd had too much to drink, as had Simpson. "What'd I hear you say?" Garrett asked.

Simpson turned and shook a finger at him. "You're cheating."

Garrett stood taller, his chin jutted forward, and he raised a fist. His brother James reached out and took hold of his arm, speaking softly. "Let's keep calm here. This is a friendly party. We don't need trouble."

Clenching the fist, Garrett hissed a response, his words brittle with chill on the sweltering air. "Don't you ever accuse a Maupin of cheating. We may be many things, but we're not cheaters. You'd better take it back now."

"I won't—"

Doc gripped Simpson's arm. "You must be mistaken. Like James said, this is a friendly party. Why would anybody want to cheat?"

Simpson yanked his arm away. "Nobody wins like that all the time."

"Garrett does," Perry Jr. said, edging his way into the circle.

Simpson swerved to face Perry. "How can he—if he doesn't cheat?"

The younger man shrugged. "He's just that good. Always has been. Only guy I know who wins like Garrett is our brother Howard."

"Look," William said. "Nobody's trying to hurt anybody. We've all had a good time. Lots to eat and drink. Maybe it's time to head in. We have some country to look at tomorrow."

Martha glanced at Garrett. He was looking at her, but she couldn't read his face. He spoke softly, as if only to her. "I wasn't cheating. I wouldn't."

She shook her head a little and then felt a hand on her shoulder. Doc. Her brother bent close to her. "We'd better go in, Martha. Been a long day."

❧

August 1844. Martha leaned back in the wide wooden chair on the Maupin porch, glad for a faint breeze on this hot day. Mr. Maupin sat next to her in the other reclining armchair, while Garrett and Elizabeth sat across from them in upright armless chairs. Garrett and Elizabeth had taken Martha out for a horseback ride this morning, showing her more of the Maupin farm. They'd accomplished a lot in the last week or so, cleaning up the fields where the rain had destroyed the crops, and putting in new plantings of corn. Despite Garrett's protests, the Poindexter men helped with everything, making the work go much quicker.

A few days ago Doc and Simpson had gone with William back to Carroll County to check again on the property there, but at Elizabeth's urging Martha had stayed with the Maupins. She enjoyed the time with Elizabeth—and Garrett. He seemed intent on showing himself a gentleman after the incident at the party. He and Simpson had remained cool toward each other but civil. Her brothers' current absence caused a mixed reaction in Martha. She was relieved to escape Simpson's tension, but she felt lonely in company she hadn't known long.

Garrett sat forward and smiled at Martha, the glitter in his eyes kindling a glow inside her. "Maybe if it's cooler tomorrow we could ride over to Millville, do some shopping. It's a nice ride." He turned toward Elizabeth. "What do you think?"

She hesitated. "We'd have to get away early and come home late to avoid the midday heat. I don't know."

A flicker lifted the corner of his mouth. "Well, I suppose you don't want to miss Doc in case he comes back tomorrow."

Elizabeth's face reddened, and Martha had to smile. The dogs, asleep on the porch, began to stir. One scrambled to its feet and bayed. The others joined in.

"What—what?" Mr. Maupin sat up with a start, and Martha realized he must have been sleeping.

Her brothers rode around the corner of the house, Doc waving a hand. "Hello, everybody!"

Commotion stirred about them as more dogs and family came outside. Young Perry took their horses, and the two made their way to the porch, surrounded by the dogs. The elder Perry didn't leave his chair but clutched his knees, head forward, showing interest in their news. Martha watched Doc and Elizabeth standing next to each other as if alone in the world. Then they seemed to notice they were not.

"So what did you find?" Garrett asked. "And where's William?"

"Same property as before," Doc said, accepting the chair where Garrett had been sitting, next to Elizabeth. "William went on home. He needed to check on his farm."

Garrett leaned on the porch post by Doc. "So have you decided?"

Doc nodded. "We have. We're buying the Carroll County property we showed you."

Elizabeth lifted a hand. "Oh, the place we stayed overnight on our way here from Aunt Hannah's?"

"Yes, that one."

"Oh, it's a lovely place." Elizabeth started to turn toward her father. "You'd like it, Pa. We'll have to—"

Elizabeth's face froze. Martha looked at Mr. Maupin. His eyes had a glassy sheen, jaw hanging slack. Elizabeth's voice resonated with fear. "Pa?"

Mr. Maupin slumped in the chair, and Martha leaped to her feet, lunging toward him. Before she could reach him, Garrett and Doc were on either side, holding onto the man's arms. Garrett glanced at Martha. "Get him some whiskey."

"I'll get it," Elizabeth said, darting away.

Martha ripped off her apron and dipped it into the water glass beside her chair. Wringing out the wet cloth, she dabbed it on his forehead. Elizabeth brought a glass of whiskey, and Garrett grabbed it, put it to his father's lips. The liquid dribbled down the sides of his mouth. Martha grasped the dry side of her apron and tried to fan his face.

"Let's get him to his bed." Mrs. Maupin had spoken.

Garrett and Doc each took an arm and lifted him, carrying him into the house and to a room at the back, Simpson staying close. Uncertain whether to follow or not, Martha let the others go ahead and inched her way to the door. When she could see into the room, they had him on a high bed, covered with a light sheet. Mrs. Maupin dabbed at his forehead with a wet cloth, and Elizabeth fanned him, while Garrett and Sarah and Perry Jr. hovered near.

Doc and Simpson stepped back to the doorway where Martha stood. An odd numbness settled over her. She glanced at Doc. "Should we get a doctor?"

He started to speak, but Garrett charged for the doorway, pushing past them. Martha turned to see Garrett plunge out the front door and disappear. Doc and Simpson trudged on outside, but Martha stayed, drawn by the room's tension.

Young Perry looked up and gave her a quick smile. "Garrett went for the doctor. Shouldn't be long. He doesn't live far."

When the doctor came, Garrett followed him into the house, strode into the bedroom, and back out to the large main room, where he began pacing back and forth, face rigid. Martha walked up to him and dared put a hand on his arm. He stood still a moment but didn't acknowledge her. "The doctor will know what to do," she said in a tone that begged he be comforted. He didn't answer, just began pacing again.

Mrs. Maupin called for Garrett and he spun about to rush into the bedroom. Martha went out to the porch to sit with her brothers. After what seemed a long time, the doctor came out. Martha stood, and he shook his head, eyes grave. Trying to swallow away the tightness in her throat, she sat again with her silent brothers. Simpson got up and wandered off, but Doc stayed with her. He would want to comfort Elizabeth, she knew, as much as she wanted to comfort Garrett.

A soft voice in the doorway roused her from the dreamworld she'd fallen into. "Martha?"

"Yes?"

"Pa wants to talk to you." Sarah Catherine.

Martha didn't move for a moment. Was she still dreaming? Why would Sarah's pa want to talk to Martha?

"Just you," Sarah said.

As in that dream, Martha made her way to the strange bedroom. The others slipped away, and she walked alone to the bedside of this strange man. He reached a shaking hand toward her, and she lifted her own hand to clasp it. The strength of his grasp surprised her.

"Miss Poindexter? May I call you Martha?"

"Y-yes."

The face, so bold and intimidating such a short time ago, looked gentle, a little wistful. "You're a good girl." His thin lips twitched upward on one side. "A good woman." He lay back and closed his eyes, as if the few words had worn him out. She waited, not knowing what else to do. Again his eyes fluttered open, and his gaze turned sharp, focusing not on her but somewhere deeper. He spoke again in little more than a rasping whisper.

"Garrett . . . is a good man. He just needs a little tug on the reins once in a while to guide him. Do you . . . understand?"

She nodded. "I think—yes."

Again the man shrank into the pillow. He became so still Martha grasped his wrist, seeking a pulse. She felt a faint throb, but his stillness frightened her. "I need to get the others," she said.

He didn't open his eyes, but nodded a little, and when she drew back he let her go. Hurrying to the door, she motioned for the others to return, and they quickly filled the room.

Then the strangest thing happened. The old man's appearance changed. He looked young and handsome, like the son beside him. A soft gasp circled the group. The man's head lobbed to one side. Sarah gripped his wrist and cried out, her wail echoing against the walls. Mrs. Maupin stiffened. A deep shudder, visible to any watcher, rolled through her, and Garrett clasped her under the arms to stop her from falling, gently helping her to a chair.

Martha escaped outside, struggling to draw a good breath, but found the air as stifling out there. Doc started for the door just as Elizabeth came out. "Ma wants a little time with him," she said. Offering an arm, Doc led her away to walk with her, to give what comfort he could. Martha wanted to do the same for Garrett, and when he came out the door she went to him, reached for his arm.

He shook his head and walked on, not welcoming her to follow. She felt a wall between them, thicker than the log walls of this house. He turned toward the back where the barns were, and soon Martha heard a galloping horse retreating into the distance. The dogs began to bay, loud, soulful cries. Martha stood on the strange porch in this strange land, alone. She had never in her life felt such intense loneliness. Tears rose.

Oh, Mama, I wish I was home.

Chapter 4

Love against the Odds

Carroll County, Missouri, Early Spring 1845

A bright warmth touched Martha's shoulders as she took a treasured moment to wander through the trees below their little cabin in Carroll County. The swelling buds would soon make leaves, but for now the skeletal shadows did little to block the sun's gentle rays. Birds thrilled to the eruption of life, calling out to each other in their sweetest spring songs.

She loved this spot, so much like the hollow below their house in Illinois. Maybe that was what gave her comfort here. She did like Missouri, though there were times she wondered at her wisdom in coming. She'd wanted adventure and freedom, but found the work came with her. She had to cook for two men and herself and keep everyone in clothes and the cabin clean with no help at all—except for the dreaded job of clothes washing, a woman's chore many men refused to do. The boys helped her with that.

She'd never actually seen her pa help with washing, but he made the boys help Ma, so they knew the routine—building up the outdoor fire, carrying water to fill the washtubs and setting one over the fire to boil, shaving the cake of lye soap into the boiling water, sorting clothes, pounding the dirty spots, stirring the white clothes in the boiling water and pulling them out with a broom handle, careful not to get scalded, wringing, rinsing, hanging everything up to dry. A terrible job.

She also milked the cow and tended the chickens William gave them. They had eggs, milk, butter, and cheese. She did enjoy making her own decisions. If she wanted to take a walk in the morning before starting dinner, she could do that. Still, the winter had felt long, the dark cabin walls closing in. Their oiled deerskin window let in light, but never enough.

She'd longed for light and joy in those dark days—and something else she couldn't quite take hold of. Doc tried to make her laugh, but he spent a lot of time mooning around himself. Simpson grew surly and snappish.

Then snow melted and trees budded. More travelers passed by. Martha's heart fluttered at each approach, and sank when she saw only strangers. Would she ever see Garrett again?

He'd said little to her after his father died. The wall surrounding him the day of his father's death never dropped. She and her brothers stayed for the burial, and left soon after. The boys wanted to get their land deal settled so they could get the cabin raised and put in a wheat crop before winter. They enjoyed a warm, sunny fall on their new land and got everything set up for the winter months—cabin walls chinked, a tidy fireplace built, a shed. Martha had thought Garrett might visit during those pleasant days, but he didn't.

Heaving a sigh, she grabbed a low branch and whispered her thoughts. "I'll probably never see him again, unless Doc asks Elizabeth to marry him and both of us go to the wedding. Everything turned so sad when his pa died. I thought he cared for me, but maybe not."

She often pondered what Garrett's father told her before he died. Had Garrett spoken to his father about her? Or was the old man just seeing something he wanted to see?

Martha had received a letter from home, the folks anxious for her return. She shook her head. "I don't want to go home, but I suppose I'd just as well."

Whether sound or motion alerted her, she didn't know, but when she squinted toward the west she saw riders. Two of them. Her heart pounded in a crazy rhythm, the pulse in her temple echoing the beat. A man and a woman. Her gaze riveted on the man—the way he moved with the horse, the steady rocking, the grace. Who else sat a horse like that?

She wanted to run out of the hollow to meet them. She imagined lifting her skirts and running up the gentle slope, fast as a rabbit, but she never let go of the branch.

They headed for the cabin, but he turned his head, a slight glance, and swung his horse around. He nudged the animal to move faster, riding straight toward Martha. She didn't move, though she suspected he would see the hammering of her heart.

Slowing his horse to make the downhill grade, he rode within a pace or two of where she stood, and there he stopped, leaning on the saddle horn to smile down at her. That familiar spark lit his clear blue eyes, and his low voice rolled off his tongue like honey. "Miss Poindexter."

She managed a smile, or thought she did. "Mr. Maupin."

"You're looking mighty fine."

This time she knew she was smiling. "I am fine, thank you."

She became aware then of Elizabeth on the horse behind him. "Martha! How are you?"

At her friend's casual greeting, Martha let go of the branch and went to Elizabeth's side to clasp her outstretched hand. "I'm well, Elizabeth. How are you?"

Elizabeth's face beamed. "I'm well. Oh, it's so good to see you. It's been such a long winter." She glanced back toward the house.

"The boys are working the field behind the cabin," Martha said. "Come on up to the house and I'll call them in. I know they'll be glad to see you."

Elizabeth reached toward her brother. "Let's get down and walk with Martha."

With a nod, he swung out of the saddle, landing lightly on his feet, and helped Elizabeth dismount. They chattered about nothing in particular on their way to the house, Elizabeth doing most of the talking.

Doc must have heard them, because he came out from behind the house drying his hands on a rag as they reached the front door. "Well," he said, a broad grin on his bearded face, "I was thinking of riding over to Ray County to visit you folks, and here you are visiting us. Must have been that bird I was talking to—he went over and put a message in your ear, did he?"

They all laughed as Doc strode right to Elizabeth, taking both her hands. Martha couldn't quite hear what they said to each other, but the gazes between them sent a glow out warm enough for all to feel.

Garrett gripped his broad-brimmed hat over his chest, glanced at Martha, and back at Doc and Elizabeth with their gazes lingering on each other as they stood beside her mare. He took a couple of steps one way, turned, looked behind him. "Simpson home?"

Doc smiled at something Elizabeth said, then faced Garrett. "He's still working in the field back there."

Garrett's jaw tightened, and a visible pulse showed on his temple. What was wrong with him? When he spoke again, his voice went raspy. "I—I'd like to talk to you, Doc—alone, if I could."

Doc had a hand on Elizabeth's fingers, neatly tucked into his arm. He gave her a long look, and nodded at Garrett. "Sure. I have some things I want to talk to you about too. Will you ladies excuse us?"

Martha would have laughed at her brother calling her a lady, if she felt like laughing. What was all this seriousness? She raised her brows at Elizabeth and received a like gesture. Shrugging, Martha reached out a hand. "Come see the cabin, Elizabeth." She drew her friend inside and pointed out the features of their humble abode. "It's small yet, but Doc has plans to make it bigger. It's all they could do for the first winter."

Elizabeth spread her arms, as if to embrace the place. "Oh, it's wonderful! You've done so much already. Curtains. Quilts."

"I brought the quilts from home. But I'm working on a new one." Martha put her hands on her hips. "What are the boys so serious about?"

Elizabeth looked down. "I couldn't say. I think—"

A loud voice from outside pierced the quietness of Elizabeth's remark. "You don't have that right!" Simpson.

Doc's answer was only partially audible. "I took . . . responsibility . . . came out . . . Missouri . . ."

Martha and Elizabeth stared at each other, eyes wide.

Simpson shouted again. "Pa wouldn't agree!"

The two young women stood in the cabin silent as stones as they listened for more, but while they could still hear voices outside, the words became only a low murmur. Then a horse's hoofbeats sounded, and Martha rushed to the door to see Simpson riding away toward the other forty-acre parcel. What had upset Simpson so much?

Before Martha could ask Elizabeth her thoughts, Garrett and Doc came around the front of the house. Seeing her at the door, Garrett smiled, the old warmth lighting his face again. "Miss Maupin." He extended a hand toward her. "Would you do me the honor of walking with me? I believe you were enjoying a walk when Elizabeth and I came and interrupted you. Could I join you on the rest of your walk?"

She took his hand. His long fingers closed over hers, and he brought her hand around and tucked it into place at his right elbow. They walked slowly across the grassy field toward the wooded hollow. The sun had dipped low on the horizon, offering little warmth, but Martha felt no chill. Garrett emanated warmth, and she dared press a little closer.

She wanted to ask so many questions, but struggled to think of a one, besides the near one that troubled her. "How—how is your mother doing?" she said finally.

"She's doin' all right. We've been busy with Pa's estate. I meant to come see you sooner."

"That must be lots of work—on top of the farm and all."

He tilted his head, nodding. "It is. I have to be administrator of the estate along with Ma. It was too much for her by herself."

"Did your pa request that?"

"He didn't leave a will." Garrett smiled at her, a subtle frown wrinkling his forehead. "That makes it all the harder."

"I'm sure it does."

"I got another piece of land next to Pa's so I can work the family farm and have a place—well, a place of my own."

Martha glanced at him, sensing an uncertainty in his tone. "That'll be nice for you—and your mother."

They walked quietly awhile, making their way down into the wooded hollow where Martha had been when he and Elizabeth arrived. Then Martha blurted the question she'd hesitated to ask but desperately wanted to know. "What was Simpson upset about? Just now?"

Garrett stopped and faced her. A breeze whispered through the bare branches, and she studied his face for the answer she sought. His eyes warmed, though the throbbing still showed in the tightness on his temples. A tenderness softened his voice. "Your brothers had a little disagreement about who can speak for you."

"For me? What do you mean?"

Garrett glanced at the nearby tree, then focused back on Martha. "Does your brother Doc speak for you? Does he have responsibility for you since you've left your parents?"

She thought about that. "I guess—yes. He told them he'd look out for me."

"So if there were decisions to be made for you, he'd make them."

Martha tried to look away from Garrett's intent gaze, and couldn't. "Yes, I guess. Doc wouldn't ask me to do anything I didn't want to, but—"

"But he'd give permission."

Martha's heart began a slow, steady acceleration, as if she were climbing a steeper and steeper hill. She knew what this was about, didn't she? But what if it wasn't?

Garrett prompted her. "Wouldn't he? Wouldn't Doc be the one to give permission?"

"Yes. Of course."

With sudden intensity, Garrett grasped both Martha's hands. "Miss Poindexter, I'll ride all the way to Illinois to ask your pa if you want me to."

Oh, Garrett Maupin, ask me, ask me.

She wanted to say it right out loud but didn't dare. Instead, she said, "You asked Doc, didn't you? What did Doc say?"

"He said he has authority for you." A smile flickered on Garrett's face. "He said he took responsibility for you when he brought you here."

"Simpson doesn't agree, does he?"

Garrett hesitated before answering. "Not entirely."

Martha almost laughed. She'd heard the anger in Simpson's voice and knew now what it was about. "Well, Doc is older. It's his say."

The crinkles formed around the corners of Garrett's eyes, setting up those starbursts within the blue, that little quirk of his lips lifting his mustache to one side. "Then, he says I have permission to ask you to marry me, Miss Poindexter. What do *you* say?"

Hearing the words at last, she managed to look away. Blood rose in her cheeks, setting them afire. Her response was scarcely louder than the breeze. "You don't have to ride to Illinois." Gazing back into his eyes, she saw his vulnerability, as if he was afraid she wouldn't agree after all, and she answered quickly to still his suffering. "I say, yes, Mr. Maupin. I will marry you."

Her breath caught at the look on his face, a sheen in his eyes like tears. His focus, so intent, reached beyond her surface into a depth within her she scarcely knew herself. He bent close until his face shadowed and the separation between them blurred. His lips touched hers, a soft warm press of flesh to flesh. The brief, delicate contact kindled a lick of fire that flared across her cheeks and swept down through her body in a sweet rush.

When he drew away, she took a sharp breath, and his brow pinched. "I'm sorry," he said. "I—"

Not wanting him to feel sorry, she answered quickly. "It's all right."

He looked away, and back at her. "I should have asked first."

She dipped her head a little. "Didn't you ask?"

His mustache twitched with the merest suggestion of a smile, the crinkles deep around his eyes. "I mean about the kiss. May I kiss you, Miss Martha?"

"You may."

His smile deepened. "I love you, Martha Poindexter."

She could scarcely breathe. "I love you, Garrett Maupin."

He leaned forward and pressed his lips to hers again, lightly, then a bit firmer. She reached up to wrap her arms around his neck and his answering embrace nearly lifted her off her feet. She didn't know if his lips pressed harder or hers, but they kissed with all the longing they'd both felt, maybe since the day they met.

Drawing his head back, he gazed into her eyes and his cheeks puffed out, like a bubble ready to burst. With a suddenness that startled her, he raised his hands to the sky and lifted his head to shout. "She's going to marry me! Miss Martha Ann Poindexter is going to marry me." With a gleeful laugh he turned and ran up the hill to a small knoll, shouting again. "She's going to marry me. She's going to marry me."

Martha ran up the hill after him, caught up in his infectious laughter, and together they ran toward the cabin. She shouldn't have run so. It wasn't ladylike, but she ran like a joyous child. Doc and Elizabeth came out, and Doc shouted back. "Elizabeth Maupin is going to marry *me!* Our sisters are going to change names, but we'll still have just as many Maupins and just as many Poindexters. How about *that?*"

He locked his arm in Garrett's and swung him around, both stepping high. Doc turned to Martha and locked arms with her, swinging her in a circle dance, while Garrett and Elizabeth danced the same. Then Garrett came to Martha and swung her. They kept up the dance, changing partners, round and round, their only music the song of birds and their own laughter, until they stopped in the exhaustion of sheer pleasure.

Doc was the first to declare hunger, and Martha put together a supper for them. In the course of their supper conversation, Martha learned Garrett had readily assumed responsibility for his sister, now that their father wasn't alive to give permission for her to marry. "I'm administrator of his estate with Ma," he said, "and she won't question my decision." Martha hoped her own parents would be as agreeable.

Simpson didn't return home. When it came time to sleep, the girls took the loft, where Martha always slept. Doc suggested Garrett sleep in Simpson's bed downstairs, but Garrett put his blanket on the floor, thinking if Simpson came home in the night and found him in his bed it might not be a good thing.

Simpson showed up about midday after the Maupins left. "Where you been?" Doc asked when they sat down to dinner.

Snuffing and wiping at his nose, Simpson studied the plate in front of him. "Camped out at the other place."

Doc leaned toward him, one hand flat on the table between them. "It'll be all right, Simpson. You'll see."

Simpson shook his head. "You're making a big mistake getting involved with the likes of the Maupins." He put a finger on Doc's chest. "I think you've been blinded by a pretty lady's blue eyes."

Sitting back, Doc chuckled softly. "You're just jealous, brother, but you keep an eye on young Sarah Catherine. She'll be old enough pretty soon."

Ignoring his brother, Simpson turned to Martha. "Remember, I'm taking you home this summer."

The words struck. "But I can't go now."

"Yes, you can. You will."

"No. I won't."

They argued back and forth until Doc put up a hand to stop it. "Hold on." He turned to Martha. "You'd better write to the folks. They'll want to know."

She blew out a hard breath. "I will."

———

Martha sat near the deerskin window making careful stitches in the delicate pink material. Tilting her head to one side, she let out a dreamy sigh and whispered to herself, "Oh my. This will be a beautiful dress. It's going to be such a fine wedding."

Tromping feet sounded on the doorstep, and Doc burst into the room, letting spits of rain in with him. "It's a wet one out there. Hope we don't have another spring like last year." He pulled an envelope out from under his coat. "You have a letter."

Martha's hand shook when she accepted the envelope from Doc's outstretched hand. She glanced at the writing, recognizing it as her mother's. Ma? Not Pa? She looked back at her brother. He gave her a gentle smile, brow furrowed, and turned to poke at the fire.

Slipping open the flap, she pulled out the single sheet of paper and struggled to hold it still enough to read. She had written her parents, explaining her case the best she knew how, telling them what a fine man Garrett was, how he had offered to ride to Illinois to ask Pa for her hand, but Doc had spoken for her. Garrett had responsibilities now that his father had died, and it seemed unfair to take him away from that when Doc could act on Pa's behalf. After all, Doc had come to know Garrett well and believed it a fine match.

Martha steadied her hands and read Ma's response.

My dearest Martha,

I am writing this for your father, as he has been unwell of late. Nothing serious, we hope, but he asked me to do the writing. We are both saddened by your letter. Did you not think your father's consent necessary before you promised to marry this stranger? If Mr. Maupin could not ride to Illinois, could he not at least write a letter requesting

consent as would be proper? Your father is not yet prepared to give
consent. But you write as if the matter were already decided. . . .

Ma's careful script blurred. Martha crumpled the letter into a ball and flung it aside, bouncing it off the soft pink fabric of her dress. The tears blinded her so she could scarcely see her brother walking toward her. He set a hand on her shoulder and spoke in a tender voice. "She wrote me too. They didn't feel my authority went so far as to consent to your marriage."

Martha looked up at him, voice choking on her words. "But we're going to have a double wedding in May. Elizabeth is already planning it. I can't back out now." She thought of Garrett, the warmth of his smiling eyes, the gentle touch of his hand that set the fires glowing inside her. "I don't want to wait." Her tone became almost accusatory as she fixed her gaze more directly on her brother. "Would you?"

He shook his head, frowning and smiling at once. "No. I can't imagine waiting longer than the month I have to."

Martha stood with resolution and marched to the small chest where they kept a little writing paper. "I'll write them again. I have to make them understand."

"Good. I'll add a note myself—if you think that'll help."

She flashed a smile at him, though tears still wetted her lashes. "Thank you. I know you can say it right, Doc. They'll see, won't they? Maybe they'll even come to the wedding. It wouldn't take long at all by steamboat."

Martha hummed softly as she swept out the corners of the cabin, trying to find solace in knowing she had less than two weeks to wait for the wedding. She wished she could be more involved in the wedding plans. Still, she and Elizabeth had talked everything over during their visit last week. Garrett and his brother Perry would be cutting logs by now for Garrett and Martha's cabin, and he'd promised to buy glass for their windows and for this cabin too, where Elizabeth would come to live with Doc.

Smiling, she chattered to herself. "How nice. Windows for Mrs. Garrett Maupin. Martha Ann Maupin. Doesn't that have a nice ring?"

She touched her fingers to her lips, recalling the pleasure of his kisses. Soon she would enjoy his kisses every day. She lifted the broom, hugged it close, and danced around the room.

"Martha?" Simpson calling her.

She hurried outside to see him getting down from his horse. He pulled an envelope from the inside of his shirt and handed it to her. Martha's stomach twisted. Ma's letter she'd been waiting for. Would they come to the wedding? Would they meet Garrett and learn to love him as she did?

Realizing Simpson was watching for her reaction, she tucked the letter inside the belt of her apron and went inside the cabin. She pulled out a plate of biscuits and set them on the table for dinner, then started for the bacon, ready to slice it. Only when she heard the boys talking in the shed did she dare pull out the envelope and open the wax-sealed flap.

She wiped her hand on her apron before slipping out the leaf of paper inside. Unfolding it, she read:

My dearest Martha,
You must come home. We are not hearing good things about the Mau-
pins. Simpson plans to come home right after the harvest, and we'll
expect you then. . . . .

"Simpson!"

Martha felt as if she'd been running across the grass and tripped on an unseen stone and the ground had come up to hit her in the face.

She stuffed the paper back in her apron belt and stormed out of the cabin, straight for the shed. A fury of heat surged through her, turning her cheeks afire. Inside, she stopped until her eyes adjusted to the dim light in the small building. The boys stood opposite the door, Doc bent over a slab of wood, rubbing it with a dark rag, Simpson leaning against the shed wall, hands on his hips.

Both looked up, eyes widening on sight of her.

She shrieked. "Thomas Simpson Poindexter! What lies have you been telling Ma and Pa about the Maupins?"

He scrunched his shoulders, tone laced with innocence. "Lies?"

"Ma says they're hearing bad things about the Maupins. What did you tell them?"

Snuffing air up his nose, he looked away from her. "I'm not the only one."

She reared her head back. *Not the only one?* "Who else?"

He jutted his chin toward her. "William agrees with me."

"William? Our cousin William Poindexter?" Her heart lurched. She couldn't believe it. "What did he say to you? Did he write to them too?"

"I could see by how he talked. Maybe he wrote. I don't know."

Her brother seemed to shrink smaller as she marched toward him, her step slow and steady, calm now as a frozen stream. "You'd better stay out of this, Simpson Poindexter, and you'd better tell your—tell Mr. William to stay out of it too, because on May sixteenth—this month—I'm going to marry Garrett Maupin and there's nothing any of you can do to stop me."

—◆—

May 16, 1845. A glorious May sun smiled on the well-wishers gathered on the broad lawn below the Maupin front porch. The heady scent of flowers rose from bouquets scattered across the porch where the brides and grooms stood. Gripping Garrett's arm, Martha could see past the minister, past the silent crowd, out to the fields that went on forever until they dissolved in the infinite blue of the sky. To this side of that infinite depth the golden gleam of new-hewn logs peeked out from a soft screen of trees. Their cabin. Garrett's and hers. Home.

She glanced at him, looking so fine in his trim dark suit, straw-gold hair glistening. The suit made him look tall and sleek. Her own pink floral dress had come out beautifully. She'd put rows of tucks in the bodice with bits of lace at the neck and cuffs, and the pearl buttons down the front that Doc bought for her in Carrollton. A headpiece of net and lace covered the rolls of dark hair piled on top of her head. She'd never felt more elegant.

She tried to listen to the words the minister was saying, but the moment outshone them. The words didn't matter. She knew their meaning. She felt it to her core. "And two shall become one. . . . What God has joined together let no man put asunder." Her hand in Garrett's arm. One body. Two souls merged into one.

Beside them Doc and Elizabeth stood taking the same vows, Elizabeth looking lovely in her blue dress, Doc rather fine in his suit too.

"Do you take this man . . . ?"

"I do."

" . . . this woman . . . ?"

Garrett's honeyed voice. "I do."

James stood next to Garrett, and on the other side by Doc, Simpson. She'd thought he wouldn't come. Out among the guests she saw William and Eliza. Whatever his thoughts or actions, he had come too. Her heart warmed to see them. Then all she saw was Garrett, smiling as he looked down at her, stars dancing in the blue of his eyes as never before, and the minister spoke the words that made them man and wife. She and Garrett kissed.

We two in a sphere alone.

Cheers rose from the crowd, forcing her attention to move out from that small sphere to a wider one that took in them all. She and Garrett turned to the other bride and groom to wish them well. Then James reached out to take Martha's hand. "Welcome to the family," he said, kissing her cheek. Brother Perry leaped onto the porch to welcome her as well, leaning toward her as if about to kiss her, but he didn't.

William came forward and gave her a long look. She searched his eyes for some answer to the doubts between them, but he didn't speak of it—not that she thought he would. "I'm glad you came," she said.

He nodded and smiled, his voice tender. "I'm glad too. I wish you well, Martha."

Her throat tightened, so she didn't know if she could speak, but she managed a whispered thank you.

Garrett broke the tension when he reached for her hand. "Come meet my brother Howard."

She would have recognized him without any introduction. The sons of Perry Maupin clearly carried the old man's mark—though each had a distinctive character. Martha realized she saw them not so much according to their likeness to their father, but their likeness to Garrett. Perry

Jr., the younger Garrett, clean-cheeked, boyish, carefree. James, the calm, dignified Garrett, carrying himself with the gentle self-assurance of an elder.

But Howard! She studied the man as Garrett drew her toward him. A dark-haired version, Howard was a thicker Garrett, gruffer—not fat, but solid, like a block of salt, hard and crusty at the edges. She wasn't sure if he deliberately wore a beard or hadn't shaved recently. While Garrett moved with the fluid grace of a cat, Howard put her more in mind of a lumbering bear. But wasn't he the only one who could compete with Garrett in the games of skill?

The family, circling around him, clearly adored him. He was telling them a story in his gravelly voice, stopping long enough to spit at his feet and pull out a wad of tobacco to bite off another piece.

He'd gone west to Platte County, Missouri, in 1840 to get married, Garrett had said, and the family obviously missed him.

When he saw Garrett approaching, he stopped his story and headed straight for his brother. "Congratulations, Garrett, m'boy, congratulations!" After a hearty handshake he turned and focused his full attention on Martha. He had the twinkling blue eyes too, but paler, more intrusive. He seemed to be assessing her, as if to judge her worth. She tried to stand tall, though tall wasn't in her makeup.

He nodded. "Little but mighty, I'd say. Am I right, brother?"

Garrett laughed. "You'd be right."

Elizabeth interrupted the greeting. "You need to sign some papers, Garrett."

"We'll talk to you later," Garrett told Howard, and as they started after Elizabeth, Martha heard Howard picking up his story where he'd left off.

On the porch, Garrett turned to Martha. "I'll just be a minute."

Nodding, she waited by the door, where she could see a man inside sitting at the table, a piece of paper in front of him. When Garrett and Elizabeth entered, he stood quickly. "If you'd sign your name right there, Mr. Maupin," the man said, pointing. "Sorry to bother you at a time like this, but I knew you'd be here." He laughed, with a friendly slap on Garrett's arm. "You said you wanted those right away."

Garrett picked up the paper and handed it to Elizabeth. "Would you read it?"

She read the short statement aloud. It sounded like a note for money. When she gave it back to him he set it on the table, leaned over, and marked an X at the bottom.

Martha's mouth dropped open. She spun around to face the long view in front of the house, not wanting him to catch her staring in shock. He couldn't write his name. Or read.

It had never occurred to her. The situation never came up. Every Poindexter she knew could read and write. Everyone in her family learned to read and write as young children. She knew some folks couldn't. But people who lived comfortably like the Maupins? Elizabeth could read. Why Elizabeth and not Garrett?

A prickly warmth nettled Martha's skin.

She could hear Garrett chatting with the man inside. Windows. They were talking about the windows. Garrett must not have cash to pay for them, but Martha and Elizabeth would have glass windows as he promised. Martha hoped he'd soon have the means to pay off this note. She moved away from the door, still trying to absorb what she'd witnessed. She didn't notice Simpson at first, coming up the stairs. "Martha?"

"Oh! Simpson."

He looked at the floor between them, then up, his gaze almost reaching her eyes. "I—uh—I wish you well."

She put a hand on his arm and tried to express her love with the tone of her voice. "Thank you, Simpson. And thank you for coming. It means a lot to me."

He shrugged. "I wanted to let you know I'm going back to Illinois."

She nodded.

"To stay," he said. "Doc doesn't need me now he has Elizabeth. It's time for me to move on."

"Please don't go on account of—"

"No, I've been thinking about this for a while."

Martha's eyes burned, and she didn't want to cry. She blinked a few times. "I will be fine—really. Garrett—he's a good man. I know you guys had a little tiff at Elizabeth's party, but it doesn't amount to anything. Too much whiskey. A little misunderstanding."

He studied the planks on the porch again.

"And I know you disagreed with Doc," she said, "but—"

"He did what he thought was right, I guess."

"Simpson!" Garrett's voice behind her. "Glad you could make it."

She felt Garrett's warm hand at her back as he reached out to Simpson. Her brother kept a neutral expression, but he did accept Garrett's outstretched hand.

"No hard feelings?" Garrett asked.

Simpson answered in a gruff voice. "I'm here, aren't I?"

Fiddle music rose above the surrounding chatter, and Garrett wrapped one arm around Martha's back to hold her close. "There'll be dancing and food. Will you stay, Simpson?"

"Maybe a while."

Garrett smiled at him, then Martha. "I'll take good care of her. I promise."

Chapter 5

Home and War

Ray County, Missouri, June 28, 1846

Stirring the cottage cheese, Martha felt an uncommon fatigue and stopped, one hand on the wooden spoon, the other on her protruding belly. Her hand bounced with a jolt from inside, and she laughed. "You're an active one, aren't you? Like your pa."

She heard a sound outside. Dogs barking? She could see out the open doorway to the dimming sky. The scent of roses wafted in from the pink rosebush Garrett had planted by the cabin door as a wedding present. Her shoulders tightened. He'd been gone all day, since early morning, and she felt his absence like a big empty hollow around her heart. He had to ride all the way into Richmond—some business on the estate—a long journey. He'd assured her he would be home by night, though. The June days were long and his big, rangy horse Jake could cover the miles fast.

Again the sound. Yes, dogs. The hounds at the big house.

She tightened her grip on the spoon. "Oh, Garrett, please hurry home."

She did love him with all her heart and soul, but she often felt alone here, since she and Elizabeth had switched places—Elizabeth all the way over in Carroll County with Martha's favorite brother, and Martha in Ray County on the Maupin place.

Her one joy in her new home was Garrett, and he did give her joy such as she'd never dreamed. The laughter, the talk, the evenings he'd sit by the fire and tell stories of his early days in Missouri in his slow, honeyed drawl. She glanced at their bed, covered in her wedding quilt, and felt a burning in her cheeks. The marriage bed in this little cabin was a happy place too. She'd had no idea there was anything so precious between a husband and wife.

Still, he was busy, trying to work his pa's big farm and his own small one at the same time. Perry helped, but Garrett carried the responsibility, and he had all that estate business to attend to.

Another sound. The gentle rocking rhythm of a loping horse, growing louder, closer. Her heart beat in time. She wanted to run out the door, race to him, pull him into her arms. But of course she couldn't do that in her condition, and he wouldn't like it anyway. "Somebody might see," he'd said the first time she went out and jumped into his arms to welcome him home.

Now she waited through all the familiar sounds—the creaking of the saddle, the jangling of the bridle, the slap of leather as he unsaddled Jake, the footsteps approaching the door. He wouldn't make her wait until he cared for Jake before he came in to say hello.

He appeared in the open doorway, and she sprang forward. When had he looked so good? His face glowed with greeting, stars glittering in his eyes. Two long strides and he swept her into his embrace, kissing her cheek, her temple, her eyelids, and homing in on her mouth. She thought she might never let go of him, never release the sweet touch of his lips, but she had to breathe.

He leaned back and smiled down at her. "Martha." Reaching out to arm's length, he laid a hand on her belly. "And company."

She laughed and pressed into him again.

He nuzzled her ear. "I thought you were a small woman. What happened?"

She smiled her unspoken answer. "Are you hungry?"

"I ate a big dinner about two o'clock and brought bread to eat on the way." A twitch of his mustache. "Not as good as yours, but it killed my hunger. I'd better go put Jake up before I tell you the news."

"News?"

He left, leaving a gigantic hole in the room, and she scurried around to put food on the table anyway in case he might want a little something. Some jerky, her own bread. When he returned he lingered by the door, his gaze wandering around the room.

"There's food," she said, "if—"

He waved a dismissing hand. "No. Not now." He glanced at her. "You remember us talking about the war." It wasn't a question.

"In Mexico. Yes. A terrible business. I hope—"

"I'm going."

Her thought disappeared like a puff of smoke. *What did he say?*

His words spilled out as if he'd been holding them in and had just unlatched the door to them. "Howard was in Richmond today, and you know Perry went with me, and—well, they're putting together a company from Richmond. We'll be the First Mounted Missouri Volunteers under Colonel Price—a fine officer. I'll be proud to serve under him, and Captain Henley. All three of us enlisted—Howard and Perry and me. We'll be mustering in . . ."

Her body froze as she stood staring at him, trying to take in the barrage of words and the charged meaning within them. But as the words came together into some semblance of order and turned into phrases, and phrases into sentences, the words started to evoke meaning. A growing horror welled inside her and exploded the ice immobilizing her. "You did *what?*"

He stared at her, brows raised, as if surprised by the interruption to his announcement and the lack of enthusiasm for it. Holding his hands out, palms together, he leaned toward her, his tone filled with earnest tenderness. "I know it'll be a tough time, but you have Ma next door and Sarah Catherine. I'm an able-bodied man, Martha. I have a responsibility to my country. For this company they need men who can live off the land. They need crack shots, and you know there's none better, if I say so myself."

She shook her head. She was dreaming, a nightmare. "What about your responsibility to *me?*" She spread her fingers over her belly. "And our child?"

He stepped forward and gently squeezed her arm, sweetness in his gaze. "If we don't look after the country—Martha, you'll be fine. You're strong. Ma will help you."

An image of his mother flashed through Martha's mind. So shadowed by her bright, sunny daughters and boisterous sons, Mrs. Maupin seemed more like a wraith than a person of substance you could actually put your hand on.

Tears rose and slid down Martha's throat, so she had no way to stop them, and they choked her voice when she answered. "I'm going to have a baby—in September—three months from now. Will you be back by September?"

He shook his head a little and took a sharp breath. "I don't muster in until the first of August. I couldn't be back by then. And I've signed up for—"

She tried to stop the sob, but it had to come out. She was going to have a baby in September and she'd never had a baby. She'd never even been at a birthing. She was frightened enough before, though she couldn't tell anyone that.

"Elizabeth and Doc aren't far," he said.

She snapped back. "They're a day's ride away."

"A short day, but—Sarah Catherine can check on you every day."

Her chin quavered as she looked up at him, incredulous. "What if I go into labor in the night? Or some other time she's not here? And what does Sarah Catherine know about babies anyway? Or Elizabeth either, for that matter?"

"Ma knows."

Ma again. Martha wanted her own ma. She looked into his shirt, her whole body shaking now with sobs. "I want to go home."

"Home?"

"To Illinois. I want to go home now."

"Martha?" An odd tone edged his voice, and she looked into his eyes. What did she see in them? Fear? In Garrett Maupin? "But, Martha, *this* is your home."

She shook her head. "I've never had a baby."

"We have midwives here. Martha, honey, women have babies all the time. We can arrange—"

"I want to go home. I need to."

"But you're my wife."

Her voice rose. "And you're going off to war, leaving me alone."

He tried to draw her into his arms, but she stiffened her shoulders, and he stood there stroking them gently. "I love you, Martha. You know that. But the war's important. I thought you'd understand that."

The more Martha thought about it, the more her need compelled her. She wanted to go home anyway, talk to the folks, smooth things over. And if she couldn't smooth things? She didn't want to think about that, but if Ma and Pa wouldn't have her, surely Louisa would. How good it would be to see Louisa. Tears began to flow down her cheeks.

A tender sadness clouded Garrett's expression, and his voice rasped. "I'll do whatever you need, Martha. If you need to go to Illinois, I'll take you." He reached up and gently wiped her tears with his fingertips.

A tug of love clutched her heart, that same tug that drew her to him in the first place, which had blossomed so rich. He always tried to be strong and certain, but he seemed uncertain now. As she stepped back from her own dilemma, a new horror struck. What if he didn't come back? War wasn't one of his games. Men got killed in wars. She gripped him, desperate to hold him safely to her. "Oh, Garrett, you will be careful. Won't you?"

He let out a soft huff. "They won't hurt me, darlin'. You can bet on that." He slipped out of her grasp and started to pace, hand on his chin. "You can't be riding now. And there's no need for a wagon. No time either. We'll have to take a boat."

"A steamboat? Can we afford that?"

"We can go as deck passengers. We can manage, and the trip won't take long. Boats run up and down that river in a matter of a few days. Water's a little low now, but it shouldn't be a problem." He turned to smile at her. "I'll check on it first thing tomorrow."

❦

Martha tucked another dress into the leather satchel Garrett had bought at Isaiah Mansur's store. Emotions tugged at her—the excitement of the trip, the hopes and fears about seeing her parents again, the dread of parting with Garrett. A year! He'd enlisted for a full year. She couldn't fathom being apart from him so long.

Picking up her one treasured book she'd brought from home, she started to pack it, then stopped and held it close to her breast. The cover was warped, the pages discolored from getting wet on their journey west, but she could still read the stories. Sometimes when Garrett was tired she read to him. It had become their custom whenever he needed to know what was on a written page, he'd hand it to her and she'd read aloud.

She recalled the evening she offered to teach him to read, and his blunt "No."

"I can," she said. "I know how. My grandpa was a teacher and I know how he taught me."

Garrett looked at her, jaw tight. "I don't need to read words, Martha." His voice softened but resonated with feeling, his eyes taking on a sheen in the light of the fire. "I know how to read. I can read the sky that tells me what the weather will do tomorrow. I can read a track in the woods that tells me what critter walked that way, or if he ran, and how long ago. I can read a man's eyes to know if he's telling me the truth. I know how to read the things that matter."

Touched by his response, Martha answered with the tenderness she felt for him. "You can learn words too."

He shrugged and looked away. "And if I do? What if I lose the other kind of reading? What if that gets lost in a jumble of words?" He turned back to her. "Some of my brothers and sisters can read—a little. Not Pa, or Ma. But I'd stand up to any of those word readers when it comes to knowing what will help me and my family survive. Have I ever failed to keep meat on our table, Martha Maupin?"

She shook her head, and he went on. "The Maupins are from good stock. Come from way over in France somewhere. But out on the frontier we took up new ways. That's the difference between living and dying out here."

The sound of a familiar bright voice brought Martha out of the memory, and she set the book down to rush outside as quickly as her ungainly figure allowed. "Elizabeth! Doc!" Garrett quickly joined them from the shed out back, and they shared hugs all around.

Garrett had something he wanted to show Doc in the shed, so the girls walked arm in arm into the house and sat beside each other on the bed where Martha was packing her things. "It's so good to see you," Elizabeth said. "You look wonderful."

Martha whisked a hand on her skirt. "There's more of me, for sure."

"Perry rode over to tell us you were leaving."

"Nice of him to do that."

"He's a good boy, Perry. I hope . . ." Elizabeth looked away, letting the thought go. Perry was going to war, like his two older brothers, and the family wouldn't rest until they were all safely home.

"How's your mother taking it?" Martha asked.

"You haven't talked to her?"

"Not really."

Elizabeth shrugged. "Ma's a little quiet. Probably from years of living with my pa."

Martha could understand how that might be, but she didn't answer.

Gazing out the front door, Elizabeth went on in a soft voice, as if talking to herself. "Pa was a hard man sometimes. I loved him dear, but I know he could be hard." She turned back to Martha. "I never saw him raise a hand against Ma, but he had a terrible temper, and he sure did beat the boys now and again." She smiled. "Us girls always got around him by sweetness, I guess."

"He was fond of you. That was clear."

Elizabeth nodded. "I'm sure he loved Ma too, but she kind of kept her place. Maybe she was afraid of him—I don't know—on account of—" Elizabeth put both hands to her mouth and gave her head a quick shake, but her sudden tension reached out to Martha.

"On account of what?"

"Oh, nothing."

"Elizabeth?"

Puckering her brow, Elizabeth glanced at Martha. "I guess you may as well know. You're part of the family now."

Martha waited a moment, then asked, "Know what?"

Elizabeth spread her hands in her lap. "It happened a long time ago. I guess it's just the way things were in the old days. People got into arguments and sometimes there were guns. I only heard the story. It happened before I was born." She paused for a long breath before going on. "When my Grandpa Maupin died, Pa was administrator of his estate, and I guess Pa's brother didn't like how he was going about it. They got in a gunfight over it and Pa shot him and killed him—John Jr., his younger brother."

Martha stared at her friend and slowly closed her mouth when she realized it had dropped open. A strange burning stirred in her stomach.

Elizabeth's low voice turned hoarse. "I guess Pa stayed around to take care of his ma until she died a couple years later, and then he cleared out of Kentucky and brought us all to Missouri." She leaned forward and looked out the open doorway. "John was married to Ma's sister, so she was widowed at a young age, had a bunch of little ones. Sad."

Memory flooded Martha. The senior Perry Maupin talking as in a dream, or memory, on a warm summer day. *We don't need any more shootings. . . . He gave me no choice. . . . What else could I do?*

Heart thudding, Martha reached out to lay a hand on Elizabeth's. "I don't think your pa meant to do it. I think he carried the regret of it to the end of his days."

Elizabeth raised her brows at Martha. "Why do you say that?"

"Something he said."

"He told you about it?"

"No. Not exactly."

The men burst into the room, stopping the conversation. Martha's gaze locked with Garrett's. What more did this man hold in his heart that she didn't know about? She was torn by love and shock and fear and longing. And she desperately wanted to go home.

———

Martha lifted her face to catch a faint breeze as she stood next to Garrett, gripping the rail of the huge steamboat churning its way down the Missouri River. Only the boat's motion created the meager drifts of wind on this sultry July evening. A different river from when she crossed it on their way west. Then so urgent. Now lazy and carefree, the late sun casting gentle pinks to reflect on the dark water.

With a soft sigh she looked up at Garrett. "Isn't it beautiful?"

He glanced her way, nodding brusquely. Being accustomed to his gaze so direct it linked somewhere deeper than her eyes, she found it unsettling that he wouldn't quite look at her. What was wrong with him? Was he angry with her for this trip? A pulse throbbed in the taut skin at his temples, and wanting to soothe him, she reached up, ready to rub her fingertips over that tightness.

He drew back before she could touch him and scowled at her, speaking under his breath. "Not here."

Pulling the errant hand back to herself, she turned and clutched the rail again with both hands. Would it be so terrible if someone saw she liked her own husband? He *was* put out with her. Did he even love her anymore? The heat swelled inside her. She wanted to remove her cloak. She'd made the flowing garment of the thinnest fabric she could find to cover her growing figure. But wasn't her dress sufficient with its high waist and yards of gathered skirts?

She wished they had a cabin so she could retreat into the privacy there and take off the cloak. The dress too. But cabins cost twice as much as deck passage, and prices were high either way during this season when the water was low. She bit her lips together. If she'd come by herself she could have had a cabin for the price of two deck passengers. Then she wouldn't be enduring this behavior of his either.

Oh, Garrett. Asking me not to show my feelings is like asking me not to breathe. And I have always *breathed.*

"Getting late," he said, backing away from the rail and picking up the bedroll and satchel at his feet. The sun had dropped below the horizon. Maybe the night would bring a little breath of coolness.

They headed toward the washroom. Deck passage didn't offer many amenities, but there was a public washroom. Deck passengers provided their own food and bedding, which meant sleeping right on the deck. Some folks brought cooking braziers for hot meals, but Martha had packed plenty of biscuits and jerky and dried fruit.

Garrett knocked on the washroom door, and a young man of maybe twelve or thirteen came out, a bucket in hand. He smiled wide at Martha. "Excuse me, ma'am. I just filled the water pitcher for you. Nice fresh water, right out of the river." He pointed inside to the washbasin. "There's a toothbrush you can use, hairbrush, comb. All the comforts of home, ma'am."

She thanked him and slipped into the tiny cubicle, while Garrett waited outside to guard the door. The toilet hole was like the ones back home, except it smelled better. Peering into the hole, she saw the water rushing beneath, the hole open to the river below. Glancing back at the freshly filled water pitcher, she pursed her lips and pulled the small drawstring bag from under her cloak. She'd brought their own toothbrush and comb.

Glad to escape the enclosure, she waited while Garrett went inside. "Stay by the door," he said, "and call out if you need me."

She agreed, wondering. What was he afraid of? Did he sense danger? Was he reading something she couldn't?

Back on the open deck, he found a place away from others and rolled out their blankets. Martha started to kneel on one side when a man threw a blanket down beside theirs, pushing their blanket aside a little to make room in the cramped space. Garrett charged forward, putting his face close to the man's, a hand on the pistol at his belt. "What do you think you're doing?"

Martha wanted to tell Garrett it was no problem, but the snarl in his voice didn't invite comment.

The stranger gathered up his blanket, eyes wide. "I'll just go on the other side of the boat."

"You do that."

Martha put a hand over her pounding heart. She didn't want to move, lest she somehow rile Garrett further. He stood, hovering, as he watched the departing stranger. Then he turned to Martha. "You better sleep against the wall. I'll sleep on the outside and make sure nobody bothers you."

Nodding, she lowered herself onto the pile of blankets—they'd brought two—and stretched out alongside a wall where cabins or other interior rooms rose in the midst of the great boat. Garrett quickly tucked his soft jeans jacket under her head, and made a pillow for himself out of the leather satchel, slipping the pistol under that.

Two blankets did little to soften the polished planks of the deck. Martha had slept on a bedroll on the floor before, but she didn't remember a floor ever being this hard. Maybe it was her extra weight. Fortunately, they didn't need a cover on this warm night. They needed both blankets to cushion the planks. She couldn't get comfortable but tried not to show it. She shifted, one way and another. The boat's whistle let out a long, mournful cry. The pungent smell of smoke gripped her nose. The baby galloped inside. A murmur of voices rose and fell. A man shouted. And laughed. The taste of jerky came up in her mouth, an unpleasant echo of their cold supper. How would she ever sleep?

Along one side she felt Garrett's body lightly touching hers. He might not want to show affection in public, but he kept in contact, as if he must know she was safe and he would wake in an instant if any harm were about to come to her. She felt buffeted by feelings of annoyance and appreciation, fear and longing. She tried to shift her position to avoid the press of the hard deck against her hip and cried out softly when the unyielding force met her other hip.

Clamping her mouth shut, she held herself still, not wanting him to know her struggle. Then she felt the gentle touch of his fingertips stroking her arm, and tears burned her eyes. Gradually, her tight muscles relaxed and she began to melt into the blankets, the hard floor only a little less rigid as her own frame stopped fighting it. She floated on the fatigue, drifting.

She marveled at those slender hands of his, so strong he could lift a log to the rooftop, or control a frightened horse, or bend a length of iron to his will, but then touch her with the same tenderness as one of those flowers he brought her last summer, when he brushed his fingertips so delicately across each petal, down to the center where he caressed the soft pollen, until the nectar rose and spilled out with indescribable sweetness. A sigh escaped her lips, and she closed them tight again, lest anyone hear, while silent tears rolled across her temples into her hair.

———

Helping Garrett collect their things, she tucked what was left of their dinner into the satchel.

"The Captain says we won't need to go into St. Louis," Garrett told her. "We can rent a horse and buggy in St. Charles and go north from there, avoid the city altogether."

Her shoulders sank. She had hoped for a glimpse of that city. She'd lived most of her life within a few days' journey of St. Louis and had never seen it.

Martha watches family from the front porch of her proper Victorian house. The young man on the horse at left is Cap. The blond girl outside the fence is Bina, the one holding the horse uncertain, but probably either Louisa or Mary. The young woman and little girl on the balcony are probably Nora and her daughter Mollie. The bigger boy upstairs would be Tom, the little one Mike. Garry is downstairs leaning on the house. This is the only picture of Martha the author found.

A ghostly image of Martha emerges, eked out of the old photograph at the top of the page by videographer Geno Edwards of Anvil Northwest despite the aged photographic paper breaking up like cracked glaze in old china.

Martha's youngest daughter, Edwina "Bina" Maupin, looks somewhat as the author imagines Martha. Bina resembles the Poindexter side, more than the Maupins. The likeness shows in online photos of Martha's brothers, especially Larry, and Larry's sons. The physical description of Martha given by those who knew her indicates she was fairly short, as were Bina and the other girls, Selena being the tallest. Martha's hair would have been darker than Bina's. Family members describe Bina's hair as blonde and Martha's as dark. PHOTO FROM AUTHOR'S COLLECTION

Martha's eldest son, Captain Henley Maupin, owned the farm for many years after purchasing it from his mother in 1888. With no photograph of Garrett, the author imagines him looking much like his son Cap. Garrett's army records and recall of friends indicate he was about five foot ten, of slight build, and had sandy hair and blue eyes. PHOTO COURTESY OF DOUGLAS COUNTY MUSEUM

During the two-thousand-mile trek across the Oregon Trail Martha was pregnant with this third daughter, Mary Jane Maupin, the author's great-grandmother. Documents suggest Garrett favored Mary along with their two older boys, perhaps because of the girl's birth in a lonely temporary cabin at their trail's end. PHOTO FROM AUTHOR'S COLLECTION

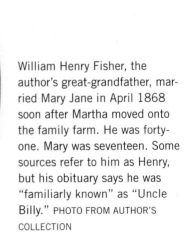

William Henry Fisher, the author's great-grandfather, married Mary Jane in April 1868 soon after Martha moved onto the family farm. He was forty-one. Mary was seventeen. Some sources refer to him as Henry, but his obituary says he was "familiarly known" as "Uncle Billy." PHOTO FROM AUTHOR'S COLLECTION

Cap Maupin had to take his boots off before he could stand on the white rug next to his second wife Adilla Peters on their wedding day in September 1893. Cap lost his first wife and child. But he soon met and married Adilla. The couple's eight children grew up on the family farm bought by their grandmother Martha.
PHOTO COURTESY OF DOUGLAS COUNTY MUSEUM

The author's paternal grandparents, Eugene "Roy" Fisher and Jennie Hager, pose at their wedding. Roy was Martha's grandson through Mary. His was the only generation not to own Martha's farm. The couple met when Michigan native Jennie, then a bookkeeper in Portland, Oregon, traveled south to visit relatives. She rented a horse and buggy, and though a skilled horsewoman, she lost control of the animal while passing through Roy's Pleasant Plain farm. The horse spooked and leaped a fence, leaving the buggy on the other side. Roy, in the house baking biscuits, heard the commotion and went out to rescue the stranded young lady. PHOTO FROM AUTHOR'S COLLECTION

The author's father, Eugene "Gene" Fisher, lovingly tended the family farm for almost seventy-five years, longer than any others among the generations of owners. This portrait was taken around 1933 near the time he graduated from Oregon Agricultural College (now Oregon State University) and purchased the farm from his Great-Uncle Cap. PHOTO FROM AUTHOR'S COLLECTION

This portrait of the author's mother, Marian Beezley, was taken near the time she married Gene and left the city to move onto the farm. The couple met in college. On one moonlit night when they were dating, Gene told her, "You haven't seen anything until you see moonlight on the Umpqua." She decided to check that for herself and enjoyed the rest of her life in that river's valley. PHOTO FROM AUTHOR'S COLLECTION

Cap and Adilla's oldest daughter, Edith, was the Maupin the author best remembers. With her love of animals, and special gift for handling horses, Edith was much admired by the young Janet. Edith told wonderful stories of the pioneer ancestors and, having no children of her own, had time to help Janet with her horse. PHOTO FROM AUTHOR'S COLLECTION

Garrett went on. "The Captain figures they must have fifty thousand people living in St. Louis now. St. Charles will be nicer. Probably less'n ten thousand in the whole county." He picked up the satchel, put the bedroll under his arm, and offered his other arm to Martha. "I'd say that's quite a plenty."

"I'd say so." She couldn't quite comprehend ten thousand people, let alone fifty thousand.

They pressed through the crowd on deck, working their way toward the right-hand side where the passengers would disembark.

When they reached the railing, she caught sight of the city and gasped. She had never seen so many houses. Buildings. Huge buildings lined up in rows. Solid structures made of brick and stone. They were beautiful. Graceful porches with railings. "Oh, look at the porches—even upstairs."

"Balconies," a man said beside her.

Balconies. What a lovely thing. People stood on the balconies, waving to the approaching steamboat, and she wondered if she should wave back. "Oh, Garrett, someday I want a house like that—with a balcony. Isn't it grand?"

Frown lines tightened his face. She'd forgotten to call him Mr. Maupin in the company of strangers, but he didn't remark on that. "Log house is good enough for me."

But Martha's enthusiasm couldn't be dampened by his gloomy outlook. The mighty boat thumped against the dock, and roustabouts scrambled to secure the massive ropes and set up planks for embarking passengers and freight.

Martha slipped into the flow of humanity surging toward the planks, her hold firm on Garrett's arm. She glanced into his face again and saw a flash of emotion in his eyes. Fear? Was he afraid as he entered this unfamiliar city? Were men as scared as women were? They just didn't want to show it? She had a feeling he would rather walk through a deep woods filled with panthers and bears than into this city of unknown things.

They stepped down the plank onto a street of cobbled stones. "Why, look, Garrett, they wouldn't even have muddy streets in the winter. Isn't that fine?"

She tried to take in everything as they walked, looking up into balconies from this new perspective below. Her head spun with the delight of it.

Oh, someday I will have a proper house with a balcony, just like that.

Garrett drew her down the street. "Let's see if we can get a room at the tavern up there, and then I'll see about renting a horse and buggy for tomorrow morning."

Martha studied the two-story building ahead. A large sign in front read, FARMER'S HOME. The place had balconies. It should do nicely.

Inside, the gentleman at the desk assured Garrett they had space available. Peering over the tops of his spectacles, the man brushed a hand over the thin gray hair on his head. "We don't have separate rooms. I think I can arrange for you to have a bed to yourselves, just the two of you. We can't always do that. Men share the beds we have, and sometimes women. But tonight we aren't too busy."

Martha sent a wistful glance toward Garrett. It would be a wonderful relief to sleep on a bed after several nights on that hard steamboat deck, but she'd hoped for time alone with Garrett. Would they have any time before he left?

The man went on. "We serve supper at six o'clock—in the dining room there." He pointed to his right, then his left. "The ladies' dining room is that way."

She had imagined a pleasant supper together, but everything would be fine.

The gentleman cleared his throat. "You can leave your things here if you'd like to go out and look around. They'll be safe. St. Charles is a nice town. Used to be the capital city of Missouri. First capital. Back in the twenties."

Garrett kept a tight grip on the satchel and bedroll. "We need to rent a horse and buggy for a few days. Can you tell me where to go for that?"

The man smiled. "I can arrange everything for you right here. That won't be any problem at all."

With that business settled, Garrett set down his bundles, and he and Martha went out to explore St. Charles until her feet hurt from the bruising cobblestones.

She dined alone in the small room with its stark white tablecloths and delicate pink floral wallpaper. The carved wood furniture didn't look solid enough to hold the weight of a man. But so elegant. Small pink rosebuds graced the china dishes. Someday she would have china dishes too—maybe with pink rosebuds.

A kick thumped inside her, and Martha smiled. She wasn't entirely alone.

———

The little black mare's hooves pounded a rhythm with Martha's heartbeat, while the buggy wheels whirred over the narrow road, sending a cloud of white dust behind. Martha could taste the grit and smell the subtle change. A growing unease clutched at her when she studied the wide rolling fields. This was beginning to look familiar. What would the folks say when she and Garrett arrived? Would they smile and reach out in warmth and hugs the same as ever? Or would they shun her? Ma's last letter had been curt, without resolution. There'd been no letter for some time.

"There." She pointed. "Turn left, just ahead there."

Garrett pulled back on the reins, turned the mare, and let her out to a trot again. Martha gripped the buggy seat with one hand, her belly with the other. The buggy had springs, but it still offered a bouncy ride on this rough track. She glanced at her husband beside her, jaw so tight. He didn't like this, did he? Not one little bit.

The fields seemed endless until she saw familiar houses at the corner, and the schoolhouse, and the tree. She pointed ahead. "Just before that tree. On your left. That's our road."

He nodded, made the turn, the track leading them out over the now rolling landscape, past the hollows where she used to play, back into the timber of giant hardwoods where the two log houses nestled, first the big house, then Grandpa and Grandma's little cabin behind.

The familiarity filled Martha with such sweet longing, she held away doubt. They stopped in front of the old family home. A dog barked when Garrett hopped down from the buggy and reached for Martha, but she didn't know the bark.

The look on her husband's face threatened to undo her. He seemed as much a stranger as that dog. Once on firm ground, she gripped his hands until she could find the strength in her legs. Then she turned and strode to the front door. Starting to lift the familiar latch, she hesitated, and instead tapped on the weathered wood, lightly, then louder.

Inside, the dog continued barking, working up to a frenzy.

Ma. Please answer.

But when the door opened, the face before her wasn't Ma's. A flood of fears washed over her. Where was Ma? What had happened to Ma? "Louisa!"

Her sister stood with mouth open and uttered a soft, incredulous, "Martha?" She shook her head. "Martha? Is it really you?"

Torn between throwing her arms around her beloved Louisa and begging for answers, Martha gave Louisa a quick, inadequate hug, and asked, "Where are Ma and Pa?"

Louisa smiled and drew Martha close for a better hug. "They're living in the little house now. I should have written you, but—didn't Ma tell you? John and I moved here last year to be closer. Pa's not well, and the little house is easier for Ma." She stood back at arm's length. "Look at you. You're in a family way." She glanced over Martha's shoulder, as if just noticing Garrett. "Is this—?"

Martha turned to see he was hanging back a ways. She reached toward him. "This is Garrett, my husband. Garrett, this is Louisa, my big sister."

He took a step closer, still maintaining a distance. "Pleased to meet you, ma'am."

Louisa seemed uncharacteristically flustered. "Come in, both of you." As she drew the couple inside, she stepped out and called, "Newt! Martha's home. And her Garrett. Go tell Ma and Pa." She offered them chairs, asked if they wanted something to drink or eat. "John's in town now, but he'll be so glad to see you."

Newt burst in the front door. "Martha!"

"Newt?" She shook her head. "You turned into a man since I saw you last. How long has it been?"

He leaped toward her, boyish as ever, and started to hug her when he saw her belly.

She drew him close. "It's all right. I won't break."

He laughed. "It's good to see you. It's been, I think, two years, more'n that."

"What are you? Fifteen?"

"Almost sixteen."

She turned to Garrett, who was making himself one with the shadows. He stood next to the wall by the sideboard—hat clutched with the satchel at his waist. Newt's gaze dropped from Garrett's face to the gun on his hip, and the boy's eyes widened. Garrett did look like a man of the West with his tan shirt and pants, though these were made of jeans fabric rather than the buckskin he often wore hunting. "This is my husband, Garrett. My little brother, Newt."

Newt heaved a sigh. "She always has to call me that. Pleased to meet you, Garrett."

"Well, you're the only little brother I have," Martha said. "And now you tower over me like everybody else."

Garrett and Newt shook hands. Then Newt darted away on his mission to inform the parents.

In the sudden quiet no one seemed to know what to say. Martha explained. "Garrett's going to the war, the Mexican War, and I wanted to be home—for the baby."

Louisa answered quickly. "Of course. You'll stay here. I know you want to be near Ma, but there's no room there, as you know, and she has her hands full caring for Pa. He gets around some. They're happy enough. Just getting older." Was Louisa making excuses?

Louisa turned to Garrett. "Our brother Larry is going also."

"Larry?" Martha said. Not Larry too. "He isn't even twenty yet."

Garrett spoke finally, his voice thin. "I was only fifteen when I fought in the war for Texas."

Martha stared at the seeming stranger in the room.

Newt returned without the former buoyancy, head low. "Ma can't come just yet."

Martha rubbed the back of her neck. Would Ma even see her? "I'll go over there."

Newt shrugged. "She said she'll come in a little bit." The words felt like a slamming door.

Garrett moved out of the shadows. "I need to be going."

Martha's breath caught. No. It was too soon.

The door opened and she looked up, expecting Ma, hoping for Ma. But it was John Bronough. Still looking fine. Dressed in suit and vest. Perfect hair. A little gray in the brown. A new line in his brow.

"Hello, John."

"Well, I'll be. Martha Poindexter. No, it isn't Poindexter now, is it? Maupin. Martha Maupin." He turned to Garrett. "And you must be Garrett."

They shook hands, firm grips, shoulders high, assessing each other. The thought of oil and water crossed Martha's mind. "I was just going," Garrett said.

"Won't you stay to dinner?" Louisa asked.

"It's a long trip, and I don't have much time. I have to muster in by August first, all the way over in Leavenworth, Kansas, and I still need to stop at home and pick up my horse."

Jake. Of course, he'd take Jake. Martha realized what a burden the timing was for Garrett, and regretted her trip had done that to him.

"It would be nice if you could meet Larry," Louisa said. "You might see him, in Mexico. He's working over at Uncle Amon's, but he'll be back this evening."

Garrett dipped his head. "I wish I could, ma'am, but I need to get some miles behind me."

Martha made a quick decision. "You need to meet Ma and Pa. Let's go on over there."

Setting down the satchel, Garrett followed her outside and down the narrow trail to the small cabin in the deeper thicket. She tried to find comfort in the happy memories of this place, but her knees felt wobbly, and a ringing in her ears crowded out happy thoughts. She'd never told Garrett about her parents' disapproval, or the harsh letters. He had readily accepted Doc's statement of his own authority. Now what would Garrett say if he knew? Would he explode in anger? Would her parents tell him?

She reached the door and knocked. The door swung inward, and Ma stood in the opening, looking small and weary, her face set in a hard frown. But her eyes. A tumult of emotion flickered across them as she looked into Martha's face, to her belly, to Garrett standing near. What were the emotions? If only Martha could read her eyes the way Garrett read men's eyes. She sought the love, the gladness, but was afraid she saw disappointment. She could easier accept anger than disappointment.

"Mama." Martha stretched out her arms for the usual hug, despite her mother's unyielding stance. She put her arms around Ma, and her mother gave her a brusque hug before stepping away, turning toward Pa, who lay on the bed at the rear of the cabin. He was struggling to sit up. Martha moved on into the room, ready to give him a hand. "Pa?"

He shook his head and sat on his own. "Martha."

"I wanted you to meet Garrett."

Pa glanced down at her huge belly, then away, his voice gruff. "A little late for that, isn't it?"

Wincing, Martha went on. "He has to leave soon. He's going to fight in the Mexican War, like Larry, and he has to get to Leavenworth soon. That's all the way over in Kansas."

"Pleased to meet you folks," Garrett said, and when Pa stirred, he put out a staying hand. "No need to get up, sir. We wouldn't have bothered you just yet, except I need to be going."

Pa looked out a window, as if to assess the hour. "Well, you better go, then."

"I'll see you later," Martha said. "Newt probably told you, I'm going to stay until Garrett comes back—over at the other house."

Ma nodded, and Martha hurried outside with Garrett, drawing deep breaths after the compressed atmosphere of the cabin. He leaned close to her, voice low. "They don't like me much."

"They don't know you. It takes them a while to warm up." Now Martha was making excuses.

He bypassed the big house, heading straight for the buggy at the hitching post where he'd tied the black mare. Pain seared as Martha felt the imminence of their parting, like the slow ripping away of part of herself. She'd been so caught up in worry over her parents' reaction she hadn't quite faced this yet. She still couldn't imagine an entire year without Garrett, but the other fear struck with terrible force. *What if I never see him again?* No. She couldn't think that.

When she looked to him for reassurance, she saw a deep scowl carving furrows in his forehead. Was he angry at her parents? At her for bringing him here? But how could he go? How could any man go off and leave his wife when she was about to have their first baby?

Leading her behind the buggy, he turned to her, taking hold of her hands, his gaze resting somewhere above her brow. Why couldn't he look at her? She felt the tears welling. She was going to cry. Desperate to keep the feelings in lest they explode out and her scatter into a million pieces with them, she held her body as tight as she could.

"Martha?" A cloud of doubt dimmed his eyes. "When I come back, you—you will go home to Missouri with me, won't you?"

She opened her mouth, but couldn't speak for a minute. "You thought—?" She gripped his hands tighter. "Garrett, I'm your wife, and I—of course I'll go home with you. I love you."

His gaze met hers, sending a shock of warmth through her, and he hugged her to him, his grip on her shoulders so firm it hurt. But she wouldn't say so. "Martha Ann Maupin, I get so put out with you sometimes I could—"

He *was* put out with her for this. She knew it. "But I had to come, Garrett."

Backing away a little he leaned his forehead toward her. "I can see that." He took a sharp breath and blew it out. "I love you more'n my own life, Martha, and if you ever left me I don't see how I could go on."

He kissed her with familiar passion, his lips lingering as if he couldn't bear to let go. She knew she was right to marry him. She loved him to the depth of her self. And she held on tight.

When he leaned away, only a little, he smiled down at her, the old lights in his eyes. "I'll see you after the war." The baby kicked so hard Garrett felt it too, and he smiled. "Both of you."

Then he unhitched the mare, climbed into the carriage, and drove away in a flurry of white dust. Standing alone, Martha watched after him, the raw tear complete. She didn't know how to bear the cruel pain or the immensity of time.

* * *

Nora's bright squeal of laughter rippled across the yard as her uncles Newt and Ben took turns to whirl her in crazy circles. The child saw the uplifted arms of her grandpa, sitting on the stoop of the little house in a ray of mottled light, and she reached out to him. "Papa." Granting her wish, Ben lowered her into his pa's welcoming arms.

Martha smiled with pleasure at the love between them. Whatever Pa might think of Martha and what she'd done, he'd accepted the seed of her action with unbounded love. As had Ma. Little Leonora had brought sweet sunshine into their lives, though a cold wall still hung between them and Martha. Whenever she tried to talk about it, they went quiet. Ma was there for the birth, more than a year ago now, tending Martha as she might tend any neighbor. When Nora came, Ma melted toward the child. "Love comes with the baby," she always said. Toward Martha a little thawing came over time, like a forgetting of the anger. In the day-to-day normalcy a sudden brightness would shine in Pa's eyes, or she'd enjoy a shared chuckle with Ma. Then like a cold gust of wind, the underlying tension resurfaced.

Martha watched now as Larry sat close to Pa, reaching a finger toward Nora in hopes of winning her over. Nora sank deeper into Pa's chest, still cautious, though a smile wavered on her rosy lips. Martha couldn't get over the change in Larry. He'd been home from the war only a few days, and he looked so thin the women kept trying to stuff him with food. It was more the eyes that struck Martha, a clouded look, as if haunted by remembered horrors.

Where was Garrett? If Larry was home, why not Garrett? The raw wound of their parting still burned, as if it would never heal without his return. The family circle helped. All her brothers were here in Woodville now except Doc. Her sister, Louisa, had been wonderful.

The sound of hoofbeats stilled the family chatter. Martha turned to look up the lane and saw a lone rider leading a horse behind him. A burst of joy shook her. She would know that rider anywhere. The horses sped up, as did the beating of her heart. But she stood, pinned to the ground, until he drew back on the reins and swung out of the saddle with the agility and grace she knew so well.

Thinking only to lift her skirts so she wouldn't trip on them, she bounded forward and threw herself into his open arms. He held her so tight she could scarcely breathe, and she tried to hold him tighter. He kissed her, long and hard, before God and family, and she didn't care what anyone thought. Garrett was home. The missing part of herself. Now she could heal.

When he had kissed her cheeks, her nose, her eyelids, and her lips again, he leaned back to smile, the stars glittering in his blue eyes. "You are a wonderful sight to see, Martha. I can't begin to tell you."

"And you." She studied his face, his cheeks so gaunt, a hollow darkness around the sparkle in his eyes, shadows of things seen which she could scarcely imagine. Like Larry. It hurt her heart to see him so.

She only gradually began to expand her focus. She glanced at the horse he'd ridden. "Where's Jake?"

Garrett looked off to the side, a sadness drawing down his features. "Lost him."

"In—in battle?" She didn't like thinking about the fighting.

"No, he ran off in the night. I don't know what got into him. I never found him. The Mexicans might have taken him. Or the Indians." He nodded toward his mount, a sorrel with straw-colored mane and tail almost the color of Garrett's hair. "The Army gave me this one to replace him. Nice horse. Rusty, I call him. And the mare—" He smiled, indicating the one he'd been leading, that one a shade darker than the other, with matching mane and tail. "She's for you. Compliments of your brother-in-law Howard. Named Sugar. 'For the little mighty one,' he said. That'd be you."

She laughed, and touched her fingers to her lips. "How kind of him. Is he all right? He and Perry?"

"They're fine. They went on home." Garrett's shoulders sank, as if from a sudden weight. "I lost my captain, though, Captain Henley. Good man. A terrible loss."

"I'm so sorry." Martha felt a weight of sadness herself—for the Captain, even for old Jake, and Garrett's pain.

"I told him if I got home safe and sound I'd name my first son for him." Garrett looked toward the family gathered in the yard, all keeping a respectful distance for this moment between him and Martha. His focus homed in on the child.

Martha clasped his arm. "Come meet your daughter. She's a happy, healthy little girl. I named her Leonora, but we call her Nora. I hope that's all right."

He nodded, following Martha. "Well, I guess we don't have to rename her since she's not a boy. We'll keep the Captain's name for our son when we have one."

Newt lifted Nora from Pa's hands and brought her to her parents. "Garrett," he said, nodding. "Glad you're back."

"Thank you. Me too."

Martha took the child. "And this is Nora."

Garrett bent his head low to look into the little girl's face. "Hello, Nora."

"This is your papa, Nora," Martha said.

Nora turned and reached a chubby fist toward her grandfather. "Papa." It sounded a little like *pom-pa* with an *m* sound in there, but it was close enough to *papa* to be confusing.

Martha smiled. "No, that's your grandpa. This is your pa." She handed the child to her father, but the tiny lower lip quivered, the chubby face wrinkling up for a good cry as she reached for her mother. Garrett quickly handed her over. Martha held her close, patting the little back. "You'll get acquainted before long. She's starting to warm up to her uncle Larry. He just got back from the war a few days ago."

The family closed around, welcoming Garrett into the fold. Louisa offered food and bustled inside to get something. Martha started after her. "I'll help."

Louisa shooed her away. "Stay by your husband. It's been too long."

Pa and Ma did say hello, but they soon retreated into their cabin, declaring a need for their rest time before supper. They did that regularly. Still, Martha wondered if they might have stayed to talk longer if circumstances were different.

Simpson hung back behind the others, and Garrett walked up to him. "Hello, Simpson."

"Garrett."

The family collected on the front porch of the big house, some on chairs, some on the steps. Larry and Garrett hit it off right away. Although they didn't talk of the war, there appeared to be an unspoken understanding between them of shared experiences, sadness, horrors. What Larry wanted to talk about was Oregon. He'd been talking about it since he got home, and Newt couldn't stop asking questions. Those two seemed taken with the Oregon fever raging here in western Illinois. Martha had seen the caravans of white-topped wagons rumbling across the meadows last spring, and she knew of folks scurrying around making preparations for next spring.

Larry sat on the other side of Garrett from Martha on the top step, arms resting on his knees. She still wasn't used to Larry's new beard that made him look like Doc, except Larry's hair was curlier. "You know there'll be land for the taking out there," Larry said. "I hear you can plant any time of year and still get a crop. And if it does snow, it'll melt in a day or two. Carrots keep in the garden all winter long. And you don't have to feed hay to the cattle. There's grass all winter."

Garrett rubbed a thumb and finger over his mustache. "Yeah, the troops have been talking about it. The Oregon Territory's ours now that the British gave it up."

"That's right, and Congress will get a land law written up before you know it."

Garrett chuckled. "When did Congress ever do anything quick?"

"Well, there's already a land law Oregon's Provisional Government put together allowing a man to claim free land."

"Is that still in effect?"

Larry shrugged. "Something will be. You can count on it."

Martha saw a new glint in Garrett's eyes and felt something stirring in herself, akin to what she felt when Doc and Simpson talked of going to Missouri. An intense curiosity about the next place over. But Oregon. It was so far.

She turned her eyes to the little cabin tucked in the woods, and tears rose to glaze the familiar image.

Interlude II

Picking my way down the narrow canyon, I felt Martha's conflict. A rush of water echoed through the tangled woods where the farm's main creek tumbled over the rocks, caught in nature's relentless tug. Fairyland, my kids called this draw, the kind of place that could make you believe in magic. Delicate ferns, grotesque mushrooms, furry moss, the water's white gossamer spray. I looked upstream—toward the source—gripped by my great-great-grandmother's story as I sought her haunting footsteps.

Even when I began my research, I knew I would need to go back to her source if I were to really understand her. I would need to see and feel the places she and Garrett had walked before. As a writer I always liked to visit the settings for my stories, not only to see how to describe them, but to feel the energies of those places. Every location seemed to have a personality. I believed that came out of the nature of the land, and out of the people who had touched and changed it. Maybe even their thoughts charged the air, the afterglow of their dreams touching us across time. Would there be something of Martha's past, or Garrett's, that still resonated?

Before I began the actual writing, I took a trip to Missouri and Illinois to find out.

Flying into Kansas City, I rented a car the next morning and drove to my first destination, Richmond, in Ray County, Missouri, arriving around noon in a dark drizzle. Despite the weather I couldn't wait to see if I could find the old Maupin homestead.

With me I had an aerial map of Perry Maupin's farm, printed from an agricultural website, and a state roadmap that was pretty sketchy on the secondary roads. After a quick lunch I headed out, feeling adventurous. No skiff of rain was going to stop this Oregonian. Besides, my time was limited. I couldn't waste an entire afternoon. I had appointments coming up, but nothing on this day. As I drove along wending back roads, I soon began to doubt myself. These roads didn't seem to match the maps. After seeing a lot of country I hadn't intended to, I backtracked. Tried a different route. It was farther, more round-about, but I finally found a road that showed on the aerial map. My spirits lifted. I was getting there.

When I reached East New Hope Road, which cut through Perry's farm—could the name be more appropriate?—a tremor washed through me. This was it. I drove slowly through the farm's center, and around the perimeter. I stopped and got out to take a picture of a pretty tree-filled hollow that must have been on Garrett's land bordering his father's. Martha and Garrett's first home together. My heart raced. I was walking on ground they'd walked long ago. It felt hallowed—at least for me.

Later, I met the three ladies from the genealogical society who'd helped me with information in Ray County—Lisa Smalley, Jenne Sue Layman, and Carol Proffitt. We spent a lovely day in the genealogical library looking through old records—ordering lunch in, laughing, searching—enjoying the camaraderie of kindred history sleuths. The most exciting item they showed me was an old ledger from Isaiah Mansur's store in Millville, Grape Grove Township, dated 1839. I carefully turned the ledger's browned, crumbling pages of neatly listed items with their prices and purchasers, including several of the Maupins—Perry, Garrett, Howard, and James.

I was delighted to find James, who'd been somewhat obscure before. Even Dorothy Shaffett in her book on the Maupins had little on him. But there he was buying goods from Isaiah Mansur's store. The Maupins bought their share of whiskey, but also skeins of silk, yards of calico, cambric, and sheeting, and many yards of "janes," the word a dialectal variation on jeans, popular for men's suits, and plenty of indigo to make it blue. They bought hats, boots, powder, sugar, coffee, coat buttons, pencils, and more. Howard bought tobacco.

When we left the library, Jenne Sue led me to the nearby grave of Captain Israel Hendley, spelled with a d, *Garrett's captain lost in the war, after whom he intended to name his first son. Garrett called the man* Henley *and may not have known his given name, because the son would be named Captain Henley Maupin. The grave of this Ray County hero lay right in the middle of a Richmond street, the lanes passing on either side with a long island in the middle surrounding the grave.*

The next day I went down in the courthouse basement to find probate papers for Perry's estate. Alone in the small room lined with narrow metal boxes holding a treasury of remnants of people's lives, I searched for Perry. Finding his metal box, I took it to a table and lifted out the age-darkened sheets—official court documents written by hand, scraps of paper with scribbled notes, appraisal lists of all he owned. When I held these in my hands, shivers ran through me.

Here I learned Garrett was administrator of the estate with his mother, Rachel. Why Garrett? He wasn't the oldest. Both Howard and James were older. Perhaps neither lived in Ray County at the time Perry died in 1844. Howard had married in Platte County in 1840. By 1850 James was in Lafayette County next door. Garrett seemed an odd choice, given that he couldn't read. Nor could his mother. The court did appoint two family friends to assist.

Garrett's absence apparently caused a little stir when he failed to file an annual settlement of accounts during probate. I saw no evidence anyone ever figured out why. On October 21, 1846, the court sent out the sheriff with a stern-sounding writ demanding Garrett "show cause why an attachment should not issue against him for not exhibiting his account as Administrator . . ." The sheriff took a copy of that writ and gave it to Rachel, reporting back to the court "the within named Garrett Maupin not found."

I let out a small laugh when I read this. Of course the sheriff didn't find him. Garrett had already left for the Mexican War, apparently without a thought to the court's desires. The paperwork was filed the following month as the writ demanded, without Garrett's help. He wouldn't be back for a year, but the required document had no signatures, or X's.

Carol was working in the courthouse that day and came down to see how I was doing. She ordered lunch for us and skimmed some of my discoveries, commenting that Perry must have been fairly wealthy, given all the stuff he had. I was curious whether he owned slaves, as one family legend suggested. Carol doubted he did, since none were listed on his appraised property and I'd never found any on the census lists, which did show slaves owned by others. She said he might have hired some on occasion. Many did.

Returning to the courthouse the next morning, I searched land documents to see what happened to Perry's farm after he died. He owned close to four hundred acres at the time of his death, having held the original land patents from the US government on several adjoining parcels. Because he didn't have a will, the property was divided among Rachel and the children.

The florid handwriting and legalese on the old deeds made it hard to follow various transfers among siblings, but all were ultimately selling their portions to a man named John Wollard. Among those were James Maupin and his wife, Anna. There he was again. With a wife. And he included her in the document, which many husbands didn't in those days, making me feel kindly toward him. The estate closed in 1849, but various land transactions continued until 1853.

That afternoon I went out with Jenne Sue to revisit Perry's property and meet the current residents, the Frazers, David and Marilyn. A bright, sunny day. When we arrived, the Frazers told me their family had owned the property for many years. I asked if it was a Century Farm, and they said much more than a century. Their family had owned it since their ancestor John Wollard. I knew that name, having seen it so many times on records that morning.

"Oh my goodness," I said. "Do you know who John Wollard bought the land from?"

They didn't.

I smiled. "He bought it from my family, the Maupins."

Their eyes widened, faces bright with surprise. We had a pleasant conversation, and they were kind enough to let me wander around the place to take pictures and get the feel of the land. The old Frazer house, dating from 1880, stood about where I guessed the Maupin house would have been, on a rise in ground overlooking fields to the south that appeared to go on forever. Huge trees shaded the wide green lawn. David and Marilyn lived in a newer house nearby, but their daughter was renovating the old one for herself.

As I strolled away from the yard, absorbing the haunting energies, I looked back to that rise of ground and squinted until it seemed I could almost make out Perry's old log house beneath the trees instead of the Frazer's frame house. I heard the faint echo of laughter. Shimmering voices. People having fun. But of course it was Jenne Sue and the Frazers. Most of it.

In Carrollton, Missouri, I happened to meet Glen Hill, who'd researched for me there—the one who found documents showing Doc and T. S. acquiring land, not Doc and Ambrose. I'd gone into the library looking for information, and a woman at the front desk kept referring my questions to a man sitting beside her, a slender fellow with thick curly gray hair. When he led me into *another room to show me some of the library's local histories and documents, I had a sudden inkling. "What is your name?" I asked.*

He bent toward me a little, as seemed his habit, and spoke in a soft drawl. "Hill. Glen Hill."

Delighted, I smiled and introduced myself. We became instant friends.

His familiarity with the records in his town made research easy. He took me to the courthouse, where he knew everybody and could put his hand on just the right deed book to answer questions I hadn't even thought of yet.

We had lunch together. Another lovely sunny day. He drove me around the county in his 1989 Buick. He said he had a newer car at home but liked driving this one. He showed me Stokes Mound near Aunt Hannah and Uncle Jim's place, and he drove over some pretty marginal roads to find Doc and Simpson's land. I saw much more country than I might have alone. At Doc's south forty, we climbed out of the car and leaned on the fence to look out over the landscape.

Glen smiled. "Hills and hollers, as far as you can see."

I gave him a warm smile in return. "Yes."

The entire countryside from there to Perry's in Ray County was all gentle rolling hills with pretty tree-filled hollows.

On my own again I found William's place on the Missouri Bottoms, rich ground, broad and flat as any table. I could see why some risked flooding for that fertile soil.

After exploring western Missouri I drove east, stopping for a weekend to enjoy the charms of quaint St. Charles with its refurbished old town. Then I crossed the Mississippi into Illinois. My primary goal in Illinois was to find Martha's parents, Thomas and Maxy Poindexter. I had a property description for their land in Greene County. At the courthouse in Carrollton, Illinois, a helpful woman in the county clerk's office showed me the site on a map, but when I went out that rainy evening to find it, I couldn't locate Woody Road, which would take me there.

The next morning skies cleared. I went for breakfast at a local restaurant, the kind of place farmers and other locals congregated, making me wonder if anyone in Carrollton, Illinois, ever ate breakfast at home. Noticing a friendly sounding group at the next table, I leaned over and asked if they could direct me to Woody Road. Sure, they could. They gave me landmarks. One drew a map on a napkin.

I drove right to it. Out past the flatter land along Woody Road I came to Martha's girlhood home, another place of rolling hills and tree-filled hollows. Did all these folks originally from Virginia seek out the hilly sites because they felt familiar?

I knocked on the door of the modern house on the property. A woman came to the door, widow of the man who'd once farmed the land. We had a nice visit, and she allowed me to walk around. The old Poindexter house was probably behind hers, on the next forty acres over, since that was the first piece acquired by my ancestor. She said she had timber in the back. When I heard timber *I thought of tall Douglas firs like those in the Pacific Northwest, but these were hardwoods. When the Poindexters first settled here, the whole landscape was probably more heavily timbered, until pioneers carved out fields for crops by cutting down trees.*

Looking toward her back forty, I imagined the log houses of Martha's family tucked into a wooded setting. I tried to see through Martha's eyes and sense her longing gaze before she turned away from that familiar sight for the last time. A lump filled my throat.

More time in the courthouse revealed nothing new on Thomas and Maxy. I came across some land deals for family members, quite a few for Maxy's family, the Woods. Their township, Woodville—or Woody—was named for Maxy's older brother Amon Wood, the most prominent family member. There were no death records that far back.

Through the historical and genealogical society, I found a gravestone for Martha's grandfather, Stephen Wood, placed in the local cemetery by the Daughters of the American Revolution to honor him for his service in the Revolutionary War, but a plaque stated his actual burial place was unknown.

Aware that Martha's sister Louisa moved to neighboring Macoupin County in 1855, I drove there to meet a researcher who'd looked for Thomas and Maxy for me in that county, in case the parents followed their daughter. She hadn't found them but suggested a few more documents. I enjoyed a small discovery. Court records showed Doc had been in the county in 1843 long enough to get into a minor scrape and get sued for a small amount of money. Another case indicated older brother Stephen had been there, as I already knew from the census. But no Thomas or Maxy.

I visited the small town of Virden, where Louisa and John Bronough had lived out their lives, John having been Virden's first mayor. They were buried in a lovely cemetery west of town. I wandered through the stones, savoring the sunny fall day with pleasant breezes rippling the bronzed leaves, but my hopes of finding Thomas and Maxy were dwindling. They seemed to have slipped out of this world like wisps of yesterday's fog in a new morning sun.

The next day I needed to get on my way back to Kansas City to catch my plane. Before leaving, I decided to make one last stop at the Greene County Courthouse. A woman directed me to indexes for the old chancery court, which heard a variety of cases in the old days. I hadn't tried that.

I scanned the list and there he was, Thomas Poindexter, being sued by somebody. I let out a muffled yelp.

The index didn't show dates on the early records, but gave box and file numbers, Box 22, File 6, for this case. Surely the documents in that box would have dates. Maybe they would show a date after 1840, indicating he lived past that time. Heart pounding, I ran into the next room to ask for assistance. The walls of both rooms were lined with narrow metal boxes, like those in the Ray County Courthouse basement where I'd found the probate papers for Perry. I anticipated the thrill of a similar find.

The woman climbed a ladder to find Box 22 on the very top row. But when she looked inside, she found no File 6. She had no idea what had happened to the missing file. My shoulders slumped. Frustration!

I recalled what a couple of genealogy ladies had said. One told me, "You'll find them." But another shook her head. "Sometimes there isn't anything to find." Anyway, my time there was up, and whatever else I learned had to be from home.

Back home I followed up on that missing file in Box 22. I called Illinois state archives to see if they might have a microfilmed copy. They didn't. But a helpful man there discussed possibilities and directed me to regional archives where I might find other information that could tell me what I really wanted to know, which was how long Thomas and Maxy lived.

Mail came from the regional offices, and I ripped the envelope open. A woman had found a voting record from Woodville precinct in Greene County, Illinois, for an 1845 election for county commissioner and school commissioner. The man at the state archives had assured me everyone voted in those days. They appreciated that hard-won privilege. The handwritten names were hard to read, but the Poindexter name tended to show up. I'd noticed that on previous searches through many a handwritten list. The woman who sent this thought one of the several Poindexters might be Thomas.

Biting my lip, I took off my glasses and stared closely as only a nearsighted person could effectively do. I wanted to make a T for Thomas out of one of those florid initials. I compared it to other names more obvious and shook my head. Thomas did not vote in this election. I called the woman at regional archives to ask if she was sure I had the whole list. She said I did, but the ornate writing had confused her. The name she'd thought was Thomas was Ambrose, one of the boys.

Gradually I began to accept what I hadn't found and considered what I had. All the boys were on that list for August 1845 except Doc, who'd married Elizabeth Maupin in May 1845 in Missouri. All were voting in Woodville precinct in Greene County, virtually on the old family doorstep. Why had they all congregated back home—not to visit, but to live there so they became voters there? What had drawn them?

I'd seen a program on public broadcasting about how scientists searched for planets in other solar systems. The planets were too small to see with the strongest telescopes, but they affected the suns they encircled, their gravity tugging at the suns and making them wobble. An image came to mind of something similar, though working in an opposite way.

I had evidence of the planets, the sons of Thomas Poindexter, and I was looking for the gravity that drew them to their center. Could I find the missing sun at the center of their solar system by the gravity on their presence?

I could see only two good reasons why Thomas Poindexter didn't vote in August 1845. He was either dead or too ill to leave his bed and make his way down to the Woodville schoolhouse where eligible voters cast their votes. Somehow I had to pin this down by looking at the planets, not the sun.

Based on the election of 1845 in Woodville, Illinois, I believed Pa was still alive in 1845 because the boys hadn't scattered yet, and they would. I thought if he had died already, they would have visited but not moved there. I thought he was ill or he would have voted. I believed Ma was alive and well in 1846 or Martha wouldn't have returned home then, and she did. The boys began to leave a couple of years later.

I concluded both parents were gone before the 1850 census because Louisa was there in 1850 and she wouldn't have let them be missed by the enumerators. So I put Pa's death at 1847 or 1848 and Ma's death soon after.

More family legend struck down. I no longer believed they had lived into the 1860s to continue their disapproval of Martha's choice, but their disapproval probably continued to haunt her. I doubted she ever saw them after that trip to Illinois for the birth of Leonora, a birthplace recorded by multiple census records that told me Martha made the trip to have the child there. When that visit ended, Martha's face turned west. The lure of new places was leading her away.

Wanderlust. It had carried my ancestors across the country, bit by bit. My father used to say, "They ran us out of France. Then they ran us out of Virginia, and then Kentucky and Missouri. Now here we are and there's no place else to go."

It might have been truer than he knew, though probably not all of it. Gabriel Maupin did flee France during the persecution of the Huguenots, landing finally in Williamsburg, Virginia. Gabriel's son Daniel trekked to the wilderness of western Virginia, pushing toward the Appalachians. Daniel's grandson John felt the lure of the unknown and worked his way to the hills of eastern Kentucky into what eventually became Clay County. Along with him came his child Perry, who would eventually father Garrett. I had no reason to suppose any of those between Gabriel and Perry fled any circumstances behind them.

Whether Perry fled Clay County after the death of his father—and brother—I didn't know. He was probably ready to leave an unfortunate scene. I learned of the incident from William Albertson, a well-respected Maupin researcher my newfound cousin Linda introduced me to on the Internet. I was trying to pin down the year Perry and his family left for Missouri, but also wanted to know when Perry's father John died. Sources gave conflicting dates.

William had all the estate papers for John's estate and was able to clarify that Perry's father had died in 1824. William said Perry stayed in Clay County taking care of his mother until she died in 1827, and left soon after, probably because of the problems over the death of John Jr.

I sent a quick reply. "So what happened to John Jr.? And what problems prompted Perry to leave?"

William's answer made me sit back in my chair. "Thought I told you. They got in a gunfight over the father's estate and Perry killed John."

I sat stunned. It took me a while to respond. I asked finally if Perry had gotten in trouble with the law, if the courts had a case against him. William said no. He'd found no case.

As I was trying to work this into my mind and into the story, I contacted the genealogical and historical society in Clay County. When I asked if the society had any old newspapers that might tell about the incident, the man said they didn't, but he doubted anybody back then would have made much of it. Folks would probably just consider it a family matter, he said, commenting on the county's notoriety for blood feuds and gunplay.

And I thought I'd grown up in the wild and woolly West.

As for the next generation after Perry, I found no evidence of Garrett wanting to run from anywhere—yet. Probably just the wanderlust. A quest for more freedom, as for so many men.

But what about the women? They might voice their opinions, but ultimately the man had a legal right to decide where the family lived. If he wanted to trek westward into an unknown wilderness, she went too. Women were keepers of home and family, though men had sole custody of the children. Free was a man's word. When applied to women it became derogatory. A free woman might be promiscuous, unrespectable, dangerous. Women weren't supposed to be independent. Martha may have pushed the limits demanding to go to Illinois. What would she say—or think—about Oregon?

Women had a central role on the farm. On the frontier, the simple need for help could blur the edges of the rules dividing men and women, but it remained a patriarchal world.

Martha's family and Garrett's had pushed west before. But a trip to Oregon would take them to the western limits of a continent. In 1846 the United States had just taken possession of land below the 49th parallel in the Oregon Territory, which had been jointly occupied by the United States and Britain for many years.

At one time the British Hudson's Bay Company was the dominant force in the region as they pursued the lucrative fur trade of the day. But American promoters began encouraging immigration in hopes of gaining possession, and as the fur trade dwindled and American immigrants poured into the area, the British finally gave it up. Guidebooks described a wondrous land, while downplaying the difficulty of the route to get there.

Land laws remained uncertain. Since 1843 people had relied on laws enacted by Oregon's Provisional Government to stake their claims, but since the United States took possession those laws lacked authority. Still, Congress was

working on a bill and people expected free land, lots of it. The Indian popula-
tion, decimated by disease brought by early traders, had decreased to the point
settlers found space and little friction at the outset.

Martha's adventurous spirit had taken her as far as Missouri, but that was
a place with towns and farms and fairly good transportation. Oregon lay on the
far side of a great wilderness with no easy access by land or sea.

Years ago I had followed that Oregon Trail with family, as near as roads
allowed. We pulled a travel trailer, our own version of a covered wagon. We
experienced the rough edge of a Kansas tornado, saw the landmarks—Chimney
Rock, Scotts Bluff—and the trip grew long. But we could only glimpse the
magnitude of what our ancestors had to overcome.

I thought about my trip to Missouri and Illinois to research Martha's story.
Hop on a plane. A day's travel. An easy day's drive across Missouri to Illinois. If
I needed to talk to someone back home, just pull out the cell phone.

It was hard for me to imagine the isolation Martha faced coming to Oregon.

Chapter 6

The Oregon Trail

On the Prairie, May 1850

Martha trudged through the tall grass where the wagon wheels had laid it down enough for her to walk. She thrilled to the strange, magnificent beauty such as she'd never seen before. Not a tree in sight. Not even a shrub to amount to anything. Just grass, waist high, covering the gently billowing land as far as she could see, and flowers in a rainbow of colors, woven through the green like a tapestry. Overhead a wide blue sky arced, clear but for a few fluffy white clouds. She felt like a small dot in the vast picture.

Spring air filled her with the sweetness of nectar in a bouquet of flavors so intense she could taste them on her tongue. The sun cast a gentle warmth, soft breezes tickling her hair, as she let her bonnet fall back. The jangle of harness and roll of wheels had become a steady song, the occasional sharp voices of command like clashing cymbals.

They were finally on their way. A year ago she and Garrett had done a lot of work getting ready for this trip. Then he got into a disagreement with the Ray County company they planned to travel with, and all that work came to a halt. He decided to wait a year. Just like that. Larry and Newt went anyway, and came back to help Garrett and Martha this year. Martha let out a soft chuckle. She could laugh now, but it wasn't funny at the time.

The weight of troubles slipped from her shoulders as she looked west toward a new land and new possibilities. She saw it in Garrett too, the exhilaration, the lust for adventure, leaving the old behind and looking to what lay ahead. Oregon. Folks sang that old hymn, "Beulah Land," and looked to Oregon. That was their Beulah Land.

This prairie seemed like a paradise, but it was just a step along the way. Newt said the grass would get taller, even higher than his head. Stories were told of Indians standing on the backs of their horses to see out. She'd wondered about Indians, but the boys had no trouble with them last year.

Ahead of her Garrett in his broad-brimmed hat and kerchief walked beside the lead yoke of oxen, hitched in two spans to their fine wagon Garrett had built. The horses followed, tied behind, where two chickens rode in a crate. Cows and a spare pair of oxen moved freely around them. The two little girls were asleep in the wagon, giving Martha this moment of freedom. She smiled. Underneath the high wagon bed, the churn rocked, the motion of the wagon doing her work for her as it churned milk into butter.

Coming onto a slight rise she saw the white-topped wagons before her, a line snaking out so long the wagons looked tiny in the distance. To the right, another line, and another. To the left, the same. Turning, she saw them behind, white dotted streaks across the green. Her little family wouldn't be lonely in Oregon. Half the population of the United States seemed to be going with them. What had Larry said? Last year some thirty thousand people came over this trail, most to California for the gold, but hundreds to Oregon too. This year folks estimated there would be twice as many.

She was glad to have Larry and Newt along. They'd brought their report back from Oregon last fall, arriving in Missouri in November after more than six months of hard travel. On their way west they fell in with a couple of experienced, fast-traveling packers carrying supplies across country, and returned east with them after a short stay in Oregon. The boys slept for most of a week when they got back to Missouri.

"Prettiest country you ever saw," Larry had said of Oregon. He conceded the trip was difficult at times, but knew a frontiersman like Garrett would do fine. The boys had put up a small cabin there. It gave Martha comfort to know it was waiting for them.

She took one long glance behind, then sighed and faced ahead again. With Ma and Pa gone, she had nothing to hold her back now. She would never forget the pain she saw in their eyes the day she went down to their little cabin and told them good-bye. Was it still the pain of disappointment over what Martha had done? Or just the pain of knowing they'd never see her or little Nora again in this life? Martha would never know.

A wave of nausea stirred, and she bit her lower lip. The sickness wasn't severe. She was lucky that way. But she knew. It had to be. She'd missed her monthly in April. By her calculation, the baby should come in December, and they should be in Oregon by then. Better for the baby—and her too—though she would be large before they got there.

She looked at Garrett, walking along in his easy rhythmic gait, and let out a long breath. He was a manly sort. He had his needs. Sometimes she had strong feelings too. Sometimes the sweetest sensations poured through her like rich warm honey. Maybe she wasn't supposed to think about that. Maybe she wasn't supposed to want that. But she did think about it, and sometimes she did want to feel that. If only she could keep the babies from coming so fast.

She shouldn't complain. She knew women who had one every year. So far, Martha's were two years apart. Nora would be four in September, baby Louisa two in December. Martha had tried to keep Louisa nursing longer in hopes that might prevent this until after the trip. Some women thought that worked, and maybe for her it did hold things off. It seemed to this time—at least until March when Louisa wouldn't cooperate any longer.

Martha watched Garrett gently stroking the ox's back. How tender he was with the animals. And with her. Maybe tonight. She would never tell a soul she thought these things, not even Garrett, most especially not Garrett. At least she didn't have to worry about getting in a family way when she already was.

The sun was dropping. A bank of darker clouds moved upward, as if intent on making the sunset earlier. The caravan appeared to speed up. Racing the sun? A gust of wind swept across the white arched wagon covers, making the cloth snap in an echoing staccato. A sense of urgency rippled down the line, and through Martha. Voices rose. Men barked orders. Garrett turned and called out behind him. "Circle up! Storm coming!"

The words repeated, down the line and all around, like ripples in a pond, growing dimmer in the distance.

Martha studied the sky. There were clouds, and a little wind. But it didn't look so bad. Still, she hurried to the wagon to help Garrett. She heard another sound that demanded her more immediate attention. Louisa crying. Garrett stopped the oxen, and Martha scrambled up to the front wagon seat and reached in for Louisa. "Come on, baby. You're all right."

The child stopped crying on sight of her mother, and Nora sat up wide-eyed beside her. "You want to get out, Nora?" Martha asked, getting a silent nod in response.

Garrett grabbed Nora and put her on the ground, his tone sharp. "Get them back out of the way. We've got to circle up."

Once the wagons of their own small company had formed into a ring, the men unhitched oxen and with the help of the women drove the animals inside what had become a corral of wagons. The bank of clouds had not stopped with swallowing the sun. They rolled across the sky like a flooding river escaping its banks. Dark, foreboding. They seemed to have weight. Another gust struck. Canvas cracked like thunder, followed by a rumble of real thunder. Lightning streaked through the black clouds. Then the wind came in earnest.

Garrett swooped up the children and put them back in the wagon, calling Martha to climb in with them. Wind hammered—one way and another. The wagon shook. Cattle bawled. Louisa cried again, her wails lost on the howling wind. One heavy gust whipped so hard the wagon rocked to one side, and Martha leaned the other way as Garrett did, lest it tip over and throw them on the ground. He said nothing, just sat clutching a child in each arm, his face set.

The wind eased and the rain began. Huge raindrops battered the heavy linen canvas Martha had sewn with such care, the sound so loud she covered her ears.

When the pounding stopped, Garrett let go of the children and climbed out of the wagon without a word. Martha crawled over to look out. What a wet, bedraggled mess. How would they ever get supper? Water began to seep through the first layer of the wagon cover. Before leaving on the trip, Martha had brushed a generous coating of linseed oil over the outer surface to rainproof it, but that wasn't enough for a storm like this. The wetness was spreading to the inner layer. That dripped, a steady sprinkle, like rain from their own low cloud. Everything inside was going to get wet.

"We might as well get out, girls. At least it's not raining outside anymore."

Where would they find dry wood for fire? They needed it for cooking and warmth and drying things off. Someone had a few sticks of wood they'd tucked low in their wagon bed. Several had dry tinder in metal boxes. With considerable effort they managed to coax a flame and soon had a fine fire. "Don't bother about cooking," Garrett said. "We have plenty of jerky and biscuits." His eyes brightened. "We've got along with that before."

The bustle of preparations stirred around them, everyone doing things the easy way on this one evening. Martha looked up and saw stars glittering overhead. A clear sky once again. On the horizon an enormous moon rose.

They ate with good appetites. Then Martha put their few utensils away while Garrett tended the animals. She tugged at the rolled mattress so she could lay it over the top of their carefully packed items, stopping to run her hand across the trunk at the center, the box of dishes, the bags of food and cookware and clothes that didn't fit in the trunk, her small bag of cut-out dresses and shirts for sewing on the way, a carefully wrapped start of lilac, a cutting from the pink rose Garrett gave her, a sack of seed grain, Garrett's treasured grindstone to sharpen tools. A heavy thing, but he wasn't about to leave that behind. "It was my pa's," he'd said, "and I'm not going without it."

Feeling the damp bags, Martha laughed at herself. Was she having tender thoughts before the rain? She shook her head.

A sweet sound floated on the air, and she drew her head out of the wagon to listen. Someone was playing a fiddle. Another higher pitched tone lay over the first sound. A flute. A glimmer of pleasure lifted Martha's dampened mood. She stuck her shoulders back into the wagon to roll out the mattress, flattening it over the bags, and realized the inside of the roll was dry. She smiled.

Outside, the music grew merrier, a tin pan drumming the beat. Newt was dancing with Nora, holding her two hands. Her face beamed, looking up at him. She'd remembered him immediately when he first came out to Missouri, and she adored him. Although she hesitated when he came back from Oregon with a beard, one word from him and she ran right to him. While Newt whirled about with Nora, Larry held Louisa in his arms, stepping to the music and swinging her in circles so she giggled with delight. Others in the company joined in to dance around the fire with them.

Garrett looked up when Martha approached. His eyes caught the fire's reflection and sent its warmth straight to Martha's heart. "May I have this dance, Mrs. Maupin?"

"You may, Mr. Maupin."

He took both her hands and stepped in a close circle to the music's soft beat, his gaze locking with hers. Martha didn't know any fancy dances, and he didn't either. It didn't matter. They felt the music, and love, and the thrill of their adventure. Out here in this wild land convention didn't matter either. They moved closer until his forehead pressed against hers, and she decided her previous thoughts hadn't been so audacious after all.

———

Martha's feet burned and her back ached when she bent over to pick up another buffalo chip for their cook-fires, grimacing as she tucked the dried buffalo manure in her apron. She looked back to see Nora trailing behind. "Keep up with Mama so I can see you. Remember what I told you. Anytime you're out of the wagon you have to be where Mama can see you. Remember?"

Nora hurried a little. "Yes, Mama. But there's a pretty rock." She held out a small pebble in her palm.

Martha looked closer. Sunlight glanced off the shiny stone streaked in varied shades of green. It looked polished, like a gem. "Very nice, sweetheart."

"Can I keep it?"

"Of course. You can put it in your pocket."

Nora kept studying her rock, brow puckered. "How did it get here?"

"I don't know." Martha cast a glance across the strange landscape. Plenty of tiny rocks speckled the gravelly sand, though not many shiny or green. The land was mostly dry and dusty. Bits of short grass. The Platte River making its lazy way between sandy bluffs, curving along a wide swath of bottomland. The shallow stream could sometimes be as much as two miles wide and a few inches deep, seldom deeper than three or four feet. No timber or undergrowth, a few scattered cottonwoods and willows. Islands and sandbars, quicksand. Muddy, warm.

A line of wagons followed the river, not so many as at the beginning, the companies having dispersed over time, some traveling faster, some slower, some taking slightly different routes. Herds of cattle ranged off the trail toward the bluffs.

Nora leaned against her mother. "Maybe somebody dropped it."

Martha looked down to see the child still scrutinizing the green pebble. "Maybe. Or the river did. Uncle Larry says the river moves back and forth on this wide river bottom. The rock might have come down the river when the channel was over here, once upon a time."

Nora's eyes lit up at the familiar story language, and Martha ran a hand over the child's soft golden hair, forgetting what that hand had been gathering. With a shudder she wiped her palm on her skirt and brushed the top of Nora's head, wishing she could brush away all the dust and filth. But a bath in that river left them about as dirty as before. "Let's pick up more chips. We need them for our fire." They made surprisingly good fuel and their smoke didn't leave a taste.

"I can pick up lots of chips," Nora said, slipping another into her own little apron, and pushing the hair back out of her eyes with the same hand.

Martha let out a sigh. "Yes, you can, and then we'd better get back to the wagon, because Louisa will be waking up from her nap." Martha wondered why Nora had to choose now to give up naps.

❦

Women's bright voices stirred around Martha as she stood barefoot in the stream, rubbing the clothes together in the water to wash away the caked mud. Thank goodness for the women. What would she do without other women to laugh with and share stories with? Much as she loved Garrett and her brothers, they didn't see life in quite the same way. Besides, out here in this treeless land, there was that critical service women provided for each other when one had to relieve herself. They would gather around with their wide skirts and create a curtain for the one in the center.

Now here she was surrounded by women doing their laundry, and all the men had gone on a buffalo hunt. Martha had seen the herd that covered the land like ants. Thousands, maybe tens of thousands. For the men nothing else mattered.

"I know Garrett has to go for one," Larry had said, eyes gleaming. "I got one last year—the most exciting hunt I ever went on."

She'd watched the hunters for a while today, sharing the thrill from a distance. The men rode right out into the mass of shaggy beasts while they thundered across the plain. She held her breath when a buffalo veered toward a rider. The buffalo fell. The man rode clear, and Martha breathed again, watching until the herd rumbled beyond her sight.

Now Betsy Cole huffed. "No, sir. They didn't have time to stop for washing. We could be down to our last rags and there wouldn't be time to slow this train, and then somebody sees a buffalo and everything stops for the hunt." She shook her head. "Men. Won't even stop for the Sabbath. Only the hunt."

Martha chuckled. "Well, I guess we can thank the buffalo for clean clothes." She twisted her face at the silty water rolling past. "Relatively clean."

"They'll smell better," Ellen Foster said.

Martha inhaled the odd pungent scent of soil and weed. "Sweet smell of the Platte."

Laughter spilled, and built, and they heard each other and laughed more, and hearing that burst into giggles until they held their sides and tears poured down their cheeks.

The sound of galloping horses stopped them. Garrett rode straight for the women and pulled up short, his eyes glassy. "We'll feast tonight," he said, lifting his rifle to the sky. A huge chunk of meat lay across the horse's withers, another across the flanks. Garrett had gotten his buffalo.

Garrett crowded their wagon in among the others waiting to cross the Platte's South Fork, and Martha stepped up beside him. When she saw the river her heart made a heavy thud and seemed to sink to her belly. This wasn't the lazy Platte they'd come to know. The sickly yellow water boiled and surged. It must have been a mile wide. She looked up at Garrett but saw no expression in the set of his face.

"Do we have to ford the river here?" she asked, hoping there might be another way.

He gave the curtest nod.

Larry walked up to him, pointing as he explained. "We'll have to take a diagonal course downstream to the middle, then turn and take a diagonal upstream. That should bring us about straight across. You have to watch out for quicksand. The water's shallow, but it can drop to three or four feet pretty sudden."

For a long moment Garrett made no response, his face like granite. Martha wondered if he'd heard, with all the noise of the stream and the shouting people and bellowing animals. Without apparent emotion he spoke so quietly she could barely hear. "Let's go, then."

She waited, watching other wagons plunge into the rushing stream, men yelling at the oxen and prodding the river with long poles, checking depth.

Garrett's sharp voice startled her, and she turned to see the fierce glare carved on the granite of his face. "Did you hear me, woman? Get in the wagon with the girls. Hang onto them and hang onto the wagon and don't let go."

His harsh tone struck like a slap, and she hesitated. He reached up a hand and for a minute she thought he might actually slap her. Physically. He had never struck her. She wanted to protest his harshness, but was too stunned to respond. The yelling and splashing and cries of children and clatter of wagons reverberated around her, and somewhere inside herself she found the ability to move.

Turning away from him, she clambered into the enclosure of the covered wagon where both her children sat crying softly. Her own tears spilled onto her cheeks.

Nora reached out. "Mama, what's the matter?"

Martha pulled the child into her embrace, and gathered up the crying Louisa, holding them both in one arm while grasping the edge of the wagon bed with her other hand. "It'll be all right," she said, brushing her face against each downy head, wetting the silky hair with her tears.

When the wagon rolled, bumping over the rocky ground, she gripped firmer, her whole body tightening against the jolting and the fear. She could see out the arched opening in the front as their faithful oxen followed Garrett down the bank. She held her breath when they stepped into the water. The wagon shuddered against the torrent, the sound crashing around them in a million echoes. The vessel slowed, sank a little, and bounced forward again. Garrett pressed through water up to his knees, stumbled, caught himself. He had the long pole in his hand, the one he always kept in the loops he'd crafted for it along the outside of the wagon bed. Now it steadied him and showed where the holes were—and the quicksand.

The pole sank, and he gave a sharp command to drive the oxen away from the spot. Glancing back, Martha saw their horses hauling back on their halter ropes that tied them behind the wagon. "Easy, Sugar," she said. "Easy, Rusty. You're all right. Come along." The chickens back there in their crate squawked so much she wondered if the horses could hear her, but they stopped pulling so hard. She kept talking to them in the most soothing voice she could make, finding comfort in something to do, until even the children quieted.

The boys were busy driving the cows. She heard Larry's hoot, and cattle bawling amid the splashing and squawking. She wondered if the chickens would ever lay another egg after this.

Garrett made the turn in the middle of the stream. She felt the added crunch of turning wagon wheels. "Almost there," she told the girls, speaking over her shoulder to tell the horses. "Almost there." Telling herself. She saw wagons ahead, oxen dragging them up out of the water, onto the bank. She saw Garrett walking in shallower water. Almost there.

Tears flowed again, dripping unheeded off her jaw. Only when they were well above the water did Garrett stop the oxen and walk back to the wagon. "You can get out now," he said, his gaze not quite lifted toward hers.

———⋄———

Martha looked up the long dry slope they had to climb. Bluffs came right to the river's edge here, so they couldn't pass. They had to go around and that meant up. She clasped a child in each hand and started walking. Both pulled back on her, and her tone turned sharp. "Come on. Walk on your own. I can't get up this hill myself and drag you too."

"Up," Louisa said, whimpering as she reached for a carry.

"No, Louisa, I can't."

Nora started to cry. "I don't want to."

Garrett called out from behind. "What's going on up there? I want you ahead of me in case the wagon slips. Get on up the hill."

Martha gave a half glance back to him, only until she saw him out of the corner of her eye. Then she looked not at the steep bluff ahead, but the trail right at her feet. Somehow she had to find the strength to get herself and her children to the top. She took a step in the dry, crumbly soil, then another, tugging at the little hands.

The sound of approaching hoofbeats stopped her, and she looked up to see Larry riding to her. "Give me the girls," he said. "It's enough for you to climb this yourself. Do you want me to get your mare?"

Martha handed up the girls, first Nora, who went on behind the saddle, then Louisa in the saddle in front of him. Martha could ride, but what if she fell? She didn't want to risk that in her condition. "I'd better walk. Thank you for taking the girls. I don't know how we'd do this without you boys."

He gave her a quick smile and moved his horse up the slope with her treasures on board. Watching them, she thought of the unseen treasure within her and began the climb again, stepping carefully to guard this one as well.

The higher she climbed, the more she could see of the incredible landscape around them. Ridges, mounds, hollows, cavities that looked as if they'd been dug out by giant shovels, scarcely a tree, no vegetation of any kind except for sparse tufts of dry grass and twists of twiggy shrubs in the deepest hollows. The poor animals. How would they ever find enough to eat? They were getting thin, their coats dull with caked mud and layered dust.

Garrett caught up with her as she neared the top. He reached toward her, and she took his hand, thankful for his firm grip when they scrambled up the last steep rise. He didn't say a word. He said little these days that didn't have to be said, as if the words might drain his energy and he had to save it all for the daily ordeals. She felt something of that herself. She could scarcely catch breath to breathe, let alone use it to talk.

Did he know the treasure she held inside her? She hadn't spoken of it yet. Could he tell? If he'd marked the days and noticed her lack of monthlies, maybe he knew. But he hadn't touched her in that way for so long, how would he? Every night they fell into bed exhausted. Maybe he read it in her, the way he read other things of nature.

When he let go of her hand she turned to thank him, but he didn't look her way. With his eyes narrowed, he was studying the track across the high plateau ahead.

The storm swept in from the west. Another met it from the east. Wind whipped the wagon covers, her dress skirts. A gust reached down and picked up a tent. Shrieks rose from the family under it. The sky turned dark, though the sun couldn't have been down yet. They had only camped early because they'd found a rare patch of grass and wanted to feed the animals before moving on to more barren country.

A streak of lightning slit the sky. Thunder shook the ground so soon after, Martha knew it was close. The cattle scattered, escaping the circled wagons and running in all directions. Someone's horses galloped after them. Mr. Cole's. He followed, yelling. "Get back here, you cussed—"

"Damn it," Garrett said, flinging a tent stake to the ground with such force it stuck, stabbed into the soil.

Martha flinched, then scowled at him. Such language in front of the children.

But before she could say anything, he stomped away, grumbling. "Damn! Son of a bitch. It'll take hours to hunt them down."

Huge raindrops began to pepper the ground, and she turned away from Garrett to get into the wagon with the children for whatever shelter it offered. Another bolt of lightning. Jumping, she looked back to see about Garrett, but he was still walking away, untouched. She had half expected to see a black smoking cinder where he'd been struck down, right there on the spot.

Martha walked. Step after step. Behind Garrett. Alongside the wagon when the girls were inside. . . . Holding Nora by the hand, pulling her along. . . . Carrying Louisa so she would stop crying. . . . Her left boot was getting a hole in it, letting the gritty dust in to nestle between sole and foot and bite in worse than the grit outside the sole. . . . Step after step.

She walked past natural wonders . . . Chimney Rock . . . Scotts Bluff . . . the Devil's Gate. The oppressive heat sucked her energy. Dust filled her nose and eyes, even her ears. Sounds dimmed—the creaking wheels. Cattle bawling. Thudding hoofbeats. Ropes squeaking. A shout. What was that? Nothing important.

She couldn't get her breath. She was three months pregnant.

Brambles tore at Martha's skirt. Her legs felt leaden, as if climbing, and she was, even if it didn't look like it. She was about to walk across the Great Divide of this continent, where the waters of the land separated— the waters on this side flowing east to the Mississippi and ultimately the Atlantic Ocean, the waters on the other flowing to the Pacific. She'd thought it would be a mountain. A ridge. A great wall to keep the waters apart.

Yet here the land spread out before her in such a gradual rise she could scarcely tell she was climbing. Wind whistled across the high desert. The sun shone warm on her back, not a cloud in the sky. Nights had been cold, though, everything white with frost in the mornings. The acrid smell of sage clutched her nose. She'd been tasting it for days. The scrubby plants dotted the landscape, along with other low, tangled brush, a spare coat of dry grass like a mangy dog's hair.

She'd seen snowcapped mountains in the distance, but no craggy peaks rose to meet them here. She heaved a sigh, thankful for that. So weary. They'd been traveling almost two months, and she'd walked all the way. On this broad stretch of ground she let some space come between her and the wagon. The girls were asleep, even Nora, both worn out. Martha needed a bit of quiet. The sounds of the train softened with a little distance. The creaking and rolling turned to a low murmur, rhythmic, almost melodic.

When would she know she'd reached the western slope where water flowed to the Pacific Ocean? Would she ever see that ocean? She'd never seen an ocean in her life. She closed her eyes and imagined herself floating on that peaceful sea, floating on a stream of wind. Her skirts whipped against her.

Opening her eyes she saw an encampment ahead, a flag snapping in the breeze above it. Was that a United States flag? It was. Her breath caught.

A rider came galloping from the encampment, coming toward her. Newt. He called out to her as he neared. "That's the pass—South Pass." He pointed behind him and pulled his horse up close. "They have sort of a post office there. We can send mail back to the States. I think we'll have us a party tonight."

Martha smiled, hands across her middle. "A party. How long has it been?" Her middle was starting to thicken. She'd have to start letting out her dresses soon. She was four months pregnant.

———

They plunged through the night to cross the forty-mile desert. It would take two days, but they had water in casks, and grass for the animals. Garrett and the boys had cut grass from a nice patch back on the edge of the desert and piled it on top of the mattress. The poor beasts would be able to eat and drink. They were getting so gaunt and weak, their hooves wearing out on the harsh ground. They kept losing their iron shoes. If Garrett ran out of iron he'd have to use sole leather or buffalo hide to protect their hooves.

The familiar creaks and groans of the train took on an eerie tone in the darkness. Martha tripped on something and caught herself. The moon shone bright, but left uncertain shadows. The endless desert bore down on her, like the endless hours. How would she stay awake all night? Walk all night? But the daytime heat had become almost unbearable, even before the desert. The men decided the only way to safely endure this dry stretch was to travel at night. The water would go further with less thirst, and they wouldn't have to suffer the killing heat.

Nights were almost as cool as in the mountains. Martha shivered and rubbed her arms. Nothing like the warm muggy nights of summer back home. What an odd country.

In the empty quiet fears rose. *Cholera.* The dreaded word echoed in Martha's head as she remembered what those strangers had said when they passed by a few days ago. So far that horror hadn't struck the emigrants traveling with Martha's family. But these fast-traveling packers brought word the disease was sweeping through companies behind them on the Platte. Had Martha's people escaped it? Would it follow? What in the world caused it?

The boys had told of cholera on the trail last year, and Martha had seen many graves along the way. The disease could come over a person like a striking snake. He could be well one day, and a couple of days later be buried beneath the alien soil. One of the girls coughed. Louisa? They were sleeping in the rolling wagon. Dust. The dust was making her cough. So dusty here. Martha put her hands to her face and shook her head. She couldn't look at that other horror. She and her family had to escape it. She trod a little faster into the night, only occasionally glancing over her shoulder.

Martha batted away mosquitoes as she sat in the shade with the girls and several other women and children outside the sturdy structure. Fort Hall. What a relief to find this semblance of civilization so far out in the wilderness. It also meant they'd covered a fair amount of their journey, but when she asked Larry if it would be downhill from here, he wouldn't answer.

The men stretched out under another tree, their talk rising in waves like the billowing mosquitoes. The voices grew louder with each round of the whiskey bottle. "Gold!" she heard.

"California has the gold."

She didn't want to go to California. Garrett had invested in farm equipment, seed grain, and cattle for farming. He hadn't spoken of California since starting this trip. He hadn't said much about anything for a while. Where was that man who could sit around a fire and tell story after story, the words rolling off his tongue like honey? She heard his laugh now, but it was the edgy laugh whiskey gave him. At least he was talking.

Night settled around them, and still the men talked. Martha took the girls to the wagon and tucked them in. She wished she could hear what the men were saying, but she couldn't leave the girls alone where the wagons were parked, outside the fort walls. She lay back beside her little ones to wait for Garrett. She would ask him all about it as soon as he came in. Her eyelids grew heavy. She forced them open, but they seemed to hold weights.

She woke, startled by a sound, and felt him next to her. He was snoring, deep, rattling snores, and the close air inside the wagon reeked of whiskey.

———❧———

Martha tramped through the choking dust, a handkerchief tied over her nose and mouth—on her way to Oregon. Not California. Oregon. No wonder Larry wouldn't talk about the roads west of Fort Hall. They were harder than before. Steeper. Rockier. Dustier. Rivers wilder. There was an occasional tree now, sometimes wooded areas even, with tall conifers and cottonwoods, the nights still refreshingly cool. But the heat of the day radiated with scorching fury.

Garrett stopped the oxen and poured water from his pouch onto a cloth, then wiped it over the animals' noses, cleaning off a little dust. They nodded their massive heads, as if thanking him, and one nuzzled him. Old Bob loved to be stroked under his chin, and Garrett obliged for a moment before moving along.

The trail here was littered with the bones of oxen and fresher dead beasts—along with discarded trunks and furniture—and another human grave.

A chill raked Martha despite the heat. The smell of death assaulted her nose.

The tattered wagon covers didn't look white anymore. Gray dust coated every surface, working its way down into every nook. Garrett had to brace the big wheels with sticks to keep the dry wood from slipping, the hubs wound with rags to hold the spokes in. Animals and people alike looked thin. So little grass. Even when they heard about grass ahead, they'd find much of it eaten off already by the companies that came through before. Now Martha worried about their own food supply. Her food bags had gone flabby for lack of contents.

They'd traded with some Indians—shirts for fish—large dried salmon to add to the meat supply. But they were nearly out of flour. How long until they reached The Dalles, where they might buy more? Garrett also traded for moccasins for both of them, since their boots were worn out. This Indian footwear did help on the gritty track.

Their company had dwindled, with many headed for California. She missed them.

Coming over a rise, she stopped, still as a post. Another river crossing. White froth surged above swirls of crashing water as it thundered between solid rock banks. "Do we—?" She shook her head. "We can't ford that."

Garrett looked ahead with the set of his jaw that seemed almost permanent now. "We'll have to raise the wagon box onto blocks, and double team. You'd better find some shirts, so we can trade for piloting." He pointed, and she saw the canoe, a couple of bare-fleshed Indians working it into the foam to cross toward them.

She put a hand over her growing middle and frowned. Could she trust those men to lead her family safely over? She was five months pregnant.

⌒ ⌒

Martha wrapped the blanket around her shoulders, shivering as she tromped through snow. Giant trees towered over her head, then gave way to piles of shale. *The last mountain to cross.* She kept telling herself that. But this was the hardest of all. They were working their way along the Barlow Road, her family traveling alone now. She thought the label *road* an exaggeration for the track they were struggling over, but men had tried to carve this track across the wild Cascade Range that divided all of Oregon's dry eastern part from the green Beulah Land on the western side.

Close on their right, lofty Mount Hood pointed its sharp coned pinnacle toward the sky. A snowstorm had surprised them in the night, giving the stony peak a fresh crown of white, but the day was warming. Martha admired its beauty, even in her exhaustion. The baby kicked so hard, Martha pressed her hand over the growing bulge. She was six months pregnant.

⌒ ⌒

A soft gasp burst from Martha's lips when she looked down the hill.

"Laurel Hill," Larry said. "The last one."

No one had told her the last mountain just dropped away on this side. This was the worst hill on the whole long trail. She clamped her arms over her chest. "We can't take the wagon. We couldn't possibly."

Larry peered over the edge. "Must be a sixty-degree slope, at least half a mile down."

If she hadn't known how long the journey was back to Missouri, she might have turned around right then. This was too much. A wide rutted gash cut through the trees, a sheer drop full of rocks and mud that ran so far down she couldn't make out the bottom in the shadows. All the things she'd packed—her trunk of clothes and treasures, the food they needed to survive—could they pack it on the horses and oxen? Would an ox even carry a pack? Could they in the condition they were in?

"Let's get the ropes," Garrett said. "We'll snub it to the trees and work it down."

Larry gave a brusque nod. "Better chain a log behind for a drag."

Martha looked at the men as if they were crazy. "What did you say?"

Garrett took hold of Martha's arm, squeezing so hard she cried out. "You're hurting me. What—?"

"We're taking the wagon down this chute, Martha, and I want you to get the girls, and then I want you to keep the hell out of the way, and don't say another damn word."

The blood rose in Martha's cheeks, and her chin quivered as she stared fiercely into her husband's eyes. Yanking out of his grasp, she turned and got her children out of the wagon and took them to a tree a ways back, where she stood and glared.

Garrett unhitched the oxen and started tying the longest ropes to the wagon, then looped them around sturdy tree trunks already scarred with rope burns. He rough-locked a rear wheel with a few wraps of chain around the tire, fastening the chain's end to the wagon to keep the hind wheels from turning. While he did all that the boys cut down a fir, and with the help of a pair of oxen drew the log over and chained it, branches and all, to the back of the wagon.

Martha held tight to her little girls, one in each hand, numb. But when Garrett brought his most faithful oxen to the front to hitch them up again, her eyes burned. Dear old Bob and Zack. So weary. Wouldn't this whole contraption just roll right over them?

Garrett turned to her. "We'll come back up for the other animals. You wait till the last. I don't want any of them behind you. Some might fall." He looked at Larry and Newt. "Ready?"

With nods all around, they gripped the ropes, muscles clenching as they pulled back, and Garrett bellowed. "Get up, Bob. Get up, Zack." The massive creatures inched to the brink and stepped over, jolting down the incline in a halting slide. The wagon tipped straight forward and skidded, men with it, slipping out of Martha's sight. Her mouth dropped open. She hurried to the edge to look, little hands still tight in hers.

The sound was horrific. Rumbling. Scraping. Rattling and squeaking. The terrible screech of the locked wheels. Men yelling.

And the sight. The wagon almost straight on end. Canvas cover trembling. The huge tree with all its branches flaying, limbs breaking off. Rocks and soppy clods flying. A boulder coming loose. Rolling. Oxen scrambling. Men digging in their heels, holding the ropes taut.

She gulped a sharp breath and took in the smell of gouged soil and bruised branches.

When a rope played out to the end, the men stopped and wrapped it around another scarred tree trunk, slowly working their way down, snubbing from tree to tree.

She watched them grow smaller, the sounds gradually fading, until the cloth-topped vessel became a miniature in the far depth. When she could finally take her eyes off the spectacle below, she looked for the trail she and her children and the rest of the animals would have to take. There, alongside the chute. It zigzagged a little, wasn't torn up like the chute, but the drop was every bit as steep and long. She looked down at her little girls, at her own huge belly, and a cold thread of fear shivered down her back.

———

September 14, 1850. Pieces of sunlight scattered like jewels on the dark trail winding through massive conifers beside a rushing stream. Huge deciduous trees grew back home, but nothing like these giants reaching straight to a sky scarcely visible through their thick boughs. Martha had to watch her step, lest she trip on a gnarled root. The wagon ahead of her jounced over them, rattling the metal pots and dishes. The rich scent of fir and cedar twined with the musk of the animals. She smiled at Old Bob and Zack, treading along at the head of the team, apparently no worse off for their ordeal on that chute. The family had made it without loss.

Newt had the girls on horseback with him, following the cows. Larry had ridden ahead. The darkness of the dense woods began to close in on Martha. Just when she thought she might suffocate, she saw a patch of sky where a few hardwoods mingled with the evergreens.

The wagon moved faster, and her heart sped with it. Were they about to see what they'd come all this way for? The rich land of Oregon? Their Beulah Land? Technically, they'd been in the Oregon Territory since they crossed the Continental Divide at South Pass, but when most folks talked of Oregon they meant the lush green lands west of the Cascade foothills. Somewhere west of these woods.

The trail widened and she moved up alongside the clattering vessel, a pound of hoofbeats just audible above the noise of the wagon. It was Larry, riding back to them, a wide smile on his bearded face. He waved and yelled. "You can see up ahead!"

A sense of lightness lifted her heart.

When they came out of the trees, she stopped and stared. Rolling prairie lay before her, rich with grass gold as straw but oddly lush. More of those tall pointy firs edged the prairie, a strange sight to her. In the distance they seemed even stranger than in the woods behind. Out where the firs lined the horizon, they impressed her as something alien. But beautiful. So this was Beulah Land. She glanced at Garrett, and his gaze met hers, a flash of wonder passing between them.

He looked forward again. "We'd better keep moving. We still have a ways to go." The cabin in Polk County was miles ahead yet, probably a good week of travel, but this was Oregon.

Even the oxen twitched with excitement, their mouths full of tender grass. When Garrett called them to go, they hurled against their yokes with new vigor as they pressed on down the gentle slope like animals headed for the barn. Martha grinned. Why wouldn't they be excited after all their suffering and want? A banquet lay before them, as far as they could see.

———

December 1, 1850. Rain battered the cabin roof of thatched fir boughs, small drips sprinkling here and there as Martha paced, her moccasins scuffing over the packed-earth floor. She hugged the blanket tighter around her shoulders and across her enormous belly. Her nightdress, thin and worn, didn't offer much warmth anymore.

Evening shadows closed in. Was it late? The drooping firs surrounding the tiny cabin made the place dark even in the daytime, with all the heavy clouds. Now the fire in the mud and stick fireplace cast a feeble light. Garrett had added the fireplace to this cabin the boys hurriedly built for them last year before returning to Missouri to lead them west.

She was thankful. This was more than many newcomers had. Some were living in hollowed trees and drafty shacks. Fortunately, she and Garrett had chinked the walls before the rain hit, even Nora helping. He'd intended to do more, but he'd spent days riding through the country, looking for the perfect piece of land to claim. They were only squatting here, like most folks new to Oregon.

Martha meandered past the girls, asleep in the little bed Garrett had made, and glanced up at their father sitting close to the firelight, working on a harness. December already. The baby jolted inside her. It shouldn't be long now. The baby had dropped yesterday. Martha knew the feeling after two of them. She knew where it was. She could feel the little feet. The head was down. Ready.

A fierce tightness gripped her belly, and a groan escaped her lips. No. Not this night. It was too dark.

Garrett looked up. "You all right?"

"Just a contraction."

He bolted to his feet. "Are you—is it time?"

It happened again, seizing her so strongly she stumbled to the bed, but before she could sit, warm water gushed down her inner thighs, puddling, and soaking into the dirt floor. She bent over the bed, clasping the bedclothes until the pain softened enough to let her turn her lumbering frame and sit.

Garrett started toward her, then headed for the door, grabbing his hat and coat. "I'll go for help."

"No!" She reached out. This was happening too fast. "Don't leave me alone."

He went to her and knelt on the floor, taking both her hands in his as he studied her face. "Is it—?"

She clutched his hands tighter while another contraction tugged. When it let go, she whispered, "There's no time. You can't leave me alone."

"But—"

"Help is too far. The baby might come while you're gone. Please don't go."

His voice rasped. "I don't know anything about—I don't know how—"

She pressed her forehead to his. "How many calves have you helped birth? And foals?"

"It's not the same."

"I can tell you what I know, what they did for me before."

She looked into Garrett Maupin's eyes and saw a stark fear she'd never seen in him, despite all they'd gone through. Her voice trembled. "You won't leave me, will you?"

"I won't leave you, Martha. Tell me what to do."

Another contraction. She gripped his hands again, digging in her nails. "Hold . . . on . . . until . . ."

When the pain eased she sat back, taking great heaving breaths, and he stood over her, waiting. "Water," she said finally. "Boil some water in a clean pan. You'll need to clean the knife."

His eyes widened.

"To cut the cord."

He nodded, and she went on to tell him what she remembered. "You'll need a little washcloth and towel and blanket. And the little strip of cloth to tie the cord. They're all in the basket in the corner, ready. Maybe—maybe some blankets to raise my head." She sat, weaving, then sank into the softness of the blankets and coats Garrett rolled up for a pillow.

Martha's sister Louisa and Ma had been there for Nora. Then when her own little Louisa came in Missouri, Garrett's ma brought a midwife, and his ma was so tender and kind, Martha regretted her earlier uncertainties. In fact, Rachel Maupin had emerged in the absence of her husband until Martha came to be quite fond of her. If only she were here now, or any of the women.

There was a woman about five miles away who had delivered several babies. She'd agreed to come help Martha when the time came. If the boys hadn't moved on, one of them could have ridden over there while Garrett stayed with her, but they'd found a place to put up another cabin, just across the county line. They were a good five miles away too.

The contractions grew stronger, fiercer. Garrett was torn between holding onto her and getting the things ready as she'd asked. She lay back during a moment of calm, and he set the basin of boiled water and knife and cloths on the crude wooden table, not half a pace away. He wiped his hands on a clean rag. "What can I do now?"

She couldn't talk, but she grabbed his hands, and he knelt by the bed and let her dig in until she thought she would make his hands bleed despite his hard calluses. She didn't want to cry out for fear of waking the girls, but she couldn't keep it in. The cries came and the pain, and he held on until she pulled back the tangled skirt of her nightdress and tried to see. The huge belly blocked her view. "Is it coming? Do you see?"

His eyes glittered in the firelight. "I see the head. You need to push it out."

Exhausted, she lay back panting. "I've been pushing. I can't—"

The pain took over again, and she tugged on Garrett while she pressed with every bit of strength she could find within herself. Sweat poured down his forehead, and he clenched his jaw as if pushing with her. Then with one long, mighty heave, she knew it was done. He caught the tiny, slimy bundle in his two big hands and looked at it with such awe, a light surrounded them in a glowing orb. A crackle in the fireplace told Martha a log had flared, but that didn't take away the illusion.

"It's a girl," he whispered, "and I never saw a finer one." The tiny fists waved and she let out a strong cry on her own.

"The cord," Martha said. "Here, hand her here."

She cradled the infant in her arms, then lifted her to him while he meticulously tied and sliced the cord. "You'll need to wash her now, and dry her, and wrap her up in the blanket." She watched as he held the tiny figure over the water, washing away the sheen of birth, and gently drying her before wrapping her in the blanket.

Tears burned Martha's eyes, and she blinked so she could watch, ready to counsel him but, more, wanting to see every part of it. He could be harsh sometimes, and those hands severe, but in this moment she loved the tenderness she remembered well.

When he brought the bundle to Martha, she moved over to make room for him. The afterbirth came, and he took that away, but when he'd cleaned everything he came and lay against the pillowed blankets with her, wrapping his arms around mother and child. The little one looked from one parent to the other with solemn eyes. Garrett chuckled. "I think we did all right, Mama."

Martha nuzzled his cheek. "Yes, Papa, I think we did."

He put a tender finger on the baby's miniature ear, and the old familiar honey filled his voice. "Welcome to Oregon, Miss Maupin. How about Miss Mary Jane?"

Chapter 7

Dark Days

Lane County, Oregon, July 1851

A hot summer sun beat down on the fertile land of their Oregon claim on the upper Willamette River, well south of the settlements of Oregon City and Portland on the lower Willamette. Moisture rose on Martha's forehead despite the cooling shade of a tall fir. Garrett was working on their new log cabin with Larry's help.

She tucked Mary Jane in her cradle, the older girls playing nearby. Here she could watch the building process and lend a hand as she was able. One day she wanted a proper house—a frame house with a balcony—but Garrett had told her this would be the finest log house she'd ever lived in, and she was thrilled at the prospect of her new home.

Newt had gone with a friend to Yreka, California, a few months ago looking for gold. For a few painful moments she'd thought Garrett would go with them. Somehow she held her tongue, and the whim passed.

Sweat glistened on Garrett's face and arms as he lifted one end of a log while Larry lifted the other. Together they heaved it atop the east wall. When they had it secured, Garrett stopped to gaze at the rolling fields, the grass higher than his waist. His voice resonated with pleasure. "Rich, Poindexter, rich." He wrinkled his face. "But damn little money."

Larry chuckled and glanced at Martha, knowing she didn't like Garrett's language.

Heedless, Garrett motioned toward their grove of dark firs. "Some folks around here laughed at me for claiming land with trees, but they come in pretty handy when you want to build a house, don't you think?"

"Can't argue with that," Larry said, wiping sweat off his face. He'd shaved his beard since coming to Oregon—Garrett too, though they both kept the mustaches.

Garrett let out a soft huff. "They laugh, and then they turn around and come asking for logs to build their own."

"Well, with six hundred forty acres, I think you can spare a few acres for trees and still have plenty to till."

Garrett raised his brows. "If you could have found yourself a wife, Larry, you could have got as much too, instead of half that."

Larry whacked a stick on a log, but only grinned.

Martha smiled. The new Donation Land Claim law was good to couples. She and Garrett each got 320 acres—with her portion separate. Garrett called it *his* claim, but it wasn't his alone.

He slapped a friendly hand on Larry's back. "Smart to come when we did too. Doc will wish he hadn't waited."

How Martha wished Doc and Elizabeth had come, more for their company than for the land they would gain. But it was true. The law said settlers who arrived in the Oregon country before December 1, 1850, could claim twice the amount of land. After that a single man could claim only 160 acres, a pair together 320.

Garrett had been camping down here since spring and had a field planted already. Now that the weather was better, they'd left the cramped cabin up north in Polk County and were all settled here with their covered wagon and a makeshift tent until they could move into the log house.

Garrett hoisted his axe. "Well, back to work. We won't get this house built if we stand around jawing all day."

Martha checked the girls and then picked up her sewing basket, finding a comfortable backrest against a tree. Such a pleasant setting—a rise in ground with fir trees behind, the soft rolling plain spreading in front. The dark-green Willamette River flowed gently beyond the trees, cutting through one corner of their claim, angular buttes on the far side of the river only partially screened by their firs. A nice creek curved its way across the property, bordered by small hardwoods—willows and alder, a few oaks and maples, another creek on the west side. For years Indians had kept wide stretches of grassland open in the valley by burning, Larry had said, though there weren't so many Indians now as in earlier days.

She was glad to have the house on high ground. She didn't know what the Willamette would do, but she'd seen enough of the raging Missouri to want some height. The whole Willamette Valley stretched for miles on either side of the river, mostly flat with an occasional butte, the Cascade Range on the distant horizon to the east, the Coast Range as far on the west. A sharp butte lay south of them, where a man named Eugene Skinner had settled. Word was, he was trying to promote a town near his butte.

That would be nice. A town, only a few miles away. Maybe Newt would come back and start that blacksmith shop he dreamed of—if the gold didn't spoil him too much. He did have a knack with metal.

She looked up, startled to see a rider coming from the north, right through the tall grass in front of the house. She hadn't heard the horse with all the pounding of the axes. She put down her sewing and stood. The girls hovered behind her skirts.

The man stopped his horse and smiled, looking from Martha to the men, back to Martha, brightness flashing in his eyes. A young man, probably no older than Larry, maybe her age. He took off his hat, the sun highlighting a reddish cast in his light-brown hair, and spoke with an accent unfamiliar to her. "Well, now, it looks like I'd be getting myself some neighbors, then. And a grand day to be putting up a house, is it?" He stretched his hands wide. "Could you be asking for better, now?"

She smiled in return, but didn't find words to answer.

He faced the men once more. "My name is John Vallerly. I staked my claim to the north of you here, the second place over."

Garrett put down the log he was holding. "I'm Garrett Maupin. This is my brother-in-law Larry Poindexter." Garrett turned toward Martha, no doubt to introduce her.

But Mr. Vallerly swung from his saddle, landing lightly on the ground, and walked straight to her, reaching out his right hand as if to shake hers, but when she put her hand forward he took hold of it and held it in his, bending toward her. "And who would this lovely lady be?" He honed his gaze on her with a sparkle in his blue eyes that reminded her of the lights in Garrett's.

"I'm—I'm Martha Maupin."

"That's *Mrs.* Maupin—my *wife.*" Garrett. Martha looked up to see a dark shadow cross Garrett's face, but the man squeezed her hand, drawing her attention back to him.

"It's a pleasure to be meeting you, ma'am. It's a grand sight to be seeing a lady like yourself." He leaned over and winked at one of the girls behind her. "And the wee ones. I'm a long way from home and family, all the way from the fair land of Ireland. Oh, and it's fair here, to be sure, but it won't do without someone to talk to, not at all, at all."

The words sprinkled off his tongue like bits of silver, until she couldn't help laughing with delight. "It's nice to meet you too."

As if spurred by her laughter, he went on. "I have my cabin built already, and it'll be a pleasure to have you come with your fine family and put a bit of sunshine into the place, will you? When you have the time?"

"That would be nice."

Another smile lit his eyes as he bent down and kissed her hand, then turned toward the men, apparently oblivious to Garrett's scowl. "Now, gents, what can I do to help?"

When he released her hand, Martha pulled it back and put it behind her, touching Nora's soft head.

Garrett and Larry hesitated, but John Vallerly soon found he could help Larry lift logs while Garrett sharpened the axe on the grindstone he'd brought from Missouri. Before long they were all working together. Mr. Vallerly didn't stop talking. Although Martha kept her distance, working again on her sewing, she heard him talk about Ireland, about the terrible famine there, about his family nearly starving and him deciding to come to America so they had one less mouth to feed, about the long trip across the ocean.

As the sun slipped low, Martha stirred the coals of their campfire, ready to put together a meal for them. She heard Garrett ask Mr. Vallerly to supper. Though Garrett seemed cool toward the man, a Maupin never turned away a stranger at mealtime, certainly not one who'd worked hard all afternoon to help him.

They ate their supper of biscuits and bacon and fresh wild berries, to Mr. Vallerly's frequent praise. "I have never in all my long days ever eaten such fair morsels as these, Mrs. Maupin," he said of her special biscuits, and she couldn't help beaming at his enthusiasm.

Martha passed a jug of cool fresh water from the creek, but Garrett lifted a hand. "Why don't you get the whiskey jug, Martha?"

She went to the wagon, where their things were stored. They'd been lucky not to need much whiskey for medicine. She supposed it wouldn't hurt to drink a little. But when she pulled it out of its place among the food bags, she was surprised to find how light it was. What had happened to all the whiskey? Her forehead tightened. Garrett. She knew it was nearly full when they got to Oregon. He hadn't consumed much on the trail. He wouldn't, knowing he had to have his faculties about him, given the dangers. But in the months since their arrival? The long, dark winter?

Shaking her head, she took the jug to where the men sat on the ground around the campfire. Her distress edged her voice. "Garrett, there's hardly any left. If we need it for—"

The sharp furrow of his brow stopped her, but he didn't comment. Turning away, he passed the jug to their company.

Mr. Vallerly smiled. "Empty, is it? Not at all. There's aplenty here. And I have a jug at my house, near full. I'll bring it tomorrow when I come to help."

After Mr. Vallerly left and Larry bedded down in his tent, Martha started to climb in the wagon, where she and Garrett and the girls slept, the way they did on the trail, cozy and warm on these cool nights. She was thinking how much she loved the cool summer evenings of the Far West when Garrett grabbed her arm and pulled her around to face him, his voice low. "Martha Maupin, I don't like you sassing me in front of strangers."

"Sassing?"

"About the jug."

"I wasn't sassing. I was just telling you."

His voice became a chilling hiss. "Do you think I can't see for myself?"

⌁

January 1853. Martha rushed through the rain toward the house, careful not to spill the warm milk. She glanced toward the river, recalling the flooding Missouri. She set the milk in the cool room at the end of the back porch and hurried inside to check the ham. Her feet felt light, heart racing as much from excitement as from scurrying. Everyone was coming for dinner. She wanted everything just right.

Lifting the heavy iron lid from the pot in the fireplace, she peeked in. The rich aroma of boiling ham enveloped her. It smelled so good she could taste it. Giving it a poke, she nodded. Nice and tender. Biscuits in the Dutch oven needed a little more time. She bounded upstairs to check on the girls. Nora, in charge of getting them dressed, was doing fine. At six she was quite a little lady. Martha didn't know how she'd manage without her.

Four-year-old Louisa insisted on helping herself, but Mary, two, was agreeable as always. Martha had already dressed baby Selena, who'd be one month tomorrow. Four little girls. Garrett despaired of ever getting a son, but they were the prettiest bevy of girls Martha had ever seen.

A knock sounded on the door. What a lovely sound. Satisfied all was well upstairs, Martha hurried down to answer it. So nice having the stairs after using a ladder for such a long time. And the floor. She loved the new puncheon floor, made of heavy slabs of rough-hewn boards. No more hard-packed earth.

Opening the front door, she saw her dear Doc and Elizabeth and hugged them both and their little boy, George, almost as old as Nora and bigger already. "Come in. Come in."

Elizabeth stepped in ahead of Doc and began wandering around the room, admiring all the handiwork. The new curtains and quilts, a nice table in the center with long benches on either side. "It smells wonderful in here."

"One of the hogs we butchered and smoked. I think it'll be a nice one. I hope so."

Doc put a hand on Martha's shoulder. "As long as you made biscuits. You did make some of your famous biscuits, didn't you?"

Martha laughed. "Of course, Doc. I knew you were coming." She heaved a happy sigh. "And everybody else. It's so good having so many of us here."

Most of Martha's family had finally come to Oregon, and some of Garrett's as well. Doc and Elizabeth came over the trail last summer, along with Ben and Simpson and Garrett's brother Howard and family.

Garrett's sister Lucinda and her family had come the year before. Newt was back from California, rich in stories, if not in gold. Poor Ben lost his wife on the trail, a girl he'd met in Carroll County and married shortly before heading west. Now he was alone, like her other bachelor brothers.

Elizabeth turned to Martha. "I think we'll see plenty more next year too. I know quite a few folks planning on it. Oregon's getting almost crowded."

Martha smiled. "Well, that'll mean more young ladies. Maybe my brothers will find wives yet."

"John Vallerly found one. They're going to get married later this month, I hear." Elizabeth lifted her brows. "But I think he has a way with the ladies."

Martha laughed and imitated Mr. Vallerly's accent. "He does, now, to be sure."

Elizabeth laughed with her, and Doc chuckled low in his throat. "She's a Ray County girl," Elizabeth said. "John Brown's daughter. Young, but nice. They're good people. They came over the trail with us."

Voices sounded outside before another knock on the door. A whole crowd of family pressed close, anxious to get in out of the rain, which was coming down even harder.

Howard's gravelly voice rose above the others. "Look what the rain blew in." He chortled and wiped drips of rainwater off his dark chin whiskers as he ushered in his wife and children.

Then Martha's brothers—Larry and Newt, Ben and Simpson—and Garrett's sister Lucinda and her husband, Garrett right behind them. They took off their dripping coats and hats and hung them on the many pegs Garrett had driven into the wall by the door.

Now his face twisted with worry. "Don't like the look of the river. It's rising fast."

A sense of urgency spurred Martha. With the help of the women, she got food on the table. Besides ham and biscuits, they had vegetables from her garden, still growing, even in January. And she'd made pumpkin cake from the huge pumpkins they grew.

As soon as people finished their cake, the men started to leave. "That was a mighty delicious dinner," Howard said, "but we need to check on our animals."

Murmurs of agreement answered him.

"We're on high ground," Garrett told them. "Bring your animals here." He turned to Martha. "We need to take everything we can up into the loft."

The next hour or so became a blur of activity. Packing things upstairs. Beds. Food. Dishes. Tools. Even the table. As family returned, some pitched in to help with that, while Garrett and others saw to the animals. More than family came. Neighbors. John Vallerly and his intended bride and her family, the Browns.

An uncharacteristic edge sharpened Howard's tone. "There's houses floating down the river. This doesn't look good."

Garrett stood looking at his brother, silent. Then he gave Howard a curt nod. "Let's bring in the animals."

Prickles chased across Martha's nerves. "Bring in where?"

"In here. In the house."

She looked around her home, down at the beautiful puncheon floor. "In *here?*"

"They'll hold the house down, and the floor's higher than anything around."

"But the mess!"

He raised his brows at her. "Less mess than a river floating you downstream. Get on upstairs and make sure the girls are safe."

With heavy steps, Martha climbed the new stairs to the loft and joined the others finding places as they could amid the treasures they'd rescued. They sat on mattresses and bundles, some on the loft floor, some on the table and benches. Martha gathered her daughters to her like a mother duck collecting her ducklings beneath her wings. She swallowed tears that ran down her throat.

Then she heard the lilting voice of John Vallerly and looked up to see him bending down to her, hand outstretched. "Thanks kindly for this, Mrs. Maupin. I sure didn't know I was helping build an ark when I came by that summer. Not at all, at all."

She took his hand, laughing, the tears in her throat making an odd snorting noise, and laughter rose in a rippling circle. The sweet young Brown girl stood behind him, smiling. Over the girl's shoulder, Garrett appeared at the top of the stairs. He glanced at Mr. Vallerly, and looked straight at Martha, face set like stone, eyes piercing. The laugh froze on her tongue, and she drew her hand to herself. Garrett vanished.

A commotion sounded below—bawling, nickering, stomping feet, shouts of men. The house shook with them. The river turned louder. The agitation took on a different feel, like trembling. The river had hit the house.

No one moved. The building's tremors echoed through Martha. Someone had set a lantern high in the ceiling, but it cast a thin glow, its soft shudder moving the shadows. The sky turned pitch-black, the dark of night blotting out all but their meager sanctuary. The surrounding danger, unseen, loomed greater. The hour grew late. People found a way to lie down. Garrett came back up and sat on an upper stair, arms resting on his knees, head low. If he ever lay down, Martha didn't notice. She leaned against the wall to nurse the baby, then gave in to fatigue and stretched out herself, little Selena cradled in one arm.

At some point Martha fell asleep, and when she woke the river was down. The house had stood. She didn't want to see what had happened to her floor.

Mr. Vallerly smiled at her. "I'm sure we're out of danger now. And don't you be worrying, Mrs. Maupin. We'll help clean that floor. They put hay down. It'll clean up fine."

◆━◆

January 22, 1855. Martha lay on the bed, panting, Elizabeth by her side. Martha had been midwife for Elizabeth last year when she had her second son, Granville. Now Elizabeth was helping her again, as she did when Martha gave birth to Selena two years ago. Every two years, regular as a reliable clock.

Another contraction clutched her.

Elizabeth held her hands, let her cling.

Martha pushed, then breathed long breaths while sweat streamed. She saw Garrett look in. He appeared content to stay on the sidelines after helping with Mary. He always kept a soft spot for Mary—from that night, Martha guessed.

Elizabeth brushed a wet rag over her forehead, talking softly, calming. "We may have lots of midwife duties after the rash of marriages last year." All Martha's brothers but Newt had found wives.

"Yes." Martha watched Garrett leave.

Elizabeth went on. "Wouldn't surprise me if Newt doesn't join them soon. Did you see him with Elvira McCord? I hope so. I like her. I'm so glad Ben found someone else."

"You were there when his first wife died, weren't you?" Martha's voice quivered.

"I saw her die in his arms. A terrible trip. And then Nancy had the baby, right out there along the Platte River." Howard Maupin's wife.

Martha batted away tears. "We didn't have anything like that on our trip west, just the ordinary miseries."

Why was this taking so long? She'd been in labor for hours.

A fierce contraction gripped her and wouldn't let go. She cried out. Garrett rushed in. Pain. So fierce. Relentless. The baby came, and Elizabeth caught it.

Moving close, Garrett reached down and picked the infant up, cord and all, and let out a whoop. "It's a boy! God damn, if I don't have a boy."

"The cord," his sister said, ready with the knife and a strip of cloth.

"I can do this." Garrett laid the infant on its mother and took the strip of fabric to tie off the thick, pink rope of flesh. Then he grabbed the knife and cut the cord himself. Giving a satisfied nod, he lifted the child again and looked into the red face as the little one wailed with gusto. Garrett just laughed. "Let her rip, boy. That's my boy, Captain Henley. Good to meet you at last."

Elizabeth tilted her head. "Captain Henley?"

"It's what I promised my captain before he died. In the war. I said if I lived to have a son, I'd name my first son after him." Garrett jiggled the child until he stopped crying and looked up at his father. The pride in Garrett's face filled the room, and it was a sizable room.

—◆—

January 1856. Martha stood against the counter in the little store in Eugene City, waiting while the shopkeeper figured up what he owed her.

Garrett wandered around the store, Cap in his arms. Nora had Mary and Selena, one in each hand. Louisa kept to herself.

The shopkeeper looked at Martha over his spectacles. "That'll give you three dollars and thirty-eight cents in credit after your purchases, Mrs. Maupin."

"Oh, thank you very much."

"Thank *you*, Mrs. Maupin. You bring in fine butter and cheese, nice eggs. No trouble at all to sell them."

Martha was doing what she could to help out, though Garrett didn't quite like it. She glanced at him, looking a little disheveled, pointing things out to Cap. She wanted to get something for Cap's first birthday later this month. Maybe she could find something for a few cents.

If only things would work out better for Garrett. They could grow anything in Oregon. Selling it was something else. Wheat was a standard for exchange in Oregon. The shopkeeper here would take wheat in exchange, but at low wholesale rates. Transporting it by wagon to better markets in Portland was out of the question due to the bad roads, and no one had dared bring a sizable boat this far down the Willamette.

So much mud. When had Martha ever seen such mud? Even here in Eugene City. Eugene Skinner's wife had named it Eugene City, but most folks called it Skinner's Mud Hole.

A bell tinkled on the shop door, and Martha looked up to see John Vallerly come in. A sudden glow lit his face on sight of her. "Mrs. Maupin." He took his hat off with a sweep and reached out to take her hand. She thought he was about to kiss her hand again, but perhaps thought better of it, letting go after a gentle squeeze. "It's a fair sight to see you on this bright, sunny January day, Mrs. Maupin. How are you getting along?"

"I'm well, thank you. How are you?"

Garrett stepped up and placed a hand on her shoulder.

"Mr. Maupin," Vallerly said. "A fine good hello to you too—and this wee one." He took Cap's hand in his two fingers and shook it lightly.

Garrett's voice sounded taut. "Mr. Vallerly."

A sudden longing tightened Martha's heart—not for Mr. Vallerly, but for his manners and his unbridled joy in life. She wished Garrett could be more refined. Happier.

Garrett looked down at Martha. "You done here?"

"I want to get something for Cap—for his birthday. It's this month, you know."

"You can do that later. Let's go." He took her arm and marched her toward the door. Nora had the girls gathered up to follow.

"But, Garrett—"

Bending close to Martha's ear, he spoke under his breath. "I don't want to hear any more. We can't afford a present for Cap."

She glanced over her shoulder. "Nice seeing you, Mr. Vallerly. Please say hello to Mrs. Vallerly for us."

He nodded, and she thought she detected an uncharacteristic sadness in his eyes, if only for a moment. The bright smile returned. "I'll do that, thank you. And a good day to all of you."

<hr/>

February 1856. Martha carried the milk out of the cows' small pasture and swung the gate to close it behind her. The gate sagged, squeaking on its hinges, and dropped to the ground.

"Oh, dear!" The thing had been getting harder to open and close. Now she had to fix it.

When was Garrett getting home? He'd gone to town again, trying to get a better price for the wheat. She hoped he had some luck. He got in such a stew over the whole business.

Teeth clenched, she tried to set the gate in position and hold it while she worked on the hazel-withe hinge on top, but when she began struggling with the hinge, the gate slipped out of her grasp and fell back to the ground, scraping her leg. "Ouch! Stupid thing."

Again she lifted it. "Why didn't Garrett fix this?" She got the hinge fastened and stepped back. The gate slumped, and fell again. She heard a horse cantering toward her. "Well, it's about time." She wheeled around, hands on her hips, and froze. It wasn't Garrett.

"John Vallerly," she said.

The lights flashed in his eyes. "Mrs. Maupin." He swung down from his horse and came straight to her. "Can I help you, ma'am?"

Her cheeks flared. She felt the heat and knew she must be bright red. But she had been struggling. Maybe he'd think it only from that. She thought she ought to protest. "I'll get it. I—"

He bent down to pick up the gate. "Here, then. I think the hinge is just stretched a wee bit." His voice, his entire manner, seemed intended to put her at ease, but her heart beat wildly. He had the gate up and swinging in no time. "There, now, that's better."

Brushing his hands together, he gave her another direct smile. "And how have you been, Mrs. Maupin? I've scarce seen you since the other day in town."

"I've been well, thank you." Such pleasant manners. Was he always so kind? She'd never experienced anyone quite like him. Americans were so gruff by comparison.

She became aware of a lock of hair that had escaped its pin and was trailing down her back. Trying to tuck it into her bun without being obvious, she wondered what Garrett would think. As if her thoughts had conjured him, she heard Rusty's nicker and looked up. Garrett rode straight to where she stood next to John Vallerly. Garrett's cheeks looked flushed, as if he'd stopped by a grog shop. His chin jutted forward.

Vallerly spoke first. "Mr. Maupin, a fine good day to you, sir. How are you?"

Garrett offered a curt nod. "Vallerly."

Bending down to pick up his hat from the ground where he'd tossed it, Vallerly smiled at Martha, a look in his eyes that spoke of concern and care, a gentle kindness in his tone. "Mrs. Maupin." He jumped on his horse and reined it around to turn away.

She called after him. "Thank you for the gate."

For once he said nothing, just tipped his hat as he spurred his horse to a gallop.

Garrett dismounted and walked over to Martha. "What was that about?"

She shrugged, inclining her head toward the errant gate. "The hinge stretched or something. The gate fell down. I was trying to fix it and—"

"You couldn't wait till I got home?"

"I didn't want the cows to get out, but—I didn't ask for help. He just offered and—"

"And you couldn't say no?"

Martha tried to find understanding in Garrett's eyes, some spark of feeling, but the old spark appeared clouded. "It didn't seem neighborly to refuse help when I needed it."

"What was he riding this way for anyway?"

"I don't know."

"Does he do that regularly?"

"He never has before that I know." She took a short breath. "Garrett—"

"Where are the children?"

"Nora has them—in the house."

He glanced at the house, and took hold of the gate, testing the hinge. "Convenient."

"What—?"

"Maybe young Vallerly ought to tend to his own wife."

"Ma!" Louisa came running out. "Ma, can you come in? Nora won't let me—"

Martha snapped at her. "In a minute."

Garrett grabbed Rusty's reins and led him off to the barn. Martha watched her husband go, his step wooden, without his usual grace and rhythm.

A stray wish whispered. *If only he could be a little smoother polished at the edges—like Mr. Vallerly.*

February 23, 1856. Martha whipped the butter paddle over the rich yellow mound. Nice butter. She'd carve off a small amount for the family and sell the rest. Maybe Garrett could take it into Eugene City tomorrow. She tightened her brow. She didn't like asking him.

Stomping feet on the front doorstep startled her. She shrank inside, wondering which Garrett Maupin would come in the door—the disgruntled one, the one who's a little too happy because he stopped off at a grog shop in Eugene City, or the one she feared most, the angry one. She wanted to see the tender one with the bright words of hope. She knew that one. She just hadn't seen him lately.

The door slapped open, and he stormed in, slinging his coat in the corner. *The angry one.* He'd been to the grog shop too. She could smell it.

"God damn, son of a bitch—"

"Garrett, the children."

But Nora was already gathering them to go upstairs. "Story time, Selena. Come on, Cap." She picked him up and followed her sisters up the steps.

Martha walked over and put a hand on Garrett's arm, desperately wanting to make things better. "What is it?"

He waved a dismissive hand and plopped onto a bench at the table. "They want to price us out of business. There's no use even carrying the grain into town. No use even planting more."

Before Martha could respond a brisk knock hammered the door. Garrett rose as if a heavy weight bore down on him. When he saw the man at the door, he swung the wooden slab inward. "Jim McCabe. How are you? Come on in."

The man hesitated, then took off his hat and stepped inside, far enough so Garrett could close the door behind him and shut out the cold. He stood tall, hat pressed to his chest, and spoke with sharp clarity. "Garrett Maupin, as Sheriff of Lane County I'm afraid I have to arrest you for assault with intent to murder one John Vallerly. You need to come with me."

A gasp escaped Martha's lips.

Garrett shook his head. "Oh, Jim, you know better than that. I never assaulted anybody, and I sure never intended to murder him."

"I'm sorry, Garrett, but I have my bounden duty." Sheriff McCabe pulled a slip of paper out of his pocket and glanced at it. "He says you overtook him out on the county road by Joseph Davis's claim, drew a pistol from your belt and cocked it, put it one foot from his head, and swore you'd blow his brains out." The sheriff checked the paper again. "He says he knocked the pistol away from the direction of his head and grabbed hold of it and in the scuffle the thing went off."

Garrett reached a hand toward Mr. McCabe. "That's not how it happened, Jim. You see, he was—"

"Well, you can explain that in court, Garrett—Mr. Maupin. Please come now."

Martha sank onto a bench as she watched the sheriff lead her husband out of the house.

⸺•⸺

March 1859. "All right, line up." Larry said, smiling at Martha's growing brood as they happily formed a line to please their uncle.

The baby began fussing in her cradle, and Martha went over and picked her up, the child's long dress cascading over Martha's skirts. "Don't cry, Baby Girl."

Hands on his hips, Larry nodded. "Stairsteps. You're still making stairsteps, Martha. Six now, plus the baby."

She laughed. "I think you're starting your own steps, Larry. How is everybody?"

"Good, good." He turned and walked toward her, touching the baby's gauzy dress. "How's she doing?"

Martha looked over at the handsome line of children—four big girls, two boys. "Why don't you go on outside to play? It's such a nice day after all the rain."

With squeals of joy, the children burst out the door and scattered into the bright spring afternoon. Little Tom toddled after Cap. Two now, he always tried to keep up with his four-year-old brother. Watching them, Larry chuckled, then sobered as he faced Martha again.

Shaking her head, she glanced at the baby. "This one isn't as strong as the others were. I hope . . ." She let the words go.

"Have you named her yet?"

"Garrett wants to name her Martha Ann. I want to name her Isabell. So we call her Baby Girl." The child's eyes closed, and Martha put her back in the cradle.

"How's Garrett?"

Martha drew a deep breath. "Seems like he's been angry since the sheriff walked him out of this house three years ago." The jury had declared him not guilty, but that didn't quite erase the shame. John Vallerly never showed his face around here anymore, but he had his own grief. His young wife died about a year ago giving birth to their only child, a boy. Martha had heard he sold his property and was leaving town. The grandparents were taking care of the child. Martha regretted the whole row between him and Garrett. Mostly she regretted the change in Garrett. Maybe it started before, but that incident seemed to set the change. "It's hard to face the neighbors."

Larry gave her a soft smile. "You're not the only one. It's rough out here in Oregon—especially Lane County. You know what they say. If you want to shoot somebody and get away with it, go to Lane County. Half the cases are *assault with intent to murder,* no matter what it's about."

"Do you think Garrett did try to kill John Vallerly?"

Larry shrugged. "Hard to say what happened. They both like their whiskey. And they can both be pretty hotheaded." She'd never seen that side of Mr. Vallerly. "I think you might as well take the jury's decision and let it go."

"I wish Garrett would."

Patting her shoulder, Larry told her good-bye and headed out. She heard his jovial chatter with the children, and the retreating hoofbeats of his horse. She felt blessed to have five protective brothers close by. A shiver raised the hair on her arms. The house felt empty. She called to the children to do their chores and started supper. Garrett should be home soon.

The children had eaten and gone to bed before she heard Garrett's horse. She tensed, waiting. Would he come in drunk again? She heard a stumbling footstep outside the door, and a stream of language that burned her ears.

The door swung in so hard it slammed against the wall, startling her. Garrett staggered in. "Son of a bitch, God damn it, can't you keep the God damn shoes off the porch?"

"Garrett! The children will hear you."

He stumbled straight to her, the stench of whiskey engulfing her. But she forgot the smell at sight of the sharp look in his eyes. His lips curled in a snarl. He raised one hand high and slapped the back of it across her mouth.

The pain seared. She let out a short cry and stood, stunned. He'd never struck her before. She backed up, hand on her mouth, and he closed the gap with one long step, putting his face so close she couldn't focus. She could almost taste the whiskey on his breath, blended with the salty taste of her own blood.

He spit out his words, slurring a little. "I'm not one of your children. I'm your husband and you'd damn well better start showing a little respect."

Her own voice sounded tinny in her ears. "You hit me."

"Damn right I did. You're too damn mouthy, woman, and I have a right as your husband to keep you in line." He started to turn away, and faced her again. "A responsi-*bil*-ity to keep you in line."

He stumbled to the bed, sat down with a thud, and leaned back in a rolling motion until he lay with one foot on the bed, the other on the floor, both boots still on. In moments he began to snore. Martha stared at him, hand on her mouth, thinking she ought to take off his boots and put his other foot on the bed, but she couldn't make herself move.

———

May 1859. Martha checked the baby in her cradle. She was sleeping but felt warm. Frowning, Martha drew her arms to herself, fingertips together. The child had been sick off and on for the three months since she was born, but not like this.

Martha heard voices outside, and her spirits rose a little. Doc and Elizabeth. Garrett came in with them. "Could I get you a drink?" he asked.

"Not now," Elizabeth said, heading straight for Martha. "How are you? And how's the little one?"

Martha shook her head, leaning into Elizabeth's embrace, then Doc's. Garrett poured himself a cup of whiskey. "Doc? Won't you have one?"

"Maybe a small cup."

Elizabeth and Doc both bent down to look at the baby. "Is she any better?" Elizabeth asked, touching the tiny forehead. "Oh, so warm."

Martha sighed. "I don't know what else to do. I sponged her down, but she's sleeping now. I hate to disturb her when she sleeps so little."

Stepping away, Martha brought out some biscuits, along with coffee for the women, and the four sat around the table, reminding her of old times. She couldn't muster the old feelings of pleasure and promise, though. The children's voices echoed outdoors, her own brood glad for cousins to play with.

Garrett turned to Doc. "How does your wheat look?"

"Looks nice," Doc said. "Things grow good here."

Garrett drained his cup and poured another. "Yeah, if you can sell it."

Doc rubbed a thumb over his cup. "Maybe now that Oregon's a state we can get a little more help. Get some roads. The steamboats didn't do much good, did they?" The first side-wheel steamer had reached Eugene three years ago, and Garrett sent wheat north. But rates for transport were so high, profits were next to nothing. With that and the uncertainty of navigation this far upriver, folks soon gave up on the idea.

Garrett snorted. "Oregon's a state all right, but a free state. At least we sent some good proslavery Democrats to the Senate." He slammed his cup on the table. "Did you know some Yank came by here the other day wanting to use my grindstone? I told him, no God damn Yankee is going to sharpen his tools on my grindstone."

Martha's brows rose. Maybe Garrett had more than John Vallerly burning his insides.

Garrett went on. "No Yankees and no Irishmen. Isn't that right, Martha?"

She felt the blood rise in her cheeks and clutched her cup to keep her hands from trembling.

Elizabeth faced Martha. "There's a woman over by us who has a way with herbs. Maybe she'd have something for your little one. Would you like me to talk to her?"

"Maybe so. I've always tended them myself, but this is beyond me. Garrett even brought that doctor from town a couple days ago, but he wasn't able to help her much."

Doc patted Martha's hand, and pushed away from the table. "We should be going. We just stopped by on our way home from town."

When they'd said their good-byes, Martha heard the baby fussing and hurried to pick her up. Taking her to the rocking chair, Martha tried to feed her, but the poor thing just shook her little head and fussed more.

The girls hovered near. "Nora," her mother said, "would you get some cool water in the pan there with the rag in it?" When Nora brought the pan, Martha sponged the child, desperate to cool the fever burning inside the tiny body. Garrett stood in the shadows across the room, watching.

Still, the child whimpered, and Martha looked up at her oldest daughter. "You'd better put some supper down, Nora. I don't think I should leave her."

Once the others had settled around the table, Nora came back to her mother. "Do you want me to hold her while you eat?"

Martha's stomach churned. She didn't see how she could eat. "Maybe I'll have a bite later. You go ahead."

Darkness pressed down on their log house. Nora put the boys to bed, while Louisa milked the cows and Mary and Selena cleaned the table. Garrett had gone outside somewhere. Martha kept rocking, rocking. She finally sent the girls to bed. She had a feeling it would be another long night. The baby's fussing turned more raspy, then quieted. A heaviness drew Martha deeper in the chair.

Martha woke with a start. She looked into the tiny face, the eyes closed, a perfect curve of eyelashes under each eye. Drawing the little one closer, Martha spoke to her in a low whisper. "I must have fallen asleep when you did." A nettling warmth struck. "You're so still."

She moved the child. Rubbed her cheek. No life. No breath. A scream rose in Martha's throat, but wouldn't come out. Garrett lay asleep on the bed beside them. She couldn't bring herself to wake him. Not now. Nor the others. Couldn't let out her despair. She rocked fiercely, clutched the baby to her breast. Pain swelled inside her until she knew it was going to explode and break her into a million pieces. And she was going to die because she couldn't live broken in so many pieces.

—◄►—

Martha stood beneath the tall fir tree at the edge of the woods on their property and watched as they lowered the tiny box into the rich, dark ground. Even the sun wouldn't look down on them on this overcast day in May. Martha was surprised to find herself standing here alive. How could she still be alive when the pain wouldn't quit swelling?

Garrett stood next to her, silent, face as rigid as that little box. He stepped forward and lifted a shovel from a pile of fresh raw dirt, took a scoop out of the pile, and dumped it onto the box. His brother Howard picked up another shovel to help. Her brothers and their wives gathered close around her.

When the hole was filled, they all walked toward the house, where neighbors were setting out food. Someone had brought the table outside. Elizabeth led Martha to a chair. Then all the sisters-in-law pulled chairs up and pressed close to Martha. She wanted to melt into their combined embrace.

She knew Elizabeth lost a child back in Missouri, but Martha wasn't there and it never became real for her. She knew her sister had lost three, two of them before Martha even left home. But Martha was young—she couldn't have been more than twelve—and Louisa seemed so strong. Sure, she cried. Everybody cried, but then she went on. How did she do that? How would Martha ever go on?

❦

July 1859. The July day wouldn't give up its heat with the coming of evening—almost like the evenings back East. Martha helped Nora put the younger ones to bed. They still needed their mother, and she found joy in each of them. Despite her doubts, she'd slowly gained feeling again.

Back downstairs she thought she heard a horse and looked, but it must have been her imagination. She was worried about Garrett. He'd taken the baby's death hard, but he wouldn't be consoled. She remembered how he was when his pa died and he put a wall around himself so she thought he didn't love her anymore. He was like that now—shrunk into himself, gone a lot, even more than before.

Another sound. Yes, Garrett. She knew the horse. Her body tightened in what had become a normal reaction. When he came in the door, she backed away, bumping into the table. His eyes looked glazed, and he started for her, stumbled, caught himself, and grabbed her by the arm.

She tried to pull away. "Garrett, you're drunk."

He didn't let go. "You're my wife, and you need to remember who you belong to."

What did he mean by that? Vallerly? John Vallerly had kept his distance since Garrett threatened to kill him—although he did express condolences when she passed him in town the other day. Why wouldn't he? It was the mannerly thing to do. The kind thing. She remembered the sympathy in his eyes. She'd also expressed her belated condolences to him for the loss of his wife. How could she not? Martha was surprised to see him, having heard he was moving away. Maybe he was back visiting his little boy. Did Garrett see? Garrett had gone over to the blacksmith shop. She didn't think he was anywhere in sight.

Garrett's voice rasped now. "I see you talking to that man, he's a dead man and you're with him. You understand? And I'd better not hear any more stories. You're my wife, Martha Maupin. You damn well better remember that or—" His words became a hiss. "—or I'll kill you."

She stared into his eyes and didn't recognize her husband in them. Was it the alcohol talking? Or did he really think these things? Where had her Garrett gone?

He latched onto both her arms, his fingers biting into her flesh, but she wrenched away and pushed the flat of her hands against his chest. "Garrett, stop. You're—"

He reared taller, lifted a fist, and swung at her face, the back of his hand whacking against her right jaw. Before she could react, the hand swung back and slapped her left cheek. She tried to swallow the cry, but couldn't. Her head spun. Pain reverberated.

He stepped back, staggered a little, and moved his right hand down to the pistol on his belt. Tears rose to blind her and she hugged herself, clawing her fingertips into the fabric of her dress. She wanted to run, hide, but she stood blinking, staring toward his hand on the gun. Would he draw it? Her knees turned soft until she thought she would crumple onto the floor.

He wheeled away and stormed outside.

Reaching for the table, she clung to it as she dropped to the bench, lowered her head into her hands, and let the tears flow.

July 1860. Martha put the baby in the cradle. Another little girl. Three months. The same age as Baby Girl when she left them. Martha caressed the fair cheek. So strong, this one. Such a treasure after the loss, born a year after. Without the nursing Martha guessed there was nothing to stop a child from coming. She remembered what Ma used to say. *Love comes with the baby.*

"Yes, little one, it does." Sometimes Martha forgot and called her Baby Girl, and the hurt stabbed her heart. "I'll always have a hole inside me, but you fill another place so full I can feel good again."

Cap and Tom came over and stood by the cradle, their faces glowing with pride. "She's a fine one, isn't she, Ma," Cap said.

Tom grinned. "Pretty Bina." They'd named her Edwina, but Tom turned it into *Bina*, so everyone called her that.

The boys darted a look at Martha, eyes wide. Their father. She heard him too. She cringed inside. "You boys better go upstairs and see what your sisters are doing."

They didn't hesitate, both turning and running up the stairs. It hurt to see them so afraid.

Martha called up to Nora. "Better come get Bina." She wondered if their boarders were with him. They had a couple staying here, Mr. Cassida and his son, probably sixteen or so. Garrett never turned a needy stranger from his door, so long as he wasn't a Yankee. Garrett seemed better when the boarders were here, but they'd been working in town the last few days and stayed there when they worked late.

She heard only one horse. Glancing behind her, she saw Nora carrying baby Bina up the stairs.

Maybe he'll be all right today, Martha told herself. *If I can just keep from upsetting him.*

Hearing him clear his throat outside the door, she slipped around behind the table and tried to appear natural, pulling a long-handled frypan off the shelf and reaching for the butter pat to coat the surface. She hadn't quite reached the butter when he came in. She ignored the sullen darkness in his eyes. "Hello, Garrett. I hope you're hungry. I thought I'd fry some—"

His voice raked her ears. "Why do I keep hearing stories, woman?" He pulled the pistol from his belt and pointed it straight at her. "I told you I'd kill you. I'm going to shoot him and I'll shoot you."

Her mouth dropped open, and she stood, unmoving, then grabbed the only tool at hand. She picked up the frypan and held it over her heart. "Garrett, don't. Please. I don't know what you're talking about."

He raised the pistol. "Why do you keep saying that, woman, when you know damn well?"

He was drunk. She heard it in his speech. But he was still a marksman. His finger touched the trigger. "Garrett, I—I love you. Please."

In a flash of motion so fast she could scarcely follow it with her eyes, he flung the pistol across the room onto the bed. It bounced from the mattress to the wall and back onto the bed. Letting out a long breath, she looked back at him. Now he held a whip in his hand. "Maybe this," he said. "What you doing with that pan?"

She held it out, ready to lower it to the table, but her hands shook and she felt it slipping from her grasp. She held on tighter, saw him move. The whip lashed out, wrapped around the pan in her hands, slashed her fingers, and ripped the pan away. It clattered to the floor, the sound echoing against her ears. She turned over her shaking hands. Streaks of bright-red blood crossed both palms.

An old memory swept past—Garrett's younger brother Perry showing everyone his untouched hand after Garrett whisked a bottle from his palm. Maybe the alcohol spoiled Garrett's aim today. He'd been drinking that day, but he wasn't staggering drunk like now. Or maybe he didn't care about her the way he did his brother.

She started toward the sideboard for water to wash the blood off when she saw motion out of the corner of her eye. The whip rose again. She lifted a protective arm as she turned away, and the lash came across her upper back. Once, twice. Another stroke. And another. Cutting. Slashing. She shrieked. She couldn't quit shrieking. Then it stopped. She heard the slamming door and looked to see he was gone. Taking a ragged breath, she crumpled onto the hard floor.

***

September 1860. The horse didn't sound like Rusty. Martha peeked out the window into the hazy sunshine. "Doc!" She ran outside. "Doc, come in. How are you?"

"Hello, little sister. How are *you*?" He got off his horse and tied it to the post, opening his arms as Martha rushed into them. Holding her for a long moment, he leaned back and looked into her face. He brushed his fingers over her cheek, slowly, as if scrutinizing it. "Are you all right, Martha?"

Did the marks show? Could he see? "I'm all right."

He stood taller and looked around. "Garrett home?"

"No."

"How's he doing?"

She heaved a sigh. "Why don't you come in and have a cup of coffee. How's Elizabeth?"

"She's fine." He stayed where he was, hands on her shoulders. "No, thank you. I don't need coffee. I just came to visit. How *is* Garrett?"

Turning away, she walked over to the small front porch and sat on the top step, waiting until Doc sat beside her. She studied the beauty of a pink rose on the bush beside the porch, grown from the cutting she'd brought across the plains—and the lilac bush out by the front path, almost a tree. She shook her head. "He's been drinking a lot. It makes him . . . touchy."

Doc nodded. "He's been in town talking with folks about the election. People are pretty riled up. If Lincoln wins, they figure the South will go."

"Go?"

"Secede. Leave the Union."

"I don't understand why they hate Lincoln so much."

Doc lifted his hands, and let them drop in his lap. "I figure we're a long ways away from the troubles back East, Martha, and it's already decided for Oregon. We entered the Union as a free state. But Lincoln— they read his speeches and debates. They think he'll destroy their way of life, end slavery. I don't know if he will, but the South thinks he'll bring the federal government down on them, and they won't have it. They'll leave the Union if he wins."

"You think so?"

"I'm afraid of it."

"I don't see why they need slaves. I never could get used to it in Missouri."

"It's different in the South. Big plantations. They need a lot of help, and if they had to pay for it—well, that'd change their economy pretty quick. They have a lot of money invested in those slaves. That's what it comes down to, Martha. Money."

She frowned, looking across the fields, the fat cattle feeding on the lush grass. "I don't know why Garrett gets in such a stew about it. Maybe it's not that."

Doc turned and took her by the shoulders, searching her eyes, brow lines sharp. "If he ever hurts you, I'll—I'll kill him."

Her heart jolted, making her voice shake. "Don't say that, Doc. Don't ever say that. Promise me you won't ever—" A sob stopped her.

He stroked her cheek. "Martha, Martha. It's all right. I wouldn't actually."

"People say things like that, don't they? But they don't really mean it?"

He gave her another direct look. "Are you sure you're all right?"

She wanted to mean it when she answered, "Yes."

⁓

November 22, 1860. The rain poured, streaking their glass windows. A dreadful weight settled over Martha. She had nothing personal against Mr. Lincoln, but she wished he hadn't won the election. His victory was making her life more miserable than ever. A rider came through with the news a few days ago on his way from Yreka to Portland. Word had come by telegraph and Pony Express and telegraph again to Yreka. Results were early but appeared set.

Garrett was in a terrible state. Every day he either went into Eugene City or to the homes of his friendly Democrats to drink and fret. When he came home tonight, would he take it out on her? It was pitch dark outside already. He should be here.

She heard him. *What will he be this time? Quiet angry or fierce angry?*

Hot tears burned. Where did her Garrett go? The one with the smile that crinkled the corners of his blue eyes and set them to sparkling like stars in the sky. Where was the tender touch of his strong, slim fingers? Even now, when he was sober she could talk to him about everyday things without him getting mean. But just a little whiskey and the meanness came out.

Will he hit me again? Strike me with the whip?

The brooding darkness of the day swept in with him, and stayed, even after he closed the door. Rain dripped off his hat and coat. He took them off and flung them against the wall.

Martha forced an even tone. "Are the Cassidas coming?"

"Not tonight."

A chill rippled across her skin.

He staggered closer, reeking of whiskey, his words slurred. "I tell you, Martha. The South should go." He focused his troubles on that, so it grew in his mind. At least it was better than other imagined troubles.

She reached up to smooth the hair off his forehead. "It'll work out."

His voice rose and he pumped his fists. "We can't live under the tyranny of the Union. With that bastard in power, we won't have any liberty at all, no rights to live as we please."

"What will you do?"

He turned toward the door. "I should ride over there and fight alongside my brothers, that's what I should do. There'll be a war now, sure, and I ought to go." He pounded a fist in his other palm.

"But, Garrett—"

He swerved back to her, reeling a little. "You gonna stop me?" He gripped the hilt of the knife in his belt. "Maybe you'd like me to go. Leave you to your sweet Irishman."

"Garrett, you know there's nothing—"

"Oh, I know he comes over here when I'm in town. What does he do? Take you right there in my bed? I know what goes on. Said he was moving somewhere else, but he can't quite stay away from you, can he?"

She shook her head fiercely. "Nothing goes on." Mr. Vallerly did stop to say hello to her yesterday when she was outside and he passed her on the road. Did someone see and report it? He didn't stop long, just went right on. He had moved away—he said so—and he'd come to visit his son. Poor man.

"Don't you be thinking about running out on me. I'll take the boys if you do—and Mary." The precious daughter Garrett had helped deliver. He always favored her.

"Garrett, you can't—"

He slapped his hand across her mouth. "Stop sassing." He slapped her again and again. Then he raised his fist and slugged it into her shoulder so hard she fell back onto the floor.

Her protest came out as if she had no power to stop it, her voice wailing, broken with sobs. "Do you think you can beat all your . . . frustrations out on me? Do you think . . . that will make it . . . better?"

She wiped her eyes to see into his face, and fear seized her. He was stepping toward her. His blue eyes looked cold as ice, his motions slow, deliberate. He reached down to grasp the hilt of the knife on his belt and slowly pulled it out of its scabbard. She scrambled to her feet. Could she make it to the door?

She lunged, grabbed the latch, gasped high crying breaths, swung the door open. His hand caught her skirt, but her leap yanked it from his grasp. She cleared the steps, ran with every bit of energy she could muster, out through the rain, into the dark. Which way? Where could she go? Which brother was closest? Newt used to be, until he moved to Eugene City. If only she had her mare, but she didn't have time to catch her. Garrett's plodding footsteps sloshed through the mud behind her.

She came to the road and turned south. Larry was closest now—maybe a mile away. So far. But what else could she do? She'd run for Larry's.

When she thought her lungs would burst, she had to stop. Rain streaked her face and clothes. She shivered, without a coat. She tried to listen. The rain peppered every surface. Would she be able to hear his footfalls? She heard nothing but the rain. How would she see to find Larry? Her eyes were adjusting a little. The road was barely lighter than the grass on either side. She'd feel it if she got off onto the grass, wouldn't she?

Finding strength from deep inside, she ran again, slower now, steadier. She had a long ways to go. Maybe he'd given up. Maybe he was facedown in the mud somewhere and wouldn't wake up until the whiskey wore off.

Tears streamed with the rain, and on she ran, until a tiny glitter shone ahead. Larry and Eleanor's cabin? The light pulled her on like a magnet, tugging, drawing her closer, close. She saw the square frame of the window now, the warmth of a fire and candlelight inside. Sobs started again as she reached the door and pounded.

She almost fell inside when the door opened, and Larry caught her in his arms. "Martha. What are you doing out in this storm?"

"Larry." Her sobs wouldn't stop, and he just held her.

Vaguely she heard Eleanor's voice. "Land sakes, my dear, what in the world happened to you? Let's get you in some dry clothes and over by the fire so you can get yourself warm."

Martha let them lead her to the fireplace, where a glowing warmth reached out, but it couldn't touch the chill deep in her core. "Larry," she said, her voice low, but steady now, "I want to see a lawyer. I want a divorce."

They both looked at her with wide eyes, the only answering sound a soft crackle of flame, and the sudden thud of a log shifting on the hearth.

Interlude III

I crouched in the grassy field below the great firs and watched a spider weaving her snare. Light from a fog-draped morning sun touched the strands and made them glow. I smiled, but sudden tears blurred my view of her. My body felt heavy when I stood and moved on. Martha's story had touched me in places I hadn't visited in a long while.

Divorce. It had seemed a foreign word to me, even in 1989. Something other people did. Yet how much worse for Martha in her day. Although not unknown in 1860, especially in the West, divorce was still rare. How could she do it? But how could she not?

I'd asked myself the same questions. Why did she stay with him as long as she did? I never experienced physical abuse. I always thought if ever I did I'd leave immediately. But often those who experienced it didn't leave.

Why? Probably many reasons, but two in particular. A belief things would get better if she could avoid whatever she was doing to invite the abuse. Or a more compelling reason: fear. If she left, what would he do? Would he be even angrier and track her down? It wasn't an unfounded fear.

But for Martha there was more. I'd looked into some of the related laws and customs of that period to get a clearer picture. Women had so few rights in her day. Men had a right to control their wives by law and tradition. A man had a duty to protect his wife, so he could control and limit her behavior. Society accepted moderate physical force to keep her in line. By the 1850s some states had liberalized divorce laws, allowing divorce for cruelty, but violence had to be severe and meet certain standards—habitual, life threatening, and not provoked by the wife's behavior.

Martha and Garrett were caught in a cultural shift. At a deep level my husband and I were also caught in a cultural shift when both genders had long been crippled by a norm that wouldn't allow either to develop their full human potential. In 1989 women were seeking full partnership in a male-dominant world. The shift was far from complete now, but norms had moved enough to make it difficult for me to imagine the crippling suffered by Martha's generation.

What did Martha stand to lose if she divorced Garrett? Loss of her children? Managing alone on the frontier? I struggled to understand her situation, how everything had disintegrated so badly. To write her story I needed to know the milieu in which she lived.

By 1860, great shocks tore at the roots of her culture. The North's rising industrial society jolted people off their familiar bearings and caused a backlash of rigidity in religion and the division between the sexes. The South remained caught in a patriarchal hierarchy that declared the lowest rung even less than human, with gender roles firmly set.

One might have hoped the promise of the West would invite a new equality and greater personal freedom. In some cases it did. But people didn't necessarily leave everything behind. Along with tools and dreams, many packed up their old habits and beliefs and doubts and brought them along. When things got tough in that unfamiliar setting—as inevitably things would—anxiety made them clutch those old ways even tighter.

Alcohol flowed freely on the frontier, the level of consumption far beyond today's use in this country, but it couldn't be outlawed when it was needed for medicine. Guns were carried regularly, but they couldn't be outlawed because they were needed for safety against wild beasts. Laws were lax. A formula for explosive times. In the run-up to the Civil War, feelings ran high—even in the Far West, especially in Lane County, Oregon, a hotbed of North-South rivalry. And Garrett, with his strong Southern sympathies, was right in the middle of it.

In the uncertainties of this new environment, people lashed out. What today we would call domestic violence was rampant on the frontier. And alcoholism. Some men took their wives' hands and agreed to a level of partnership unknown in the day. Others couldn't. Or wouldn't. The temperance movement didn't arise out of thin air. There was a reason women came together to encourage laws against overindulgence. They were tired of being beaten.

Alcohol may not have caused the abuse, but it was often involved, especially in times of stress. It appeared to reduce inhibitions for those bent on maintaining control, especially when so much seemed out of their control. Garrett showed signs of a man in the grip of alcoholism, with a hair-trigger temper, struggling to master a difficult new world. That didn't excuse what he did. Nothing could.

When I learned what he'd done, I had trouble taking it in. I got a glimpse when I read Gloria Atwater's website. Later, when Linda Noel sent me copies of the divorce documents, the information shocked me. I never knew about the divorce filing before starting the research for this book. Linda came across that while digging around in the courthouse for information on the family. That and the court cases against Garrett.

But the first time I saw the documents, I still didn't really know these people despite their blood flowing through me. Aware I was as much related to Garrett as to Martha, I did wonder how I could write him as a sympathetic character. Of course, my goal in this project was to know Martha, and as I continued the research I became acquainted. I began to care about her as a person. I felt a growing link.

When I wrote my outline and came to the chapter on those dark days in Lane County, I looked at the documents again to be sure I had the timing right. Now that I'd come to know Martha—and Garrett—the information hit me like a body blow. I cried. I had forgotten how bad it was. I needed to add more violence to the scenes I'd planned.

Once I began the actual writing, I moved into the events of Martha's life as I would with any novel. I saw through her eyes, walked in her shoes, and in those early scenes I fell in love with Garrett right along with her. But I knew what was coming.

I might be pouring out words on my laptop or walking or taking a shower or driving to town, and a scene would come to me. I'd burst out crying—for the poignancy in that part of the story, but more, for where it was leading.

I dreaded writing about the dark days, had trouble getting my mind around it. How did a man hit a woman with his fists? Where on her soft body, when she was almost always pregnant or nursing?

I recalled a time earlier in this project when story ideas were flooding me in the wee hours. They tended to do that, entering during that period on the edge of sleep before the doubts of an awakened mind rose, as if messages were coming from somewhere—or someone—outside myself.

I woke late one weekend morning after such a flood when my five-year-old granddaughter, Calliope, climbed into bed with me. I told her I hadn't slept well because a lot of ideas were coming to me about my story of Martha. My voice cracked with the emotion of some of those messages, and I wanted to explain. "I felt sad for her when she was going on the boat to Illinois because her husband Garrett was going to go away to war and be gone for a whole year. I knew how she felt because your Grandpa Wally went to war for a whole year, and I didn't know how I could stand to see him go."

"Why?"

The simplicity of her remark stopped me, but I responded finally with a depth of feeling. "Because I loved him very much."

"But you divorced." *Matter-of-fact.*

"Yes."

"Why?"

I took a deep breath. "Because . . . because things turned bad between us, and the love . . . faded."

She thought about that. "But he came back."

"What?"

"From the war."

"Yes, he did. And Garrett did."

Now sadness gripped my heart. With such fierce love, how could it *disintegrate so badly? If I could have called back to Martha, I might have told her about the positive side of being single again—finding new strengths, abilities, personal growth. But she couldn't hear that now.*

Chapter 8

Shifting Ground

Eugene City, Oregon, November 23, 1860

Martha looked across the broad wooden desk at the lawyer's kindly face. A low flame quivered in the lamp on one side of the desk, giving scant light as it sent up a whiff of smoke to blend with the scent of old leather and musty papers. The man's words resonated in the small wood-paneled room. "Now, Mrs. Maupin, how can I help you?"

The compassion in his voice undid her. She sobbed. "Mr. Ellsworth, I think . . . I want a . . . divorce." She put a hand to her mouth, trying to hold back the convulsive sounds, and blinked hard. "I'm sorry."

"Not at all." His eyes warmed, and he reached into a desk drawer, pulling out a folded handkerchief and handing it to her.

She wiped her eyes and blew her nose as delicately as she could.

"Take your time," he said.

She sat straighter. "I'm all right."

"What is happening that makes you think you want a divorce?"

"My husband has been drinking so much lately. He comes in drunk, nearly every night."

"Would you say grossly drunken?"

"Oh, yes. Grossly, yes."

Mr. Ellsworth scribbled something on the paper in front of him and looked up at her again. "And what else? Is there more?"

"I can't say anything but he gets put out with me. He got in a fight with Mr. Vallerly, our neighbor. The sheriff arrested him for that, but the jury let him go. Maybe it wasn't as bad as Mr. Vallerly said, but they did have a fight."

Again the man made a note on his paper.

"He uses terrible language in front of the children," she said, "the most vile language."

The man nodded, and she went on. "I'm afraid for the children, afraid he'll take them away." She clutched the handkerchief to keep her hands from shaking.

"Has he hit you?"

Martha looked into the lawyer's face and swallowed before answering softly, "Yes."

"With the flat of his hand?"

"Yes."

"With a closed fist?"

She hesitated. "Yes."

When the lawyer stopped to write something down, she opened a scarred palm. "And the whip."

He peered up at her. "The whip?"

She looked away from the intensity of his gaze, over at a bookcase on the wall. "He's good with the whip. He can snatch a bottle from your hand with it, or a pistol, or a pan." The scene came to her, making her eyes brim with tears again. Her voice rasped. "I picked up a pan to defend myself. I don't know why. He whipped the pan right out of my hand, slashed the whipcord across my palms." She held out her hands, where lines of pink still showed on each palm. "Then he lashed out and whipped me across the back. I turned away so it hit there." She reached over her shoulder to touch the old wound.

"Did it cut your back?"

"Yes. I guess the fabric of my dress helped, but it tore, and my back bled and got awful welts."

"How long has this been happening?"

Pinching her brow, she tried to think. "He's been getting drunk since the case with Mr. Vallerly. That was 1856—four years ago. There were times before, I guess, but that's when it got bad."

"And he's been hitting you since then?"

"No, that's more recent. It's been going on—I don't know—maybe two years."

"How long have you been married?"

"We got married in May 1845. How long is that? Fifteen years?"

Mr. Ellsworth wrote that down. "And he's only hit you in the last two years? Never once before?"

She shook her head. "Never. I remember well the first time. It was such a shock to me. The hands that—" She couldn't tell Mr. Ellsworth how terrible it was for her that such tender hands as Garrett's could be raised to give her pain.

"Has he harmed you in any other way?"

"He draws his knife and threatens to kill me with it."

"Often?"

She looked down at the handkerchief her hands were kneading in her lap.

"Mrs. Maupin." The lawyer's gentle voice made her glance up, though not quite into his eyes. "You're not the only one who experiences these kinds of things. I know it's not easy to talk about, and it is brave of you to come here. But if I'm to help you, I need to ask these questions. Does he do this often?"

Surprised at the man's words, she met his gaze and nodded. "Often, yes. And his pistol. He pulls it out of his belt and says he's going to shoot me—says it often."

She told about last night when she ran for her life, out into the rain, finding shelter with her brother Larry—the terrible night that convinced her to see Mr. Ellsworth.

"Have you given him cause?" the man asked.

"Cause?" She sat back in her chair, as if physically struck by the question. "I sometimes speak my mind. The slightest word fires up his anger these days. He's like a tinderbox—upset with the troubles back East, the election and all. He worries about money. I try to keep the children quiet, cook good meals, keep the house and barn clean. I help as I can. I make cheese and butter to sell, and sell eggs."

Mr. Ellsworth lifted his chin and seemed to study something on the wall behind her. He faced her again. "Have you given any other cause?"

"Other?" Martha felt confused for a moment. In a flash of memory, she saw John Vallerly's smiling face, and the heat rose in her cheeks. "He accuses me of infidelity."

"Toward the marriage bed?"

"Yes, but it isn't true, Mr. Ellsworth. I have never been unfaithful."

"Is there a specific accusation? Or generalized?"

Her face felt so hot it must have been glowing red. "Generalized, mostly."

Mr. Ellsworth waited. Life seemed to stop moving in the small dark office. Finally he spoke. "Everything said in this room is only between you and me, except where you agree to place it before the court, but I need to know if anything might come up from Mr. Maupin's side of the question."

She answered so softly she wondered if he'd heard. "He accuses me of infidelity with Mr. Vallerly, but nothing has ever happened between us. Mr. Vallerly has always been kind and considerate. Nothing more."

"Thank you, Mrs. Maupin." The lawyer again wrote on his paper.

Martha felt much too warm in the stifling space and wished she could shed the coat she hadn't wanted to give up when she first came in.

Mr. Ellsworth leaned back in his chair and set his hands on the desk, fingertips together. "I will try to help you, Mrs. Maupin, but there are some things you need to know. With the abuse you describe, I can probably convince the court to grant you a divorce. But a man has custody of his own children unless the law takes that away. Mr. Maupin may be able to retain that right."

Martha leaned forward, gripped the edge of the desk. "But I'm their mother. I'm the one who takes care of them."

"Not without him. That's another story altogether."

"But my brothers—I have brothers living right next door to me. I have them."

He took a long breath. "It's not the same. I don't know what the court will do. Of course, we'll make the best case we can, but I can't promise you that you'll be able to keep the children."

A cold spike pierced her breast.

Mr. Ellsworth's voice sounded tinny against the ringing in her ears. "And now we must keep you and the children safe until the court decides. Would you be able to stay with one of those brothers?"

"I—I can stay with my brother Larry and his wife, Eleanor. They live close to our house, so I can still tend to things. The children too. Larry fetched the baby for me—she's nursing still—but the others are at home. Nora's watching out for them. She's fourteen and very capable."

The lawyer pursed his lips. "Maybe close isn't the best idea right now. Do you have a brother a little farther from your house?"

"Newt. He lives here in Eugene City, but his house isn't large."

"Good, good. We'll see about getting a house for you in Eugene City too."

Martha took a deep breath that burst out in a sob.

———

November 26, 1860. Martha hugged her children to her and smiled at the sheriff. "It's good of you to bring them, Mr. Meador. Thank you so much."

"It's my duty, ma'am—by order of the judge. Good evening, ma'am." The merest smile lifted his lips, his dark mustache and beard making his chin a long vee. "And good luck to you."

Newt's wife, Elvira, let him out the door, while Martha went to each of her children to plant a kiss on every forehead. "I've been so worried about you. I didn't think it would take so long." She'd left home Thursday night and here it was Monday already. Having to wait through the Sabbath made everything take longer. After seeing the lawyer Friday while Elvira watched Bina, she'd come over to Newt and Elvira's and stayed. She'd signed the papers this morning.

Elvira bustled about, looking in her food cupboard. "Have you had supper?"

"We have," Nora said.

"How about biscuits and milk, then? Would that be good?"

Cap grinned. "I'd like biscuits."

Martha gave him another hug, and little Tom, leading them to the table. When the children were all sitting, Martha looked at Nora. "Was your pa home when the sheriff came for you?"

Nora shook her head, looking down at the biscuit in her hand. "He hasn't been home much—except to sleep. I fix him supper, but he doesn't eat it. Maybe he'll eat tonight. I left him something."

Martha sighed. "That's a good girl. I'm sorry I had to leave you with all that."

Louisa tugged her mother's sleeve, a biscuit halfway to her mouth. "When are we going back home? Somebody needs to cook for John and his dad."

Martha raised a brow at her second daughter. *John and his dad.* Not Mr. Cassida and his son? Had she taken a shine to young John? He was a likable fellow, but Louisa was only eleven—twelve next month. He wouldn't see her as more than a child. "Have they been staying at the house?"

"Last night they came." Louisa ducked her head, studying the floor before almost meeting her mother's eyes. "When will we go back?"

"I don't know."

Elvira poured more milk for the boys, who'd emptied their cups. "You can stay here however long you like. I'll put down some more blankets upstairs, and you can sleep up there with Nelly and Perry. They'll love having you. They must be sound asleep now. I don't hear anything up there." Newt and Elvira's children. Nelly was four, Perry two.

Martha shook her head. "We're going to crowd you right out, Elvira. Mr. Ellsworth wants to arrange for a house for us in Eugene City, but I don't know."

"Well, there's no hurry."

When the children finished their biscuits, Nora started to gather them to follow Elvira upstairs, but Martha laid a staying hand on Nora's arm. "I'll put them to bed, dear. I've been missing that."

With Elvira's help fixing blanket beds, Martha tucked in each of her treasured little ones, even Louisa and Mary, who were getting to be big girls. Her breath caught when she kissed Mary. Would Garrett try to take her away? Mary and the boys?

Back downstairs Nora waited at the table, and when Elvira busied herself picking up dishes, insisting on doing that job alone, Nora turned to her mother, speaking softly. "I don't want to go back. Do we have to?"

Martha sat beside her. "We'll see."

Nora's eyes filled with tears that edged her rising voice. "Why would you want to?"

Martha felt her daughter's pain compounded with her own. How could he hurt them all this way? What could Martha do to take away the pain? "I have to do what's best for all of us."

"Isn't it best to leave?"

"I don't know, but we're here now." Martha gave Nora a one-armed hug. "You've been carrying a lot for a long time."

Nora lifted her cup and spoke into it. "I hate him."

Martha squeezed tighter, her own tears wetting her lashes.

She heard voices outside, and the door swung in. Newt came in with Larry. They both smiled at sight of Nora. "Is everyone here?" Newt asked.

Elvira folded her arms, jaw forward. "The sheriff brought them all."

Newt let out a heavy breath. "That's a relief. Everybody doing all right?" He gave Nora a direct look.

Elvira answered again. "Everybody's fine."

Newt and Larry sat across the table, and Elvira took a place at the end. "I just got a restraining order," Larry said. "Garrett came over to the house yesterday. Made Eleanor uneasy. She and the children are over at Doc and Elizabeth's tonight while I'm in town."

Martha leaned toward Larry, a hand at her throat. "He's been to your place?"

Larry nodded, glancing at Nora.

"You can talk in front of me," Nora said.

Larry patted the girl's hand.

A sudden sparkle lit Nora's eyes. "Ma says we might get a house in Eugene City. I'd like that."

Martha looked from Larry to Newt. "That depends on what Mr. Ellsworth can get the court to do. I'm sure Garrett has some money, but—"

"We can all help," Newt said, "all five of us."

Larry clapped Newt on the shoulder. "That's right. I know Doc will, and Ben, and I think Simpson too."

How lucky she was to have such brothers. But she didn't want to take from them. They had families. "I don't know how Elizabeth would feel about it."

Newt gave a soft grunt. "She's your friend. She probably knows better than any of us what you're up against."

Larry leaned back, face twisted in thought. "You might write to our sister back in Illinois. John Bronough's well off. He could help."

"Maybe," Martha said, "but I hate to ask Simpson. He tried to talk me out of this marriage." The remembrance started a new flow of tears that filled her throat. "Maybe he was right. And Ma. But I loved Garrett so much—*love* him, I mean."

Elvira responded, her voice crisp. "Maybe so, but you need to look out for yourself and the children now."

When everyone else had gone to bed, Martha sat by the fire and drew the papers out from beneath her bodice. Mr. Ellsworth had written out copies of the Complaint and Affidavit she signed that morning, and she wanted to look at them again to be sure they were right. Even as she unfolded the sheets of paper, she heard soft snores in the room behind her. The others must have fallen right to sleep.

She scanned down the page to the terrible words, as if reading about some stranger she didn't know.

But the plaintiff complains that the said defendant . . . has since his said marriage contracted the habit of gross drunkenness so as to have become for and during the last four years habitually grossly drunken and further complains that during the said time of four years he has been guilty of harsh and cruel treatment. . . .

Martha looked up, into the lowering fire. She watched the soft licking flames, heaved a sigh and skipped to another passage.

That during this past two years he has struck this plaintiff angrily and violently, with his fists and with a whip, has often drawn a knife and threatened to take the life of this plaintiff, has threatened frequently to kill her by shooting and . . . he compelled this plaintiff to leave their house by his violent threats and actions and remain absent from the house although during a severe rain storm. . . .

Martha's body stiffened. The memory threatened to break in, but she pushed it back. Words seemed to rise from the page.

And the plaintiff further alleges . . . guilty of personal indignities . . . obscene language . . . false accusations of infidelity . . .

Rubbing her eyes, she lifted the Affidavit to read it before the fire died, taking her light.

That defendant has often threatened if any proceedings for divorce were commenced against him he would remove the children and especially the two boys and Mary Jane beyond the reach . . .

Memory crashed through her protective wall. She dropped the papers to her lap and wept.

———

July 1861. Martha ran the comb through Selena's hair and straightened her dress, then smiled at them all. "You look wonderful."

Tom tugged at her skirt. "When's Uncle Newt coming?"

She picked the boy up and held him close. "He'll be here soon." Quick footsteps sounded outside the door. "That must be him now."

Newt and Elvira had promised to take the children for a small picnic by the river. It would be good for them. They had so little to do here in town since school was out for the summer.

She let Newt in, and the children clustered to him. They loved their uncle Newt, always full of fun and ideas. "You sure you won't come?" he asked Martha.

"It's tempting, but I think I'd better keep Bina home. She needs a good nap."

"You got a letter." He handed Martha an envelope.

The Bronoughs. She ripped it open, but there was no letter. Only a bank draft. A hundred dollars. It slipped out of her hand and Mary picked it up. Mary's brows rose when she saw it. "A hundred dollars. We're rich."

Cap ran over to look at it and began jumping. "We're rich! We're rich!"

All Martha could think was that her sister Louisa hadn't written a letter.

Cap quieted and took hold of her hand. "Don't cry, Ma."

Was she crying? She quickly wiped the corner of her eye. Did her own sister fault her?

Cap reached his little arms around her skirts to give her a hug. "It'll be all right, Mama. We're rich."

His kindness brought more tears. How could she ever give up this child? Or Tom? Or Mary? Or any of them?

Cap turned, reaching for his uncle. "We'd better go."

Newt smiled at him. "Man of the house already. How old are you? Sixteen?"

Cap giggled. "I'm six, Uncle Newt. You know that."

"Oh, that's right. I remember." Newt looked up at Martha. "You all right?"

"I'm fine. Have fun."

The house echoed with their squeals and laughter when she closed the door. Bina whimpered, and Martha picked the child up to rock her. In moments she was asleep and Martha laid her in the cradle in the single bedroom of the little house.

Taking up her knitting, she sat in the rocker again, but she didn't knit. She rocked slowly, her thoughts adrift. How would they ever manage here in Eugene City? The one hundred dollars would help a lot. But why didn't her sister write?

Her thoughts turned to the troubles back East. All those states dropping away—one after the other. Men fighting, brother against brother. She wondered how Garrett was taking it. Would he ride all the way back on that terrible trail to fight in this dreadful war between the states? How would she feel about that? She didn't even know. He kept them in firewood and supplies as the court demanded until their case was decided, though she never saw him. One of the boarders always brought things for him. What if Garrett left for the war? Maybe if he left she could be assured of keeping the children. What would she do if the court let him keep them? When would she know?

A sound broke into her thoughts. What was it? Again. A knock on the door, louder this time, but still soft. Setting down the knitting, she went to answer it. When she opened the door, her heart jolted and she stepped back. Garrett stood in the doorway. She couldn't move as her glance took in the whole of him. He wore a clean jeans suit, sandy hair slicked back, hair and mustache trimmed, a sheen on his face from scrubbing, hat in hand.

His low voice raked against her ears with its familiar tenderness, only the slightest rasp betraying his distress. "Can we talk?"

She felt like a stone, incapable of speech.

He dipped his head a little. "Can I come in?"

Her hands rose in front of her, as if acting on their own.

A new intensity charged his tone. "I won't hurt you, Martha."

She didn't smell whiskey on his breath. With currents raging up and down her, an explosive ringing in her head, she stepped back from the door, making room for him. He nodded, a subtle bow, and stepped inside, closing the door behind him. Still she remained standing, not offering a chair, and he stood a couple of paces away from her, hat clutched now in both hands.

He looked straight at her, and she instinctively looked for the sparkle. She didn't see it, but there was something else she couldn't quite read—warmth, fear maybe.

Taking a sharp breath, he spoke evenly. "I've come to tell you how sorry I am." The words went raspy again. "I love you, Martha. I need you." He waited, and when she didn't answer he went on. "I don't want to lose you. Please. Don't go through with the divorce."

Martha crossed her arms over her breast and bit her lips together.

He took another deep breath, looked away from her and back again. "I know I was rough with you."

Rough.

"There was so much going on—the troubles in the States, the crops bringing next to nothing, our baby."

Martha pressed harder against a pang in her chest.

He ran a hand over the top of his head and grasped the back of his neck. "When our baby—when we lost our Martha—our Baby Girl—I didn't know how to make it better for you. I didn't know how to make it stop hurting." His eyes glistened.

She'd been so caught up in her own pain. She'd supposed he grieved in his own way, knew it in her mind, but not her heart.

Looking down at the floor between them, he spoke in little more than a whisper. "Then when I got rough with you—I don't know what happened to me. I just—" He faced her again, eyes pleading.

The currents swept up and boiled out, putting a sharp edge in her tone. "Yes, you do know, Garrett Maupin. The whiskey. That's what. You go to the grog shops. You bring whiskey home and—you do know."

He lifted his hands to her, palms up in supplication. "I'll do better, Martha, I promise. Please come back and I'll show you. What do I have to do for you to come back?" His voice softened. "I need you, Martha. I *love* you."

She looked into his blue eyes. When he was sober they were the clearest, finest eyes. Maybe his pain hid the sparkle. She didn't doubt the suffering she saw in them now, but how could words take away all the suffering he'd inflicted on her? Could she ever trust him enough to love him again?

Another's words echoed in her head. *We'll make the best case we can, but I can't promise you that you'll be able to keep the children.*

If she went through with the divorce, Garrett might keep custody of the children. Would he do better so she didn't have to risk that?

She stood as tall as she could and looked him straight in the face, her tone unyielding. "You can't ever hit or threaten me again." She waited for his response. What if he refused her conditions and demanded the children?

"I won't, Martha. I promise you, I won't hit you or threaten you ever again." He twisted his hat, squeezed it.

"And no grog shops. And no whiskey in the house."

"None?" He tilted his head, face contorted in disbelief. That appeared to be a problem for him, but he heaved a long sigh. "Anything—if you'll come back."

And if he broke his promises? What would she do? Walk out? What would happen to the children then?

⬤ ⬤

March 1862. Martha looked out the glass window of her house to the rolling fields of grass, the grazing cows. A fine log house, built with such promise. She rested her hands on her growing belly—fruit of her reunion with Garrett and his gentle side—his gift of flowers, his gentle touch. He'd been trying, but it wasn't easy for either of them.

Her emotions, always more volatile during pregnancy, reeled one way and another. She felt joy in the budding life, fear of the situation. If she hadn't been afraid of losing the children, she wouldn't have come back to

Garrett. She wanted to love him. She did love him, but not the same way as before their troubles.

He no doubt felt her resistance, tried to overcome it, but he was a man who liked to be in charge. He was frustrated about that, about the restrictions he'd agreed to and about a war across the plains. So the tension erupted in small ways—more swearing, harshness with the children.

She saw him coming to the door and backed away from the window. He came in grumbling under his breath. "Damn Yankees. We need to crush the bastards. But what can I do way over here? Should have gone when it started. Damn, son of a—"

"Garrett Maupin, your language. The girls are upstairs. They'll hear you."

He gave her a sharp look, a touch of defiance in his pose. Language wasn't part of their bargain. It should have been. She saw a little sock on the floor near him and went over to pick it up. When she stood, her face came close to his and she smelled the familiar odor of whiskey. She'd thought she smelled it a time or two before. Now she had no doubt.

Frowning, she gave him a direct look. "We had an agreement."

"Yeah?"

"You've been drinking, Garrett."

He spread his hands wide. "You said no grog shops, no whiskey in the house. I didn't break that agreement. You can't ask me not to have a cup with a friend in his house when he offers."

Martha glared at him.

"I have work out in the barn," he said. "Where's Cap?"

"Outside with Tom."

"Where's Nora? I need a hand out there."

"She's gone riding with her friends."

He put his hands on his hips and huffed. "How about Mary?"

"She's upstairs, but why don't you ask Louisa? She's a good help and older than Mary." They were all older than Cap—always his father's first choice, though the boy was only seven.

Louisa and Mary came down the stairs. "Louisa," Martha said, "why don't you go help your pa? Mary, you can help me start dinner."

Garrett frowned, but he didn't contradict her. Starting for the door, he stopped short and pulled an envelope from his shirt. "I almost forgot. You have a letter."

When Garrett and Louisa left the house, Martha smiled at Mary. "Why don't you get some potatoes while I look at my letter?"

Mary turned and ran out back to the cool house, and Martha sat on the bench by the table. She saw the name *Bronough* on the outside, and her heart fluttered. Pulling out the letter, she saw the familiar handwriting of her sister.

"She wrote me," Martha said. "Oh, thank the stars, she wrote me."

"Please forgive me," Louisa had penned. "I would have written before, but we lost our three-year-old Mary about the time you wrote. . . ."

Looking away from the page, Martha placed a hand on her belly and whispered, "Dear Lord. How does she bear so many losses? Poor Louisa. I can't. Not again."

Thundering hoofbeats sounded outside, and Martha got up to see. Nora was riding hard toward the barn ahead of several other riders. Nora's horse jolted to a stop at the barn door, heaving shuddering breaths, hot and winded, sweat dripping from its flanks. Martha hurried toward Nora, but Garrett got there first.

Anger charged his voice. "What the devil are you thinking? You trying to run him to death?"

"I couldn't—"

He yanked Nora off the horse, set her firmly on the ground, and slipped the bridle off the horse in one smooth motion. Before Nora could move, he grabbed her by the arm and struck her across the rear with the bit end of the bridle until her shrieks filled the air. He pulled her about and shouted in her face. "Don't you ever let me see you run a horse like that again!" Snarling, he drew the reins around the horse's neck and led it into the barn.

Nora ran toward the house crying, but Martha caught her by the arm. "What happened?"

Nora could hardly speak. "I couldn't stop the . . . the horse. We came by some horses. In a pasture. They started to run, and my horse ran too. I tried to stop. I couldn't. I wasn't racing. I hate him, Ma. I hate him. Why did you have to come back here?"

"*I* didn't have to come back." No, Martha didn't have to, but given the uncertainties of custody, she had no way to be sure the children wouldn't have to.

Nora's eyes widened, as if she understood her mother's meaning.

"Go in the house and wash up," Martha said. She walked over to where several speechless girls still sat on their horses. "You'd better go on home now, girls."

When they left, Martha went out to the barn where Garrett was rubbing down the horse. "You should listen to what your daughter is trying to tell you," she said.

He kept his gaze on the animal's back. "I won't have my own daughter abusing a horse like that. And I'll discipline my daughter as I please. It's my right as her father."

Martha recalled the story about Perry beating Garrett over a horse. "Like it was your pa's right to beat you when you didn't take care of one of his fine horses? And how did you like that, Garrett Maupin? What did you do about it? You ran away, didn't you?"

He gave her a quick look. "That's no business of yours, woman. Any daughter of mine is going to learn how to treat a horse." He turned toward Martha, the brush still raised in his hand. "And you'll be quiet about it, or—"

Was he going to strike her, despite his promise? She didn't back down—for Nora's sake. "If you'd taken the time to listen to her, you'd know—" Martha's voice rose. "—she couldn't hold the damn horse!"

Silence echoed in the barn. Garrett gaped at her, and she stared back. She'd never said that word before. How did it come out? Had she heard it so much from Garrett she just picked it up naturally?

"Martha Poindexter Maupin!" he said.

"Well, Garrett Maupin, if I didn't hear that word so much, it wouldn't be so quick to pop out, now, would it?" She turned and walked out of the barn, headed for the house.

Early summer 1862. Martha sat rocking baby Emma while Elizabeth busied herself sweeping the hearth. The child was burning with fever. Even the sponging hadn't done much to cool her. Memories scraped across Martha, dug in, clawed old scars. Doc had ridden to town to fetch a doctor, and Elizabeth stayed to help. Garrett was out in the shed hammering. Erratic blows. The occasional clatter of wood. He'd offered to go to town himself, but Doc had insisted Martha might need him.

Muffled sounds stirred upstairs. The children were all in bed, if not asleep. The smell of supper's bacon hung in the air.

Martha tried to nurse the little one, get some liquid in her. Elizabeth brought water and tried to give her that. The child wouldn't take anything. Sighing, Elizabeth drew a chair over from the table and sat beside them, leaning close. "Do you want me to hold her awhile?"

"Maybe a little later." Martha looked into the child's pink face and spoke softly, more to herself than to anyone else. "Did I let him back into my arms just to pierce my heart again?"

Elizabeth shook her head. "Oh, my dear friend, don't say it."

Martha's own cheeks warmed. "I shouldn't speak so personal. I wasn't thinking."

Elizabeth huffed. "Don't worry about that." She lifted her brows at Martha. "How are things with Garrett?"

Taking a deep breath, Martha let it out slowly. "He's trying. It's not easy for him, but he's trying."

Elizabeth let out a short laugh. "He's probably the most trying man I know."

A snicker bubbled out of Martha, and they both had a giggle.

Martha's throat tightened. "Odd that people can laugh at times like these, but maybe you need to sometimes if you're going to keep from breaking apart from the terrible strain."

"Isn't that the truth."

Still Martha kept rocking. She tried several times to set Emma in the cradle, hoping the poor child would sleep better, but every time the baby cried again. When darkness settled over them, Elizabeth held out her arms. "Why don't you let me rock her, see if you can sleep a little. You need your strength."

Martha shook her head, struggling to keep her voice even. "I can't sleep. I went to sleep with Baby Girl and she—"

Author Janet, beneath the offshoot of the double oak, looks out over the hillside below her house, to the river, Pleasant Plain, and the mountains beyond. Martha had never seen such mountains before she traveled to Oregon. PHOTO BY ROBIN LOZNAK

William, Janet's son-in-law Robin's golden lab, enjoys the magic of this fairyland creek that spills down the canyon Martha's house once faced. PHOTO BY ROBIN LOZNAK

Old oaks scatter across the farm's hill pastures—Oregon White Oak and California Black Oak—in this shot taken above Janet's house. PHOTO BY ROBIN LOZNAK

A garden spider awaits her breakfast on a foggy morning by some Douglas firs on the farm's mountain, her handiwork creating jewels of light. The Douglas fir is the area's primary timber tree. PHOTO BY ROBIN LOZNAK

An early morning sun peeks through some old Douglas firs, uphill from a spot on the valley floor near Martha's house site. PHOTO BY ROBIN LOZNAK

Facing page, top: Janet walks through the grassy field in front of the old barn built in the 1930s shortly after her father acquired the property. Martha's earliest crop on this rich river bottom was probably wheat. PHOTO BY ROBIN LOZNAK

Facing page, bottom: This white hawk, or one like it, appeared early in Janet's search for her great-great-grandmother, and returned at significant stages in the project, like a haunting presence. Bold, yet elusive, the exquisite creature finally swept into the camera's view on a bright May morning, just in time to appear in Martha's book. PHOTO BY ROBIN LOZNAK

Viewed from the uphill side, the old barn overlooks the valley floor with prune orchards and a corner of the white antiquated prune dryer showing below. A small pear tree can be seen standing alone in the field to the right. Martha's house sat close to that pear tree. Janet vaguely remembers the house, which was taken down when she was six or seven. Martha's sturdy pioneer rose that came across the Oregon Trail moved again and still lives today by a shed that once housed Janet's family. PHOTO BY ROBIN LOZNAK

This herd of Roosevelt elk ranges across the family farm, here leaping into a bank of fog, as into an unknown world. PHOTO BY ROBIN LOZNAK

However dark the winter, spring on the farm means new calves. PHOTO BY ROBIN LOZNAK

Janet's grandchildren, Alex and Calliope, float leaves down a creek coming out of a grove that stands like nature's cathedral near her house. The youngest generation on Martha's farm, these two follow a living stream into the future. PHOTO BY ROBIN LOZNAK

"Oh, but, Martha."

"I'll be all right. You get some sleep."

Elizabeth set a comforting hand on her arm. "I'll rest here awhile."

The darkness deepened, pushed back only by the low fire on the hearth. Fatigue bore down on Martha, but she fought it. The child slept fitfully, woke fussing. Martha tried again to feed her, but she wouldn't take the nipple. Even when Martha squeezed milk into the rosebud mouth, the baby spit it out, shaking her head.

Martha bent nearer the infant, voice hushed. "Oh, my child."

Elizabeth sat slouched in the chair beside her, chin on her chest, sound asleep. Garrett hadn't come in. Martha rocked. When would her brother get back with the doctor? Did she hear a horse? Or just the rocker? She felt a change in the baby. An odd weight. Martha stroked the little cheek. No response. Felt for a heartbeat. Rocked more fiercely. A wail rose from somewhere deep in her memory and slashed across the air. The world went dark.

—◦—

December 1862. Whatever warmth Martha had rediscovered seemed lost forever. The repetition of loss cut through deep ruts of old pain, like a rake across a raw wound that could never heal. Now she began to smell whiskey on Garrett's breath nearly every day. She couldn't even react to that. It almost surprised her anyone could see her. She felt like a ghost walking.

Nora cooked and cared for the younger children. All of them helped. Martha would start a task and forget to finish it. Garrett was gone much of the time, although once school started, he did drive the children to school in the old wagon. It was a couple of months or so before she allowed his tentative overtures, but she found no feeling.

Now on this cold winter morning, she realized she hadn't had a monthly in a long time. How long? She'd experienced morning nausea for weeks and accepted it as part of the miserable condition of her life. She put her hand over her belly and let out a long moan.

Mary came at a run. The girl cupped her mother's cheeks in her hands. "Mama, what's wrong? I'm here, Mama. What happened?"

Martha's voice rose to a shriek. "I don't want any more babies."

"Are you going to have another, Ma?"

Martha could only nod as sobs overtook her.

Mary smiled, her tone gentle and terribly grown up. "You'll feel better when you see the baby, Ma. It'll bring the love. You always said the love comes with the baby."

Martha clutched her child's arms. "I don't want any more babies. I don't want to feel that hurt anymore. If I have to bury any more babies you might as well bury me, because I won't live anymore. I won't."

Nora rushed in from outside, spun around, and raced out of the house. "I'll get Aunt Eleanor."

Watching the empty doorway a moment, Martha turned back to Mary. "How old is Nora?"

"Sixteen."

Martha let out a groan. "I've been pregnant or nursing for seventeen years. I don't want any more babies."

⁓

April 1864. Martha focused on little Garry, safely strapped in his chair, while the men at the table commiserated about the war. "You sure did bring the love, sweet boy."

She brushed her fingertips over his rosy cheeks. His big dark eyes looked right into her, so bright and happy. He'd smiled early, shining light on her weary soul. Hard to believe he was nine months old already.

Raised voices drew Martha's attention. What had been a tense situation before the war had become extremely volatile. While the war raged in the East, people in the West suffered an impotent rage. Many wished they could be fighting for their chosen side, but the war was far and the way between treacherous. The Cassidas were here tonight and a couple of the Bunches, shirttail relatives of Garrett's uncle Jim.

When the men got up to leave, Nora came downstairs, moving quickly to her mother's side. David Bunch stepped over to give them a slight bow. "Good night, Mrs. Maupin, Miss Maupin. Thank you for the biscuits."

Garrett let the men out and strode back to where Martha and Nora stood. "Good news," he said, beaming. "David Bunch just asked me for Nora's hand in marriage."

Nora cried out. "But, Pa!"

Garrett ignored the interruption. "He's a good man. A good Democrat."

"But I don't want to marry David Bunch. I want to marry—"

"I know who you want to marry." A fierce frown creased Garrett's brow, and he bent down to look straight in his daughter's face. "I won't have any daughter of mine marrying a damned Republican. You'll marry David Bunch, and I don't want to hear any more about it."

Nora stormed out of the house.

Martha grasped Garrett's forearm. "Please, Garrett. She doesn't love David Bunch. Besides, isn't he some kin of yours?"

"He's not blood kin, but he's been part of the family and I couldn't think of a better man for my daughter."

"Let the girl marry who she loves, Garrett."

"And let her ruin her life?"

That stopped Martha a moment, but she went on. "Then let her wait. Don't force her into something like this when she doesn't want it. Doesn't her happiness count for something?"

He set his jaw. "She will marry David Bunch."

"Garrett, please."

For a fleeting instant his eyes clouded. But he spoke with chilling softness. "This is my right as her father."

The chill touched Martha's response. "You may have the law on your side, but it isn't right, and some laws need changing."

He tilted his head, brows high, and sauntered outdoors.

Cap edged up to his mother. "Are we having a war here?"

Martha smiled. "Just a family disagreement."

"No, I mean a Civil War. Here in Oregon."

"Oh." She put a hand on his shoulder. "Only back in the States. They're fighting mostly in the South. But people here come from the States, some from the North, some from the South, and they take sides."

"Is Missouri in the South?"

"It's in the middle. They didn't leave the Union, but some folks there tried to."

Cap thought a moment. "What about Illinois? What about Uncle Stephen?"

"Illinois didn't leave the Union. It's a Northern state. Uncle Stephen may have joined the Union army. Aunt Louisa thought he might."

"What did Pa say about that?"

Martha shook her head. "We'd better not upset Pa by this kind of talk."

A knowing look came over her young son's face, and he nodded soberly. "I won't say anything, Ma." His eyes came alight, and he spoke in a rush. "Did you know Pa can take his whip and just whip it out and take a gun right out of a man's hand? He did it when we were on our way to school and somebody had a gun out and Pa—"

"I know how Pa can use his whip." A sting shivered across her back, like a memory of the flesh. "Let's don't be talking about that either."

～

November 17, 1864. Martha scrubbed the table, lips clamped tight. Rain pattered the roof, the sound thrumming right across her. Maybe Nora would be happy. But how could politics be so important when it came to matters of love? Martha had tried to make it a happy wedding—flowers, good food. All the family came, and many friends. Larry witnessed, along with Nora's pa. But the sadness in Nora's eyes sapped all the joy for Martha.

Now she kept scrubbing, casting a dark look once in a while at Garrett as he piled more logs on the fire. Sighing, she decided she'd better stop before she made a hole in the wood. Nora and David would be here soon. Time to set out plates. A light knock on the door, and Nora opened it. Martha hurried over to give her a hug. "How are you?"

Nora didn't have to answer. Her downcast eyes answered for her.

Garrett came and gave David a hearty handshake. "How are you, my boy?"

The man lifted one shoulder. "Sorry we haven't been here sooner. We've had us a busy week since the wedding getting the cabin set up the way Nora likes it."

Martha called everyone to dinner, and they came pouring in, some from upstairs, some from outside. The Cassidas were there too. When everyone sat down, young John Cassida gave Louisa a warm smile.

Something in that smile alerted Martha. The boy had been staying here with his father for several years now. Martha was pretty sure Louisa was sweet on him, but he'd never paid much attention to her.

"How old are you now?" she asked John.

"I'm twenty, ma'am."

She nodded. A man. Louisa was fifteen, a few days shy of sixteen. He'd better not be looking at her yet. But wasn't Martha sixteen when she got married? The thought didn't help.

Garrett's conversation with David caught her attention. Something about leaving? What did Garrett say?

"It's nice country here," David said, "but it is wet in the winter, all right."

Garrett stroked his mustache with thumb and forefinger. "Yeah, and I miss Howard." Garrett's brother Howard had moved to eastern Oregon last year, leaving Garrett without one of his strongest allies.

"You think the climate's better over there?" David grinned. "For Democrats?"

Garrett chuckled. "Probably is. Too many Union folks here in Lane County."

Martha hadn't noticed a lack of Southern sympathizers, but there were plenty who sympathized with the North too. They fought it out in the newspapers and sometimes on the streets. Somebody shot at the editor of the Republican paper, but didn't hurt him. Troops even came down from Vancouver and put a small cannon in the corridor of the courthouse to help keep a lid on it. Was Garrett thinking of leaving? He hadn't said a word about it.

"Time for us to go too," he said, answering her unspoken question.

"To eastern Oregon?" David asked.

Martha clutched her throat. "Across those mountains?" She remembered coming across that high desert country on the trail west, and the mountains between. And that horrible chute.

Garrett raised a brow at her. "No, south to Douglas County. It's not so far, and the climate's more to my liking. I like the rich land here in western Oregon, but I want to live amongst my own kind. Lots of folks with Southern leanings down there, I hear."

David grinned. "Not so many Yanks?"

"That's what folks say." Garrett turned to Martha again. "We can sell our claim here. Robinson's been asking about your three-twenty, Martha."

Her half was all they had left, since they lost the other half in a sheriff's sale when they couldn't pay off the note they took out on it. The incident hadn't helped Garrett's humor.

A sharp knock on the door startled her. "Who could that be?"

Garrett's back stiffened, his jaw clenching. The knocking thudded again. Martha's heart thudded with it. Garrett stood and answered the door. "Mr. Haley," he said, letting the man in.

Mr. Haley? Martha recognized him. Sheriff William Haley. Her body went rigid.

The man stood pencil straight and spoke in a brusque monotone. "Mr. Maupin, as Sheriff of Lane County it's my duty to inform you that you are under arrest for assault with intent to murder committed on one Godfrey Anchez on the fourteenth day of November. I need to take you into town."

Currents whipped through Martha so fiercely she thought she might explode with them right there on her chair at the table.

Lord help us, not again. I don't even know who Godfrey Anchez is.

———

December 13, 1864. Martha rode with Garrett and three of her brothers out of Eugene City. Doc, Newt, and Larry had come into town with her for Garrett's appearance before the judge. For a hefty bond of $1,200, the judge had agreed to let him out of jail until sentencing in April. This time the jury had declared him guilty of the crime.

Garrett stroked his horse's neck and took a long, slow breath. "Air is mighty sweet out here after almost a month in that damned hole."

"I'm sure it is," Larry said, riding beside him.

Martha and her other two brothers fell in behind. They rode in silence until they were out of town. Garrett looked around, as if assuring himself no one was near, and spoke, voice low. "We're leaving for Douglas County."

She took a sharp breath. "When?"

"Now. As soon as we can get out of here."

"And ride all the way back up here to go to court in April?" Larry asked.

"I'm not going to court in April."

Martha moved her mare up beside Garrett. "But we just signed the bond. They found you guilty. You have to appear in court in April." She and several of his friends had signed it.

He scowled at her. "They won't follow me to Douglas County."

"But—"

"Look, Martha, it's true I got in a fight with this guy, and maybe I said some things that made him think I was going to kill him, and it's true I had a pistol on me, but I wasn't gonna use it. I never laid a hand on him."

The boys started to argue with Garrett, but he didn't want to hear them. "I have no choice," he said. "Besides, I think I'll get along better with folks there. Been thinking about it anyway." He prodded his horse and galloped ahead.

The boys stayed close to Martha. Doc scowled. "I don't like it. You'll be pretty isolated down there. We won't be there to look out for you."

She swallowed at a lump in her throat. "If he's bent on going, I don't know what else I can do."

Newt leaned toward her, a sharp edge in his tone. "There are choices."

Larry slapped his saddle horn. "That's right. You almost made a different choice four years ago."

Martha gripped the reins tighter. "And have him take my children away?"

None of them had an answer to that.

She shook the reins to speed the mare to a lope. Her brothers kept pace until they caught up with Garrett. "How soon do you want to go?" Martha asked. "I need time to pack."

Garrett lifted his chin. "You have tonight and tomorrow. We're leaving tomorrow night."

Doc looked at each of his brothers. "We can bring our wives tomorrow to help." The others nodded.

The lump filled Martha's throat again. *Tomorrow night.* How would they ever manage?

The tattered wagon cover whipped in the wind as Garrett climbed onto the seat. The same wagon that brought them all the way over that terrible trail from Missouri. The same cover. Only this time Garrett had hitched his heavy farm horses to the front. Martha's family stood nearby. Elvira dabbed a tear.

John Cassida strode up to the wagon. "Pa and I will start with the livestock first thing in the morning." He looked inside where the children sat on mattresses and blankets piled over all their earthly things they could bring. Martha could follow the link between the gazes of young John and Louisa. The young man's tone softened. "I'll see you in a few days."

Louisa's good-bye was barely audible.

Martha turned toward her dear brothers—all five were there—and her wonderful sisters-in-law, and their children. How could she bear to leave them? They'd been her solace and joy, and protectors, for so long.

Garrett flicked the reins, and the horses started. The wagon rolled out onto the narrow track, and Martha turned to wave at everyone. In the dimming light of dusk, her brothers and their families didn't seem clear enough. She squinted to see better, but too soon they melted into the shadows. A turn in the road, and she felt cut off, alone in the world.

Garrett leaned toward her and whispered, "Something going on between our Louisa and young John?"

She shrugged. "He's a good Democrat."

He let out a huff. "When we get to Douglas County, the Cassidas better find a house of their own."

Garrett drove to the nearest ferry. He got down to lead the horses on, but the rest of the family stayed inside. An easier crossing than many on that long trail west. Still, it brought back memories. As they drove off on the other side and headed down the long road, more memories crowded in. The creaking wagon. The jingling harness. The steady plop of the animals' hooves. The jolting of the springless wagon seat that had made Martha walk the trail west. Tonight she had to ride, given how hard Garrett pushed these horses. They moved considerably faster than the old oxen.

As dusk deepened, the moon shone through a break in the clouds. A light drizzle spit into the wagon. She watched the moon. A dark finger of cloud reached for it, and a terrible dread came over her.

"We'll travel until we reach the county line," Garrett said, "then camp for the night."

"How will you know?"

"I'll know."

The drizzle on her cheeks turned warm as hot tears spilled.

Chapter 9

Scattered Pieces

Douglas County, Oregon, April 1865

The sweet spring air filled more nooks in the small cabin with every whisk of Martha's broom. She went after every suffocating particle of dirt accumulated over the long dark winter, determined to let the cleansing brightness in. Rugs and blankets billowed in the sun outside.

They'd found this place to rent while Garrett looked for land to buy. A man named Charles Henderer had a couple of extra cabins on his large farm near the village of Elkton, having bought three claims together. He rented one to the Maupins, the other to the Cassidas.

Martha stopped sweeping and leaned on the broom. Here she'd tried to put their lives together, wondering if she could ever pick up the many pieces that seemed scattered to the winds. How could she bring back the love and trust while building defenses? At least she'd found relative calm after the wars of Lane County.

Garrett was supposed to be appearing in court in Lane County soon, but he didn't seem to have plans for going. Last month, late March, Martha and Garrett had taken a quick ride to Eugene City to close the sale on her portion of their Lane County claim. Mr. Robinson had paid them $2,400, a nice sum. Martha hadn't rested easy the whole trip. She'd worried about Garrett going into the city for fear the authorities would keep him, but he'd assured her his bail was still good until April. Today, with money in his pocket, he'd taken Cap out to look for properties. Garrett wanted to take Cap everywhere, and Cap loved it. At ten, the boy stretched to be the man his pa wanted him to be.

She had her own conflict about whether Garrett should go to court. She knew he should, because the court had ordered him to. But what if they put him in jail? What would she do then? She gripped the broom handle tighter. What if she'd never gone back to him? Well, she wouldn't have Garry, would she? He was almost two now, a pure delight. She sighed. She wouldn't be pregnant again either.

If Garrett went to jail, she couldn't stay at the Henderer farm. Garrett paid the rent by helping farm the land. He'd also found work hauling freight from Oakland to Scottsburg, making good money. That seemed to make him happier. He hauled wool, surplus grain, and other produce to market through Cyrus Hedden's store in Scottsburg and brought back manufactured goods the farmers needed. Garrett was gone a lot, which had its good side and its bad side.

Lifting the broom again, she targeted some heavy cobwebs draped high across the log wall. She heard a horse nicker. Garrett and Cap already? They hadn't been gone long. The creak of a wagon sounded. Not Garrett and Cap. They didn't take the wagon.

Stepping outside, she squinted toward the oncoming vehicle. Several people filled the open wagon bed. As they neared, she recognized the driver. Ira Wells, one of her new neighbors. And Anna, his wife. And the Kents, Levi and his wife, Mary. Martha smiled, seeing them. The two families lived next to each other a few miles to the south.

Mr. Wells called out. "Hallo, Maupins."

Martha's children had gathered behind her, Tom and Bina jumping with pleasure to see company. The Wellses and Kents had brought some of their many children.

Martha spread her hands wide. "Welcome. Good to see you. Come on in. I'm in the middle of cleaning, but that gives us more room."

Laughing, the men jumped down and began helping wives and children. The two women spoke in delightful accents, Mary Kent's Scottish, Anna Wells's German. No sooner had little feet hit the ground than the young ones were running to play with Martha's brood, even Louisa and Mary joining in their fun.

Martha led the adults inside and reached for a pitcher on the sideboard. "Can I get you something to drink? Or a bite to eat?"

Mr. Wells lifted the basket in his hands and set it on the table. "Thank you, no. We just drove over to see how you're doing."

Martha put down the pitcher. "I'm afraid Garrett and Cap are out looking at properties."

"Any good prospects?" Mr. Kent asked.

"Nothing yet. Garrett's so busy with freighting and work here on the Henderer farm, he hasn't had much time."

Anna Wells began pulling bags out of the basket. She smiled at Martha. "We bring some treats for your children. We cannot stay long, but we look in on you now and again. Yes? We must go to Elkton now, for the mail."

Mary Kent's pink cheeks rounded. "Aye, it's only a wee bit, but we want you to know if there's ever anything as you'd need, we aren't far away."

The men nodded their agreement, and Martha wished she could hug every one. "Thank you so much. The children will love these." What lovely people, and how desperately she needed their friendship. "Garrett will be sorry he missed you."

"We'll see if there's mail for you," Mr. Wells said, "and stop by again if there is. Do you have any mail you want to send out?"

Martha clasped her hands together. "That's so kind of you. No, nothing to go out, thank you."

When the families were all back in the wagon, heading off for Elkton, Martha and the children stood waving a long good-bye. Martha wished they lived closer. They made her feel less isolated. If she had trouble she couldn't run to their house on a rainy night, but it was a short ride by horseback. One river crossing—with a ferry.

She felt terrible thinking this way, but she recalled Doc's warning. "Find friends. Know where you can go for help." Of course the Henderers lived close, and the Cassidas—over in the other rented cabin—but Mr. Wells had a warm, fatherly manner that tended to wrap around a person. Garrett hadn't shown signs of trouble. But he seemed tense much of the time. The old warmth couldn't easily return with thoughts like these.

Martha lifted her shoulders and went back to the house and her broom. When she heard horses again, she peered out the doorway and smiled. Cap rode ahead of his father, calling out. "Ma! Ma!"

She strolled outside, and when the boy came near her, he pulled his horse up short and took several deep breaths, face flushed right through his blond hair.

"What is it?" she asked. "What did you want to tell me?"

He took one more gulp of air and burst out with it. "Ma, they shot the president. Somebody shot President Lincoln, and he's dead! And Lee surrendered. The war's over."

Garrett drew his horse beside Cap's. "It's a terrible thing."

Martha put a hand over her heart. "Oh my. It surely is. Whatever you may have thought of him, it surely is a terrible thing to shoot a president."

Garrett tilted his head, one brow up. "I mean, it's a terrible thing Lee surrendered. We've lost, Martha. The Yanks have taken away our liberties, and we'll be nothing but slaves to them. Don't you see? They come in and take our property—" He shook his head.

Martha pressed a hand to her forehead, trying to take that in. "Well," she said, "it's good the war is over." She didn't know about the rest. It seemed odd to talk as if they were slaves when slavery had just ended for others. But to kill the president. What a horrible business.

Garrett spoke softly, yet with fierce resonance. "This war may never be over. They may not be fighting it in the field anymore, but it's not over."

Martha wanted to argue. With such hard feelings on either side, though, she couldn't quite convince herself Garrett was wrong.

May 1866. "Why don't we all go," Garrett said. "It's going to be a nice day. Do you good, Martha. We can drop the younguns at school and go into Elkton to the post office, maybe visit some folks in town."

She held the baby close, nursing him in her rocking chair. The thought of visiting did have appeal. Though Elkton had no stores, only the post office, it had grown into quite a village, three hundred or more people, and she'd developed friendships there. But the thought of keeping after her two little boys on a long outing had less appeal. She brushed a finger over the baby's cheek. "This fellow does better at home, and I've been wanting to get out in the garden. I'd better keep him and Garry here."

Garrett rested his gaze on her and nodded. "I'll go into town myself, then."

"Can I go to the post office?" Tom asked. "They have treats there."

"And miss school?" Garrett gently tweaked the boy's ear. "No, you'll have lots more fun at school. Maybe learn something too. And Ma packed you a nice lunch."

As the others scurried around getting ready, Louisa hung back. "I want to stay home," she said to her mother. "I think I've had enough school. I'm seventeen, Ma. I'll be eighteen in December."

Martha pursed her lips. "Where's John working today?"

"At Mr. Henderer's. He's helping Mr. Fisher build that barn. Why?"

"I just wondered why you'd rather stay home than go to school. You love school. And the term's almost over."

Louisa leaned closer to her mother, voice low. "John and I want to get married."

Martha feigned surprise at Louisa's announcement.

"John's working up courage to ask Pa," Louisa said.

Putting a hand on her daughter's shoulder, Martha smiled. "I think it will go well. Your pa likes John."

"Well, after what happened to Nora—"

"It's not the same. That was politics."

Louisa hugged her arms to herself. "I'm glad Nora and David moved down here anyway, so we get to see them and the baby."

"Me too." Martha had midwifed for Nora's baby girl born in March. Little Mollie. Like Martha, Nora had insisted on being close to her mother for this first child. Now Martha was a grandmother. Her own little Mike, born last December, was only three months older than his niece. Would Martha go on having babies, even younger than her grandchildren?

Mary rushed in. "Louisa, you have to go to school with us. Come on. We've missed way too much already."

They had. Only during these long days of spring with plenty of daylight did Martha allow the children to ride the many miles on horseback. They seldom got a wagon ride, since Garrett was usually gone with the wagon hauling freight. In the short days of winter, Martha tried to keep up their lessons at home, though Garrett sometimes took Cap in to school on a Monday and left him all week, letting the boy sleep in the schoolhouse.

Louisa finally relented, and Martha followed them out to the wagon, the baby in one arm, little Garry in hand. Garrett sat on the high seat, reins draped over his long fingers, and looked down at Martha, as if reading her. "Don't worry. I'll take good care of them. I always do."

She nodded, unaware she'd looked doubtful. He turned the horses, and she watched them go, filled with a mixture of relief and concern. She welcomed the peace, but would she ever relax when Garrett drove away with the children? She shivered in the morning chill. Fog still lay on the valley floor, but that should mean a fair day. As soon as the fog lifted and let the sun through, the morning ought to be fine for gardening.

Meeting expectation, the day turned nice by midmorning. Martha set the cradle in the shade by the cabin, put Mike in the cradle, and settled Garry nearby with some toys. "All right, Garry, you play here by Mike and I'll do a little work in the garden. That's a good boy."

He gave her one of his shining smiles, and she brushed a hand over his downy, light-brown hair. "I'm a horse," he said.

"You stay right here in the barn, then, horsey."

"My barn." He tucked his head behind the cradle.

Martha ambled over to the garden, only a few feet from the cabin, and got down on her knees to pull weeds. "Goodness, how they've grown since it warmed up."

She breathed in the spring air. The sweet aroma of upturned soil mingled with the scent of flowers on the gentle breeze. Birdsongs and Garry's horsey nickers rose above the distant tap of the hammers on Mr. Henderer's new barn. A glorious day.

She was just making some headway on the weeds when Mike began to cry. Brushing her hands on her old apron, she went over and picked him up. "What's the matter? You can't be hungry again." She jiggled him, finally settling him down, and heard Garry squeal. She turned to see him galloping across the yard. Her heart jolted. "No! Not that way. The well." It wasn't fenced off and the stone rim wasn't high.

She set the baby in the cradle and ran toward Garry, every motion feeling slow, as if the air were thick. He was at the well. He climbed, leaned over the edge. "Horsey needs a drink."

She shrieked. "No! Stop!" She lunged, grabbed for him, but his shirt slipped from her grasp and he toppled, fell. She watched in disbelief as his small form dropped and splashed into the dark water at the bottom.

With one quick glance to be sure Mike was safely in his cradle, she grabbed the rope that held the bucket, the other end tied to a stump. Checking the knot, she gave it a hard yank to be sure it held firm and fed it out into the well. With her knees on the stone rim, she swung her feet around, clutched the rope with both hands and reached a foot down to dig her toe into the inner wall, then the other. She lowered herself, hand over hand on the rope, toes against the inside of the rocky wall to slow her descent.

The rope scraped her palms as she slid, lower, lower, desperate to see her child in the ever-darkening depths. There. She saw him, bobbing, heard his choking coughs. Her feet entered the water, and she slid faster until she could touch him. Pressing both feet against the wall, her back opposite to hold herself steady, she let go of the rope with one hand and reached down to scoop him out. She laid him over her lap, made by that awkward position, and holding him just above water level, she slapped him across the back to help him cough the water up.

He coughed and cried and coughed more. Finally he only cried. He seemed to be breathing all right. Now she had to pull them both up. She needed two hands. "Hold onto me, baby." Her palms already raw from the slide down, she winced when she gripped the rope tight and pulled. She couldn't gain anything. She couldn't lift their combined weight. She tried to get traction on the wall with her feet, to inch up with her back, but made no headway.

Gasping for breath, she raised her head and yelled as loud as she could. "Help! Come help! Please! Help!"

She paused to listen. Nothing.

She tried again to pull them by the rope, tried to work her way up with feet and back. She worked at it until exhaustion forced her to stop and rest. Tears started, and she broke down.

She could not lose Garry. He was the one who brought sunshine back to her soul. If she lost him, her light would go out forever. She'd just sink into the water and drown with him. But she couldn't. She couldn't let him die. He'd saved her. She would save him.

She yelled for help again. Tried again. Yelled again. How long before Garrett came home from town? How long could she hold herself this way? Her whole body shook. She felt herself slipping. The dark water so close.

Her ears rang. Heart thudded. Pulse echoed in her head. So still in the deep. All the little sounds escalated. Another sound. A shout? No, the rope squeaking. No, it was a shout.

"Hallo?"

She called back, her voice so hoarse she wondered if she could be heard. "Here! Down in the well. Here."

She looked up to see the face of John Cassida peering down the hole, his face in shadow, the clear blue of the sky behind him. "Mrs. Maupin?"

Tears burned, but she had to hold back a little longer.

"Just hold onto the rope," he said. "I'll pull you up."

She clung for the life of her child and herself and rode the rope to the top. John grasped them both at once and pulled them over the ledge, onto the ground. She sank onto the blessed hard soil and wept, her child in her arms, his little back spooned against her front.

"I thought I heard something," John said, "but I wasn't sure. Then I heard it again and I had to check."

Martha slowly raised herself up and sat on the ground. "John, you're a good man, and you will have my daughter's hand, if I have anything to say about it."

He ducked his head and grinned.

She still held Garry close, reluctant to let go. "Sweet boy, you better be glad your ma has stout lungs. I may not be strong enough, but my lungs are."

John started to laugh, tried to stop himself. But when Martha burst out with a chuckle, they both gave in to laughter, until Garry's bright giggle added a high echo.

August 4, 1866. The sun hadn't risen yet on this early Saturday morning when Martha set out breakfast for Garrett and Cap.

"Gonna be a hot day," Garrett said, biting into a biscuit. He smiled at her. "You do make the finest biscuits, Mrs. Maupin."

Returning a quick smile, she forked a few slices of fresh fried bacon out of the pan and set them on his plate, then some for Cap.

The horses snorted out front and shook their harnesses, making a jingling sound. Garrett had already fed and harnessed the team while Martha cooked breakfast. They had a long trip ahead. They were about ready to go to Oakland for the first leg of the long haul from Oakland to Scottsburg. Garrett had spent the day yesterday gathering sacks of wool from farms in the neighborhood, making part of a load. He'd get the rest of his load in Oakland, then start back, stopping briefly at home before continuing on to Scottsburg.

He'd insisted on taking Cap with him, and Cap was thrilled. As they munched their bacon, Garrett glanced at the boy. "You're gonna be a real help today, son. You're eleven now. You can help drive the horses."

Cap's young face glowed. "Really?"

"Sure. You know how."

Martha's chest tightened. She bit her lip and turned to slice bread for their noon lunch. She needed to have that done by the time they finished breakfast. She didn't want to hold them up. "You'd better camp if it gets late. It's a long trip for one day."

Garrett lifted his eyes. "We will. But we have a light load as far as Oakland. We'll make good time. Should be in Oakland by noon. Besides, the sooner we get this load to market, the sooner we get paid."

They gulped down their breakfast all too fast. Garrett grabbed his wide-brimmed hat and set it on his head, running thumb and forefinger over the brim. Cap did the same with his, same set, same thumb and forefinger across the brim. Her chest constricted again.

She followed them outside, handed Garrett the cloth bag with their lunch. He stowed that under the seat and boosted Cap onto his high perch.

"Here's the list of things I need," she said. "For the house, and the children."

Garrett turned to take it from her hand, tucking it into the pocket of his pants. He stood looking at her, and she caught a glimpse of the old sparkle. Maybe the light from the cabin's open door? A warm feeling reached out like a flaring coal on the hearth. His blue eyes looked clear in a face like leather, carved by time and pain. A confusion of love and sorrow and regret rode on that line of sight between them and reached right down to wrap around her heart, wrenching it so fiercely her breath stopped.

He bent down and touched his lips to hers, gentle, then firm, kissing her in a way he hadn't in a long time. She wasn't sure she wanted him to kiss her like that, but she remembered a young Garrett with a ready smile and eyes that could light up the night sky, and she kissed him back with a hunger for something lost, something wished for.

Then he slipped away and climbed onto the high seat. "Good-bye," he said, his tone soft. "I'll take good care of him. Don't worry."

He spoke to the horses, shook the lines, and the wagon rolled out the gate and onto the road. Martha watched them go, until she could scarcely see them in the dawn light. Cap did look small on the high wagon seat. She hoped he'd be all right. They came to where the road followed a bend around the hill, and the hill appeared to cover the wagon, a little at a time, like a curtain drawing closed.

Even when they were out of sight she watched. Taking a deep breath, she looked away and went into the house, picked up the milk buckets, and headed to the barn to milk the cows and do chores before Mike and the other children woke.

The morning dragged. Such a long morning after that early start. The children seemed restless. Martha stood facing them, hands on her hips. "Why don't we go blackberry picking?"

Their eyes lit up, a murmur rising in agreement. While Martha made up a picnic lunch, the girls gathered buckets, and they soon headed toward the river where the best berries grew. The day had begun to warm. The rich scent of wild blackberries thrilled the senses. Careful to avoid thorns, they reached into the thick bushes and picked. Several in the bucket. A couple in the mouth. A perfect blend of sweet and tart. Thorns grabbed at Martha's skirts and raked her hands.

Wincing, she remembered to warn the children. "Watch out for rat-tlesnakes." The pesky things could surprise and scare the life out of a person. She didn't know anyone who'd been bitten, but heard they could kill a grown man, let alone a child.

She couldn't keep her mind off Cap. She imagined him on that high seat, the long ride, rolling into Oakland. Quite a town. He would enjoy a bit of candy from the store. Could they make it there by noon? Even with the light load? It was more than twenty miles to Oakland. Then on the way back, they'd have a full load to slow them down. Garrett always pushed himself to do more than two men, but it would be a long day for an eleven-year-old boy.

A thorn prick brought her mind to herself. Perspiration dripped from beneath the rim of her bonnet onto her forehead. Her dress was stick-ing to her. The heady bouquet of summer grew intense—blackberry and river, a touch of wild mint, a subtle essence of dry grass. Bees and cicadas buzzed. The children's voices turned whiny, and they began arguing.

She looked at the sky. Near noon. They'd all eaten an early breakfast. "Let's have our picnic," she said.

They readily stepped away from the bushes and traipsed down the slope to the river's edge, sitting back in the shade of a large tree overhang-ing the water. Martha laid a cloth on the ground and set out the bread and cheese, one bucket of berries in the center. They were just finishing when John Cassida and Mr. Fisher rode over.

Louisa walked up to John as he dismounted. Martha smiled at the looks between the two. She was glad Garrett had agreed to the match. The wedding was set for September thirteenth, just a bit more than a month away. Several of Martha's brothers and their wives planned to come, maybe all of them from Lane County. She hoped so.

Mary's bright laughter caught her mother's attention. The girl stood talking to Mr. Fisher, who was standing at the edge of the shade, hold-ing his horse's reins. Billy, wasn't it? Billy Fisher? She supposed his given name must be William. Mary chattered with animated gestures, always the outgoing, friendly one. Billy Fisher seemed a kind, gentle man, good with young people, the way he bent toward her, attentive to every word, and threw his head back to laugh at her stories in an amiable way.

"Well, John," he said, running his fingers through the curly hair above his ear, the hair dark but for a trace of gray at the temples, his chin whiskers grayer still.

John nodded. "Back to work."

With good-byes all around, they got on their horses and galloped away. Louisa watched them go. So did Mary. Martha frowned and shook her head.

After the youngsters played in the water for a while, they carried their treasure of berries back to the cabin. Martha stirred the fire and put the berries in one pan, some wax in another. Soon the smell of cooking blackberries wafted through the cabin. A tantalizing sweetness. While they cooked she pulled down whiskey bottles she'd gathered. Giving the bottles and their corks a fresh washing, she set them out on the table, and placing the pan of hot fruit beside them, began dipping out berries, slowly working the fruit down the bottle necks with a wire. Once she had the bottles filled, she drove the corks into the openings and dipped the necks into the hot wax to seal.

"I hope they keep," she said as she lined them up on the shelf. "Sometimes they ferment and blow the cork out, but we'll have most of these next winter when we're short of fruit."

Louisa giggled. "I remember that one blowing last year."

When the day began to cool and they'd had their supper, Martha went back to wondering. Where were Cap and Garrett now? They should be well on their way home, but she didn't expect them before dark. The August days were still long. Dark would be late.

She sent Tom and Bina out to bring in the cows, and before long the tromping and bellowing told her the cows were coming into the barn. "Louisa, why don't you wipe up the table while I go out and milk."

Gathering the buckets, Martha headed out, glancing toward the bend of the road as she made her way to the barn. She took one bucket and sat next to the first cow, pressing her forehead into the soft, warm flank while she gripped the teats, one in each hand, and pulled in an even rhythm. The white milk whooshed into the bucket, a steady song of plenty, the sweet familiar smell of milk and cow soothing her worried mind.

Another rhythm beat in the distance, growing closer, louder. Galloping horses. She sat straight, knitted her brow. An odd current rippled through her. Why would Garrett be galloping the team after such a long haul?

"It must not be them. It's too early anyway."

Holding still, she tried to follow the sound. Maybe someone going to the Henderers'? No. They were coming this way.

She set the milk aside so the cow couldn't kick it over and went out to see. She gripped the edge of the barn doorway when she saw two horses coming toward her, a small figure on the back of the lead horse. Their horses. Their team. But no wagon. And that was Cap, riding one horse, leading the other. Fear struck her heart. "What—?"

For a moment she couldn't move. Then she ran toward him. He rode straight to her, the horses trotting now. Sight of his face sent another bolt into her. Tears streamed down his flushed cheeks, making rivulets through the grime, and he was sobbing. The horses stopped beside her, blowing heaving breaths. Bareback, Cap slid off and crumpled at her feet.

She bent down, dropped to her knees, and wrapped her arms around him. "What, Cap? What happened?"

Looking into her face, he tried to speak. "Pa—" Sobs stopped him.

"What happened?" Louisa asked. The girls clustered around them, and Tom.

Martha shook her head. "Take the horses, Louisa. Mary, you help her. Rub them down. Give them a little water. Not too much. And walk them. Just walk them slow and easy for a bit. Selena, you watch the little boys."

All the while, she sat on the ground, keeping Cap close in her arms as he cried. He tried again to speak, but couldn't.

"Take your time, son."

He sat straighter and gulped a big breath. "The wagon . . . turned over."

Martha closed her eyes, saw it in her mind, the horror of an overturning wagon. She saw it again and again. Rolling. Over and over.

"Pa—" Cap said. She turned all her attention back on the boy. His small frame jolted with another sob, and the words poured out, as if the dam had broken. "The wool fell on Pa. I couldn't get it off. I couldn't get him out. I got the horses loose and rode for help, but we were too late. Pa—" He broke down and wept more, then shook his head. "Pa is dead."

His words hit a wall—a shield—in Martha, and would not come through to her mind. Then they slowly crept past her defenses, worked their way in and struck with searing force. She heaved a great shuddering sigh and slumped against her son.

"Ma?" He looked into her face with such despair, she had to put her thoughts on him.

Holding him to her breast, she patted him on the back, her cheek nestled against his tousled hair. "We'll be all right, son. You're all right."

He cried more, blubbering through his weeping. ". . . my fault . . . couldn't keep them . . ."

"No, son." She tried to console him with the tenderness of her voice. "It wasn't your fault." She had no idea, but she couldn't have him believing that.

"The rein came right out of my hand. I don't know how."

"Where was your father?"

"Beside the horse—or the wagon. I'm not sure."

She tried to move back from her own pain to visualize it. "Did he have his hand on the rein?"

"I don't know. Maybe. He fell, I think. Tripped on something. The horses got over to the edge of the road, and the wheels got on the edge where it—" He snorted up tears.

Tripped? Martha shuddered again.

She heard more galloping and looked up, almost expecting to see Garrett, riding after his boy. The sun had set, graying the world. But when the rider came close she recognized him. Their friend Ira Wells. She scrambled to her feet, and Cap stood beside her.

"Hallo," Mr. Wells said, pulling up his horse and swinging to the ground. "I was on my way home from Elkton when I saw your horses and a single rider. What happened?"

A chill had moved into Martha, despite the warmth of the summer evening. A large cold spot surrounded her heart until it robbed her of feeling, but she managed to tell Mr. Wells what Cap had told her. The sympathy in his face almost poured warmth on the coldness, threatening to thaw it and let her feel. But she forced her gaze away from him.

"The man that helped me promised to take Pa into Oakland," Cap said. The boy looked up at her, a frown creasing his young forehead. "Should I have gone with him, Ma?"

She set a hand on her son's shoulder. "No, there's nothing more you could have done."

"I'm surprised you were able to unhitch the horses," Mr. Wells said. "You're a brave lad." He looked at Martha. "I'll ride to Oakland first thing in the morning and see about him."

"Thank you so much. You're a good friend." She and Garrett and the children had visited back and forth with the Wellses and Kents many times over the past year or so and they'd all become good friends. She managed a trace of a smile, and noticed Selena standing close, Mike in one arm, Garry in hand. "Selena, why don't you take Cap to the house and give him something to eat."

When the children were in the house, Martha spoke to Mr. Wells again. "I need to let my brothers know."

"I'll get word to them."

She lowered her voice. "I want to know if Garrett was drinking. Don't try to protect me, Mr. Wells. I want to know the truth."

He gave her a subtle nod. "You'll have it."

Interlude IV

I stood in a world of dappled light and long tree trunks reaching for the sun, a forest floor of delicate green undergrowth. Brief glimpses of the outer world showed, as if through tall, narrow windows. The small creek trickled at the bottom of the sharp vee between slopes. Grief welled in me, my own revisited through stepping into Martha's. I sought solace here in this natural cathedral near my house.

Spring warmth enriched the scent of life and decay mingling around me, the carpet of last year's leaves nourishing the new. Life out of death. Rebirth. In this new-green world, the rough brown tree trunks stood out bold against the paler colors. Their trunks arced to form a towering cathedral roof. Those on the near slope tilted toward those across from them, coming together and crossing, as if to weave their verdant tapestry overhead, every tree working to build a new cathedral roof of living green, each new leaf a tile of life.

Most were hardwoods—big-leaf maple, oak, dogwood—a few tall, straight firs at the border. I crossed the creek and was making my way up the other steep bank when a sound drew my attention to the open field beyond the grove's upper edge. Something had become aware of me first. Elk. Their thundering hooves shook the ground. A herd of twenty or so, about fifty feet away. Sleek, powerful bodies, burnished golden in the late afternoon sun, surged in a flow, as one, sweeping across the hillside. My heart thundered with them.

Afterward, quiet echoed.

I was reminded of a picture my photographer son-in-law Robin had taken of these magnificent creatures that roamed across our land. It showed the herd as it was beginning to move out, the leaders leaping a thin wire fence into a bank of fog, as into the unknown.

A shiver ran through me. How did we ourselves dare such a leap? Whatever the relationship, the loss of a commanding presence like Garrett, or my father, had a powerful impact.

I listened for the distant hoofbeats, and as I let the glory of the woods wrap around me, I wondered how Martha felt about these special places. She wouldn't have been familiar with cathedrals like those in Europe and America's large cities. But this grove, with its long narrow windows out to the world, and its near-Gothic arch of trees overhead—this was a cathedral to me more than any man-made structure could ever be. Had she found comfort in places like these as I did now?

My heart ached for her. After twenty-one years with Garrett, she must have careened between grief and relief. All the turmoil. The divorce filing, the uncertain reunion. The court cases against him. Moving to Douglas County— just ahead of the law.

I had visited Martha and Garrett's Donation Land Claim in Lane County, beautiful farmland. Even with half lost, there were still 320 acres, most of it tillable. They did manage to sell the remaining half, but it must have been sad to leave something like that behind, given the hope and promise when they acquired it.

Nobody in the family talked about the real reason for the move to Douglas County. Florence McNabb, family chronicler, said Martha and Garrett's kids talked about the family leaving the Willamette Valley because it was too wet and unhealthy. They didn't know the rest, or didn't want to.

The law in those days wasn't the law we knew today. If you could make it into the next county, they wouldn't bother to come after you. Garrett made it into the next county with Martha and the kids and he was apparently a free man, whatever he might have done in Lane County. A case continued, with the court trying to get the bond money for Garrett's failure to appear, vehement arguments going back and forth.

Yet despite all the pain, it would have been hard to imagine life without such a presence. It certainly was hard for me to imagine the farm without my dad.

I recalled the night my father died. It was late when people from the funeral home arrived to take him, and several in our family found places to sleep overnight in the farmhouse. The morning broke, bright and sunny, a beautiful March day. We looked out the kitchen window to the apple tree across the nearby creek. A new black calf stood on wobbly legs beneath the tree, his mother gently licking his back. The first calf of the season had been born in the night.

Now, watching out the long narrow windows of the natural cathedral, looking the way the elk had run, I wished I could share with Martha the hope I found in this place and in the wonderful creatures who lived here with us. After the long dark night, there would be a bright new morning.

And new calves.

Chapter 10

Into the Unknown

Douglas County, Oregon, August 1866

Martha pressed her hands against her chest as she stood outside their cabin at the Henderer farm, watching the sky turn a brilliant red-orange. She didn't notice the creaking wagon until she heard it close by and turned. Ira Wells drove in through the gate, his horse tied behind. He came from the east, where clouds billowed pink in the glow. Drawing the horses to a stop, he inclined his head toward the wagon, and she went over to look in the wagon bed. A long, thick figure wrapped in heavy blankets stretched across the planks.

"He won't keep long," Mr. Wells said. "I need to take him over to Charlie's and put him in the cool house. Do you want to see him first?"

She shook her head.

Mr. Henderer rode up. He lifted his hat and gave a quick bow, speaking in his brisk German accent. "Hello, Ira, Mrs. Maupin. I can take him to the cool house. The Cassidas will help. You rest here, Ira."

"Thanks, Charlie. I appreciate that."

Mr. Wells slowly climbed down from the wagon, lifted his hat, and wiped the sweat off his forehead. Fatigue lines tugged on his face, aging him beyond his years. He was only a few years older than Garrett. Another month and Garrett would have been forty-five.

"Let me get you something to drink," she said.

He smiled. "A fresh drink of water would be highly appreciated."

She went straight to the well and dipped the bucket, bringing up fresh, cool water, pulling the rope hand over hand. When she heard the wagon roll away, she looked up for a minute. She never did tell Garrett about Garry falling in the well, and John said he never would. Biting her lip, she poured water into the cup on the stump and took it to where Mr. Wells sat on the ground, back against a tree. He took the cup from her hand and drank the water down.

"More?" she asked.

"That'll be plenty, thank you."

She sat on a stump near him. Louisa and Mary came over, but she told them to tend to chores. "I'll talk to you later."

Mr. Wells heaved a sigh. "No one was there to see it happen, and it happened so fast I don't think Cap knew what went on. But I've been able to piece the story together a little and have a fair idea."

He paused. "It happened in Green Valley. A man passed them not too long before. I met the fellow in town. He noticed Garrett walking by the horse on the right, a hand over one rein. His first thought was that the father was minding the rein while letting the boy think he was driving."

Mr. Wells glanced at his horse nibbling on a tuft of dry grass. "Then Garrett hung back until he was beside the wagon."

Martha watched the man's face. He seemed to want to look everywhere but at her. "Don't leave anything out."

Mr. Wells cleared his throat. "The fellow noticed a bottle in Garrett's hand."

Martha's shoulders tightened, and he went on. "In town they said Garrett had bought some whiskey at the store and had a bit to drink."

"A bit?"

"Quite a bit. He was staggering a little when he left town, and he had a bottle to take with him."

"The bottle that man saw."

Mr. Wells glanced at her. "Yes. I think when he walked beside the horse, sneaking a drink now and then, he must have stumbled. Cap remembers the rein being yanked out of his hand. Garrett must have flailed his arms out to stop the fall, got hold of the rein, and when he fell he yanked on it. The horse responded, pulled to the right, the wagon rolled onto the soft edge of the road and over it went, right on top of Garrett. They found him under a six-hundred-pound bale of wool, smothered."

The scene swept before Martha with horrible clarity, but a cold emptiness pushed back feeling. Silence settled over them as color left the sky and dusk deepened.

"It's not Cap's fault," Mr. Wells said, "if he's thinking that."

"He needs to hear that from you."

"He will. I think I'll spend the night at the Cassidas'. Anna's not expecting me home before tomorrow."

"You'd be welcome here."

"You have enough now." He rubbed the back of his neck. "I sent word to your brothers."

"Thank you. That means a lot to me."

"A reporter in Oakland is sending the story to papers in Eugene City and Portland. He let me look at a copy. It says Garrett was killed by the wool, that another man was driving."

"Another *man?*"

"I didn't tell him different." Mr. Wells's voice dropped. "It also said Garrett was intoxicated."

A shudder slunk down Martha's spine.

Mr. Wells turned to face her, eyes warm. "I did like Garrett. When he wasn't on the whiskey he was smart, had a fine sense of humor, loved his family—loved you."

She looked into her lap. "He loved the whiskey more."

"No." The certainty in Mr. Wells's tone brought her gaze back to him. "He didn't love the whiskey. The stuff got hold of him. It does that to some men. Another man can drink when he likes and let it go when he likes. But for some the whiskey takes hold and they have to have it. I've seen men even get sick when they can't get a drink."

Martha pondered that. Maybe someday she could accept it. Not now. And there was a lot more Mr. Wells didn't know.

He leaned forward, as if to emphasize what he was about to say. "Garrett was a man who liked to be a master of things, and a man like that can't love anything that makes a slave of him."

Martha stared back, surprised at the words.

The smell of fresh-cut earth reached up to Martha from the deep hole in the ground. She stood alone at the edge, waiting. A light breeze stirred the morning air on the knoll above Mr. Henderer's long valley, but the day was warming already. It would be a hot day. The tall golden grass rustled. She'd gotten used to every blade of grass turning gold in the summer here, unlike back home where it stayed green. But Oregon had green grass all winter, a fair compensation, and the gold held its own beauty.

Glancing into the dark-brown depths, she shuddered and looked up, across the valley to the river and the hills beyond. Men had dug the hole early today. People would be here soon.

She wondered if her brothers would come. They must have mixed feelings about Garrett, and it was a long ride. Voices drew her attention. The children, walking up the road. Louisa, holding Mike. Mary with Garry in tow. Selena, Cap and Tom side by side, Bina. Nora and David with little Mollie. They trailed out along the dusty track, past a screen of scrubby oaks, then out in the sun again and through the gate.

John and his pa followed, then Mrs. Henderer, Ira and Anna Wells, Levi and Mary Kent, Billy Fisher, and another man she didn't know. Probably the circuit rider Mr. Henderer asked to officiate. The stranger wore the typical long, double-breasted black coat of his calling, the divided tail flapping in the breeze.

Once through the gate they had a gentle climb up to the knoll. They all gathered silently around Martha, faces solemn, an occasional soft smile of sympathy. The clip-clop of horses echoed. Martha clenched her hands. Was it Mr. Henderer with the wagon? Bringing Garrett?

No. There were riders, several of them. She let out a soft cry of recognition. "The boys." Without further thought, she hurried down the trail, almost running, and met them at the gate. Larry, Newt, Doc. "And Elizabeth!"

Her brothers hopped to the ground and while Doc helped Elizabeth down, Larry and Newt drew Martha into a shared hug. Then Doc and Elizabeth. Even when they stepped back, Elizabeth clutched Martha's hand. "How are you doing?" Elizabeth asked.

"I'll be all right. I'm so glad to see you all."

Doc patted her arm. "Eleanor and Elvira send their love—and Ben and his Mary—and Simpson."

Martha batted her eyes at threatening tears. "Simpson didn't have much fondness for Garrett." She looked at her brothers circled around her. "I know you had your moments with him too."

Newt smiled gently. "We're here for you, Martha."

Elizabeth gripped her hand tighter. "I loved my brother with a love that won't die in spite of everything. I had to come. Besides, you're like a sister to me and you need us now."

The tears rolled into Martha's throat, turning her voice hoarse. "How is Simpson doing?" He'd lost his wife, Mary, almost six years ago and took another wife named Mary.

The brothers shrugged, brows up. Doc answered for them. "This Mary's the same in name only."

Elizabeth shook her head. "We already have more Marys than the Bible in this family. Too bad he couldn't have found another name."

Her remark tickled Martha, and a short laugh erupted, lightening the moment. "We'd better go up. Mr. Henderer will bring him soon."

The boys tied the horses to the scrubby oaks, and together the five climbed the hill. Just before they reached the top, Martha heard the hoof-beats and the creak of rolling wagon wheels. She stopped to look down toward the Henderer house. Two fine pale-gray horses pranced this way, pulling a wagon, Charlie Henderer driving, a long wooden box on the back.

She climbed the rest of the way to the edge of the hole and watched as the horses drew the wagon through the gate, onto the hill, proceeding with short, mincing steps. Time slowed. Each lift of the horses' feet appeared suspended. Dust floated around them, hanging on the air. Bees buzzed. Her ears rang. The horses grew, inch by inch, as they neared. Their great muscles bulged with the strain. Manes fluttered with the toss of their heads. Huffing breaths, a rattling of harness, the snap of wheel on rock. Louder. Closer.

The wagon shook the ground. Stopped. Men strode to either side and lifted the coffin, while Mr. Henderer clucked at his animals and drove out from under the raised box, circling away from the group clustered at the dark gash in the earth. Only half aware of the retreating wagon, Martha watched the men step to the hole and lower the box with ropes.

A fine coffin. Mr. Fisher had made it, planing the boards smooth, polishing every edge, a work of great care.

The preacher lifted his chin and spoke, his words rippling on the air, touching Martha's ears, but not quite coming in. A warm breeze ruffled stray hairs on her neck and set up tears. At the appointed time, she bent down and picked up a handful of dirt, dropping it on the finely crafted box. Backing away, she felt the strong arms of her brothers, one on either side.

A hand slipped into hers. Cap. Comforting her? Or seeking comfort? She squeezed the hand and drew him close. Men picked up shovels and began to scoop from the pile of dirt on one side of the hole and toss it in. Scoop after scoop. Filling. Covering. A fierce tremor shook Cap and echoed in her. Doc's arm tightened around her shoulder. "Do you want to go?" he asked.

She nodded, turned away, and trod down the path, a firm grip on Cap's hand. They walked in silence toward the house. Then Newt spoke softly. "You're welcome to come back to Lane County with us."

She frowned. Lane County didn't have good memories for her. Things weren't perfect here, but she'd found friends. Still, she had no home of her own. She didn't know what she would do. Mr. Henderer had told her she could stay as long as she liked, but she knew he needed the help of his renters to maintain his large farm.

"You can stay with us," Newt said. "Elvira wanted me to tell you that, and I agree."

"I have eight children still at home. You don't have room for all of us."

Doc cleared his throat. "Louisa's getting married next month, isn't she?"

Martha glanced back to see Louisa and John well behind them, but spoke in a whisper anyway. "I don't know if we should go on with the wedding so soon after—"

Elizabeth leaned close to Martha, answering in the same low voice. "I see no reason not to. We don't have to rest on convention out here. It won't help anybody's grief to hold back those two."

Martha smiled. "You've noticed how they look at each other."

Elizabeth let out a puff of breath. "In two minutes I picked up on that."

"So." Newt's grin rounded his cheeks. "That brings it to seven children."

Martha shook her head. "Eight with me. You don't have room for eight of us, Newt. We have to make our own way."

He lifted his hands, palms up. "Just think about it. You don't have to decide right now."

She breathed a sigh. "I will. And I do appreciate the offer."

Levi Kent, walking beside them, turned to Martha. "You could move to my farm. We have an extra cabin we could spruce up for you. Charlie Henderer does need a man to help at his place."

Cap piped up. "I can fill in for Pa and work for rent."

Martha put a hand on her boy's back. "Mr. Henderer wouldn't agree to that, and neither would I."

Louisa caught up with them and locked an arm in Larry's—her favorite uncle. "Will you come back for the wedding next month? I know it's a long trip, but you were planning to before this happened."

Doc patted her shoulder. "We'll try. Some of us will come."

Larry shook his head. "Too bad Garrett couldn't have waited till after the wedding." The others raised their brows at him, and he went on quickly. "Well, too bad he died at all, but you know what I mean."

"I know," Martha said.

They reached the house, and she stopped in amazement. Neighbors had brought tables and set them out in the yard, every table heaped with food. Martha wasn't sure she was ready for this, but the warmth of family and friends soon enveloped her.

⁓

September 1867. Martha stood on the lowest fence board, gripping the top rail as the cattle moved through the narrow gate. Their new dog kept close, darting around to turn any cow that threatened to bolt. Mr. Fisher had given her to the boys—Lady, they called her—young but not a pup. A mixed breed, tan and white, slight bodied with sleek hair and floppy ears, she was a good herder.

Martha yelled at John and Cap. "Don't push them! I have to count."

While the cattle poured through in ones and twos, she kept a tally. "Twenty-five, twenty-six . . . forty-one, forty-two . . ."

Dust boiled around them, choking her, making her eyes water. Cows bawled. Hooves thudded. One calf almost snuck by on the far side of a large cow. The smell of cow and manure filled her nose until she could taste it.

"Fifty-six, fifty-seven."

One of the massive creatures struck the fence with its broad side, jolting it so Martha's foot slipped. Her skirt caught on a splinter. She yanked it loose, tearing a hole in the fabric, and scrambled back up. Silly skirt. She couldn't lose count.

"Fifty-eight, fifty-nine." When the last cow ran through, Martha called out. "Sixty!" She backed off the fence, mumbling to herself. "That should be right. We had forty-five when we left the Henderer place to come over here to the Kents'. We saved fifteen heifers."

"You got it, Ma?" Cap asked, sounding like a man as he strode toward her. He walked with a rhythmic step, nimble as a cat—like his pa.

"I count sixty."

He gave her a nod. "That's right, then."

"Yes. I'd better finish filling out the papers. You can let the cows out." She tried to shake dust off her skirt as she walked to the house. Taxes. She'd filled these out for Garrett before, but never had the responsibility.

Inside the small cabin, she sat at the table where she'd left papers strewn across the top. Finding the line on the tax form, she marked down *60* after the word *cattle*. The rest were easy. She had eight horses and eight hogs. She checked the tax roll from the year before. With a value last year of $1,370, she'd paid $21.92 in taxes. The extra cattle this year would increase her value, though she had seventy dollars in debt to offset it.

Voices outside distracted her from her work. Her children began pouring into the cabin. The older ones. Nora and David, Louisa and John. Mary, with Billy Fisher behind her. Had he come to visit Mary again? Much as Martha liked the man, he was too old for Mary. Probably closer to Martha's age—not that she had any wishes in that vein for herself.

They all greeted her, still laughing from some previous conversation. She couldn't help noticing the difference between Nora and Louisa, how Louisa looked at her new husband with impish delight. Nora scarcely looked at David. Martha's attention turned back to Mary and Mr. Fisher. Mary definitely had lights in her eyes when she looked at the man, and he gazed on her as a boy might gaze on candy.

But Billy Fisher was no boy. Why was Mary attracted to him? Was he a father figure, taking the place of the father she lost?

He'd been a great help to Martha and her family. She appreciated him for that, and it was nice of him to give the boys a dog. He built barns for a living and was capable with tools. He and John Cassida had become good friends. He'd served as a witness at Louisa and John's small wedding. Newt and Larry came for it, but no one else from Lane County.

Mr. Fisher sat across the table from Martha. "How are you doing, Mrs. Maupin?"

She patted a hand on the papers. "I think I have all my numbers. I need to get this turned in."

"I can take it if you like. I have to go into town."

"Thank you. That would be wonderful."

He leaned forward. "Cap says you're wanting to move."

She lifted her hands and shook her head. "We can't stay here. We need a place of our own, but I don't know how we'll afford it." She wondered what had happened to the money from their Lane County claim. Could they have spent all of that? "I could sell the cows, but that's a little like eating your seed corn, isn't it?"

He smiled. "You might be able to get a loan. I'd help if I could."

"I know." She rubbed the back of her neck. "Would anybody loan to a woman?"

"Maybe if Cap asked."

She nearly choked. "Cap! He's just a boy."

"He's twelve, almost thirteen—and mature for his age."

Martha sputtered a little. "And I'm mature for my age too."

Billy Fisher's face twisted from a near smile to something like a frown. He stroked his chin whiskers, looking thoughtful. "Maybe you could talk to Mr. Ozauf over in Scottsburg. He might be willing to loan you money if you have a place in mind."

Cap plopped down beside Mr. Fisher. "Why don't we go look at the Shadrach Hudson claim in Kellogg? Howard Martin has it now. You met him. He's a friend of the Wellses. Pa and I went over there once. Looks like a nice place, but we didn't see much of it."

A crushing weight pressed down on Martha's shoulders. So much responsibility. She looked into her son's eager face. "If the weather's nice tomorrow maybe we should take a look—if he's still wanting to sell."

Cap's eyes glittered, small star-bursts twinkling in the blue. "All right!"

"Good idea," Mr. Fisher said, pulling her attention away from those bright eyes. He shifted on the bench, glanced at the tabletop, and looked back at her. "Could I speak to you, Mrs. Maupin? Alone?"

Heat welled from inside her, the room much too warm. "Let's go outside."

They walked out under a spreading oak and stood in the cool of its shade. When he didn't speak, she prompted him. "What can I do for you, Mr. Fisher?"

"I'd like to ask for Mary's hand in marriage."

The dreaded words struck like a blow to her middle. Momentarily angered by the blow, she faced him, her tone hard. "You're too old for her."

He bent toward Martha, hands out, fingertips almost touching together. "I know, but I love her, and I believe she feels the same."

"How old are you?"

"I'm forty—but I'm strong and healthy, and I'll be good to her."

"She's only sixteen, Mr. Fisher. Sixteen." Memory hammered at the back of Martha's mind. Sixteen. Like her when she got married. And Garrett was old for her at twenty-three. She remembered the pain of her parents' disapproval, and her insistence on going ahead despite their wishes.

She studied Mr. Fisher's face, wanted to read it as Garrett claimed he could do. Why wasn't Garrett here to handle this? He wouldn't allow it, not for this child he'd helped bring into the world, not for his precious Mary. Mr. Fisher had a kind face, gentle gray-blue eyes, but age lines already etched his brow.

"I will take good care of her," he said. "You can count on me."

"She'd be a young widow."

He looked over Martha's head. "It's hard to predict those things."

Her mouth twitched with a flickering smile. Was that a kind way to point out her own situation? "You can make a pretty good guess." She looked toward the river, to the mountains beyond, and met his gaze again. "I will not stand in the way of my daughter's happiness—if that's what she wants."

———

A narrow road cut into the riverbank leading to Howard Martin's farm, the Donation Land Claim of a man named Shadrach Hudson. Martha rode beside Cap, both silent. Opposite the river, high bluffs loomed, overgrown with trees and shrubs. Just past a thicket of firs and hardwoods on the riverside, the bottom opened into a narrow valley. A log cabin hunkered against the trees, facing an open field. A dog barked, and Mr. Martin stepped out onto the narrow stoop. "Hello. What can I do for you?"

Martha rode straight to him and stopped her horse. "Hello, Mr. Martin. I understand you want to sell this property. We'd like to take a look at it."

"Hello, folks. You want to come in a minute?"

"Could we look first?"

"I'll get my horse."

The three rode down the long valley, which broadened as they went. The hill, becoming less steep, opened out to pastureland above. Mr. Martin had planted wheat on some of the river bottom, but brush crowded fields on all sides.

"How many acres of bottomland?" Martha asked.

"Almost eighty." Mr. Martin turned to Cap. "It's fine soil. You can grow anything you want here. And you have another two hundred forty on the hill—most of it good pasture."

He went on, extolling the virtues of the place to Cap, as if Martha wasn't there, and Cap sat as tall as he could in the saddle. She let them ride ahead as she soaked in the beauty. Eighty acres wasn't nearly as much tillable land as she and Garrett had in Lane County, but it was enough.

Her pa never had more than that at any one time. And this still had all the hill land.

They rode from one end of the narrow valley to the other, where the field pinched to a near vee again. There they could look down on the river. The water narrowed between rocks that lay like huge cobblestones on either side, the crashing sound of rapids a constant backdrop to the soft voices of Cap and Mr. Martin. On the far side sheer rock cliffs dropped to the river's edge, the jagged cliff faces mottled with moss of varied greens, firs and a few hardwoods hanging on where they could take hold. A crown of firs topped the cliff, a fringe of tall willowy trees at the bottom, their leaves starting to turn gold.

Martha watched the churning white water, then turned to look at Mr. Martin's mountain.

"Can we go up the hill?" she asked.

Mr. Martin looked at Cap. "Have you seen what you need to down here?"

Cap shrugged. "Sure. Let's go up."

Martha stifled a smile. Mr. Martin led them about halfway back up the valley to a narrow track cut into the hillside, only a little wider than an animal trail. A gentle rise. As they started up the trail, Martha pressed her horse closer to Mr. Martin so she could make herself heard. "Is there any tillable land up here?"

He glanced over his shoulder at her. "Not really. Maybe the upper field." He went on talking to Cap. "It's hilly, but the grass grows like everything and the cows get fat as pigs."

"That's good," Cap said. At almost thirteen, the boy was starting to get a hint of hair on his upper lip. It made him look like a man. He wasn't large, but wiry like his father.

Mr. Martin said something else Martha couldn't quite hear.

She dropped back, shaking her head. At a bend in the trail, she stopped and looked down the long slope. Just below was the lower field where she'd watched the white water in the river. The rapids were clear from up here too, their sound bouncing up the hillside. A beautiful spot.

Turning away from the view, she saw the others were getting ahead of her, but she didn't try to catch up. Mr. Martin wasn't interested in selling her this property. He was trying to sell Cap on it. Following them up the steep track alongside a sharp gorge, she let the wonder of the place wrap around her. Mr. Martin might think he was going to sell to Cap, but the land spoke to Martha.

Where the trail opened out, a soft ridge curved up to a wide, spreading field that ran all the way to the crest, maybe half a mile distant. Oaks dotted the lower part, but the upper field was open grass with only a little low brush below a line of firs at the top. It wouldn't be hard to clear. She heard Cap's excited voice. "You could grow grain there," he said, as if he had the knowledge of an old farmer.

Martha nodded, pleased at his exuberance. She would need his help.

She nudged her horse and rode over a gentle rise across a saddle of land to a broad overlook. Her breath caught. She could see the valley, the river, a plain on the far side, and mountains beyond. A breeze stirred, like a whisper saying, "Come."

April 8, 1868. Martha rushed about, trying to make the dismal cabin presentable. Mr. Ozauf had agreed to the loan—after Cap arranged it. One thousand dollars. At least they let Martha sign the documents for her own farm—because Cap was too young. She let out a wry laugh.

Stabbing the broom bristles against the floor, she shook her head. She supposed she ought to be thankful the place had a wood floor, but the dirt was so caked and ground into the planks, it might as well be packed earth.

"I need a proper house. If only Mary had waited, we could have built a fine house and had a lovely wedding in it."

She heard horses, people's voices. Selena and Mary rushed in. "We need to get changed," Mary said, bolting up the ladder to the loft, Selena hurrying after her.

They'd been setting up tables in the yard. Martha stepped out of the cabin's gloom into the bright sunshine. She smiled, seeing the girls' handiwork. The tables looked beautiful. Plates full of food. Sprigs of blossomladen branches. More blossoms adorning the small porch, lining the posts and the roof edge, like a bower. The sweet scent embraced her. She'd never thought it could look so nice.

The horses and their riders came into view, and she called out. "Newt! Doc! Elizabeth!" The little dog Lady ran out to meet them, and Martha started to follow, when she saw Mr. Kellogg riding with them and decided she ought to wait. As mother of the bride she needed to present herself with a certain amount of decorum. Lyman Kellogg, whose family gave her new community its name, was Justice of the Peace here and would officiate today.

She could scarcely contain her excitement when she saw Larry and Ben also, and their wives, and Newt's Elvira. And Simpson! Even Simpson had come.

Nora and David came behind in a small wagon, Mollie snug on Nora's lap. Then the Wellses and Kents in their big wagon with all their children. And Louisa and John, Louisa heavy now with her first child, due next month.

Mr. Kellogg rode up to Martha and tipped his hat.

"Welcome, Mr. Kellogg," she said. "It's nice to see you again."

"Pleased to see you, Mrs. Maupin."

As he dismounted, Martha noticed she still had her dirty old working apron on over her nice dress. She reached back, trying to be inconspicuous, and yanked at the tie. Ripping the apron off, she excused herself and darted back in the cabin to tuck it out of sight.

Face flushed, she smoothed her dress, tidied her hair, and stepped back out. More people came—the Dimmicks from up at the corner, other people whose names she couldn't remember. So many had come by to welcome them since they moved in last week.

Billy arrived, looking smart in a wool suit, a meticulous tie at his neck, curly hair trimmed and slicked straight above his ears. He'd outdone himself. A fine man—if not for a child like Mary. Martha even had to write a note for the county clerk consenting to this marriage because Mary wasn't quite eighteen.

Mr. Kellogg approached her now. "I believe it's time—if you're ready."

Martha smiled. "I'll tell the girls."

Inside, she leaned on the ladder and called up to them. "Are you ready?"

Mary's bright voice. "Yes."

Martha wished she could be as calm. She went outside and took her place in front of her brothers, Cap on one side, Tom on the other, the younger ones on the shoulders of various uncles. Selena came out the door and stood beneath the bower of blossoms. John Cassida marched up and stood opposite her, leaving space between.

Mary emerged. She looked beautiful, dark ringlets framing her face, cheeks aglow, large blue eyes sparkling with her father's fire. Billy walked up the path and took her hand, as Mr. Kellogg moved forward.

A soft breeze carried the scent of flowers and lifted Martha on their sweetness, back to another time, another wedding. She couldn't take in the words, only the meaning of the moment. The love, the determination in the face of disapproval, the denial, the hope. She felt Garrett's warm hand as they stood together on that wide porch in Missouri, looked into his warm eyes, felt the love to her core.

Then Billy kissed Mary, jolting Martha back to this moment. The couple moved out into the crowd of well-wishers. Martha tried to smile. This wasn't what she wanted—especially for this daughter. She wanted a strong young man full of the exuberance of youth. But she would never do to Mary what her parents did to her. Even if they had reason.

She felt a hand on her shoulder and turned to see Larry smiling down at her. "Nice place here," he said. "But remember, you're always welcome in Lane County if this doesn't work out."

Her back stiffened. "Do you doubt my ability to make it here on my own?"

"That's not what I'm saying, Martha. I wish you well."

"We all do," Doc said, and the others voiced their agreement.

Martha suddenly remembered the special napkins she'd embroidered for the occasion. How could she have forgotten? Where were they? Upstairs in the small trunk? "I forgot something," she said, rushing away from her family, into the dark cabin. She stopped inside, unable to see after the bright sunlight outdoors. As her eyes adjusted she walked slowly to the ladder and climbed.

The loft was even darker, only a trace of light coming from the open door below and the one window covered in oiled deerskin. Martha needed a glass window. She knelt on the mattress on the floor and opened the trunk. The white napkins with her careful white embroidery lay on the top. She picked them up and ran a finger over the stitches. Sounds of revelry drifted from outside.

They carried her again to that other wedding a long time away. Tears burned. Martha hadn't cried—not really—in the nearly two years since Garrett's accident. She didn't dare start. A sob jolted her, and she clutched the napkins to her breast.

She rode on the familiar sounds, the sweet scent of the blossoms, back to the love on that long ago day. When did she lose Garrett? When did it begin? Did she lose a part of him on that terrible trail? Did she lose a part of him the day John Vallerly walked onto their new property and jealousy slashed its searing fire into their lives? Did she lose a part when he first reached for a bottle instead of her? Did she lose a part the first time he raised a hand and struck her across the mouth, slamming her words back into her head?

She'd been losing him bit by bit for such a long time—like a repeated tearing away of flesh from flesh. With each tear the layers of scar tissue had grown over the raw wounds, blunting feelings—until this moment when she saw this child they brought forth together leaving her for a union Martha could not embrace—and every old wound lay open again.

Another sob erupted. Martha crumpled onto the bed and the powerful emotions converged. Grief, held at bay too long, overtook her. Grief for Garrett. For Mary. For herself. For parents she would never reach to heal the rift. For years lost. She couldn't hold it back any longer. There, alone in the dark loft, while others celebrated, she wept, the pain pouring out of those raw places in deep, jagged moans.

A shout of laughter penetrated her darkness. She raised herself up and sat, gulping deep breaths until the sobs ebbed. She felt drained but somehow refreshed. Grabbing the top napkin, she wiped it across her wet face. Her eyes probably looked all red and puffy. How could she go back outside? But she had to. It was Mary's wedding. With the wet napkin clutched in one hand, she picked up the others and climbed down the ladder.

The water pitcher sat on the sideboard across from the door. She set the stack of napkins on the sideboard and poured some cold water from a pitcher into a small bowl. Dipping her wadded cloth in the water, she pressed it over her eyes. A footfall creaked the doorstep. She didn't want to turn that way, didn't want to be seen yet.

"Martha?" Elizabeth, her voice edged with concern. "Are you all right?"

Still facing away from the door, Martha took a long breath. "I was feeling a little . . . disheartened for a bit."

Elizabeth came to her side and put an arm around her shoulders. "I can only imagine."

Martha smiled, reaching for a towel to dab her face. "I forgot the napkins I made for the wedding."

"Oh, these?" Elizabeth lightly touched the pile of napkins. "They're beautiful. You do such fine work. Do you want me to take them out to the table?"

"I can go—if I—do I look all right?"

Elizabeth peered into her face. "You look fine. Only the slightest moisture in your eyes, and the mother of the bride is supposed to have water in her eyes. It's tradition."

They both laughed until Martha felt tears well again. "You know I always get teary when I laugh hard. I guess we've been having ourselves a good laugh, haven't we?"

"I'll say."

Martha gathered the napkins and strode to the doorway, chin high as she stepped back out into the April sunshine to enjoy this celebration that would last all day and into the evening. Friends and family would pitch their tents in the narrow field and probably revel all night.

Chapter 11

Her Own Farm

On the Farm, April 1869

Martha lugged the pan of dishwater out the cabin door and tossed the water onto the native shrubbery by the corner of the building. A beautiful spring day. Weather seemed to warm earlier in Oregon than back home. Leaves coming out already. Blossoms. It did her good to get outside. That cabin closed in on her so.

She sighed, clutching the pan against her apron. She needed a proper house. They'd been on this farm of hers for a year now, and she was forty years old. It was time. Billy was a builder. She wanted to talk to him about it. He and Mary had found a place over on Pleasant Plain, right across the river, but a good three miles around by the ferry. Glancing toward that river barrier, she wondered how Mary was doing. No sign of babies yet, but the girl did seem happy.

Maybe Martha would see them at the Dimmicks' next Sabbath. A circuit rider was coming through, and Mr. Dimmick had ridden over to invite Martha's family.

"Might be nice hearing some preaching and seeing folks. Been a long while."

Sometimes she told her children the old stories—Moses, Daniel and the lion, David and that giant—lots of fine stories. She'd known them since childhood when she used to hear Grandpa Wood tell them. He was both preacher and teacher, and sure could spin a tale.

The Dimmicks, her nearest neighbors by road, lived up at the corner a little more than a mile away, where Martha's road met the main route running south from Elkton to Oakland. Mr. Dimmick had the ferry there, he and another fellow.

She supposed this little farming community of Kellogg could turn into a town, with more people coming all the time. They had a post office, anyway. Her sister Louisa in her last letter wrote that railroad men were building across the country. They expected to have it done soon. That ought to bring the people. Folks said it would take six days to cross the plains by rail, a trip that had taken Martha's family five months.

"Imagine that. Riding along in a comfortable seat instead of walking all those miles. Six days." She shook her head and stood marveling at the idea.

Caught in her thoughts she was startled to look up and see Cap coming across the field toward her, his stride easy, graceful, charged with determination. The hair rose on her flesh, and she brushed her hands over her arms, smiling. From a distance he might have been mistaken for his father. How often had that happened? It never ceased to affect her. The dog at his heels scooted ahead to greet Martha before Cap got there.

"Need the big ax," Cap said. He and Tom were clearing some brush. He paused by his mother and put his hands on his hips, brow wrinkled. "A tree from along the river fell right out into the wheat field."

She set the dishpan on the porch and followed him out back where they did their wood chopping. The axe was stuck into the chopping block. "Our wheat fields look good, though," she said. They'd cleared a couple of fields for planting.

Cap grunted, sounded like his father. "Yeah, but this place is in terrible shape. Didn't anybody ever take care of it? Looks like Shadrach Hudson didn't do much more'n he had to so's he could prove up his claim, and I don't know what the others did."

"Well, it's had five owners in less than twenty years."

Cap pulled the ax out of the cut tree stump and hefted it over his shoulder. "No wonder it's in bad shape."

As they walked back around to the front of the cabin, she looked up the long narrow valley. "Maybe our family can keep it a little longer." She set a hand on her son's arm, stopping him. "Maybe for those other owners it was just a piece of land, a piece of business. Not something to care for—to love."

Cap lifted his chin to face her, one brow up, the corner of his mouth twitching, not quite making a smile, as if unsure he wanted to accept his mother's sentimental notion. He started to walk away.

"I'm thinking I should talk to Billy about building a proper house," she said.

He turned back to her. "What kind of house?"

"A frame house, like the Dimmick place up at the corner."

His eyes grew wide. "You should talk to Billy, all right."

<hr />

Martha sat across the table from Joe Roberts in the cramped cabin. Billy had recommended the man. "I can build a fine strong barn for you," Billy had said, "as fine as any barn in the country, but I don't do the kind of work you want on your house." He told her Mr. Roberts had built the Dimmick house, and Martha had agreed to speak to the man.

Joe Roberts put her in mind of a charming Irishman she'd met years before. The twinkling eyes. The words spilling off his tongue like silver in the delightful brogue. The brimming enthusiasm of his youth. But that was eighteen years ago. Martha wasn't a girl anymore, and that other Irishman wouldn't be young now either. Sometimes she wondered what had happened to him, if he ever remarried. But she didn't want to wonder about that today.

"I understand you're from Ireland," she said to Mr. Roberts.

"I am." A trace of melancholy thickened his voice. "A fine place, Ireland. She still tugs on me some, but this land has a nice tug too."

"It does."

He brushed a hand over his reddish-blond hair and scribbled some lines on one of the shingles he'd brought in. "So you'd be wanting a parlor—like so, is it?"

She leaned forward to see. He'd drawn the outlines of a plan and was tapping his stubby pencil on one square. "That's the parlor?" she asked.

His eyes brightened with his smile. "That'd be it, ma'am." He pointed out each of the other rooms. "If I understand what you're telling me."

"Yes, yes."

"And the front." He picked up another shingle and quickly sketched the front of the house, a sharp gable facing forward, the long line of the roof extending beside. "We can put some scrollwork on the roofline here."

"And a balcony." She looked up at him. "I want a balcony. One you can stand on."

"A balcony, is it? Well, then." He scribbled a few more lines, and there it was. A fine balcony coming out from that front gable, with a pretty little rail. It was only a rough sketch, but in her mind she saw the house in all its splendor.

She laid a hand over her heart. "That's beautiful. Will you do a big drawing on paper?"

"Not as such." He tapped his temple. "I think I'd be getting a fair idea in my head. Have you decided where you want it?"

"I've been giving that some thought."

He waved toward the door. "Looks like you have flat land aplenty here. It won't be mattering much. Just keep back from the river a little."

"Yes, I definitely will do that. I know what a river can do."

He lifted his brows, nodding. "We can get lumber from the Gardiner mill, over by the coast."

"Isn't that awfully far? I have plenty of timber here."

Again his brows rose. "I'm sure you do, ma'am, but you'd be lacking the sawmill. We can bring lumber down by boat to Scottsburg and then haul it here by the military road. About a twenty-six-mile haul, but you'll be having the finest lumber. That's what you'd be wanting for a fine house like this."

"Well, if you're sure."

His eyes sparkled. "Mrs. Maupin, this house—it's your dream, is it? I'll make you the house you've been dreaming of. You can be counting on that."

"How soon can you start?"

"As soon as we get the lumber."

———

The gentle spring sun warmed Martha's back as she strolled around the gentle rise. Budding scents wafted on the air. She had walked the length of her bottomland and back. This was the highest ground on the valley floor. Here she would build her house. A proper house. With a balcony. Like the ones in St. Charles.

From this spot she could see the hills wrapping around the bottomland. The house would look out on her mountain, across the road. She walked toward the roadway and turned to imagine the house's face as Mr. Roberts had drawn it. Then she walked back and stood about where the front porch would be, to contemplate her view. Scrub oak and lone firs sprinkled the steep slope that dropped to a canyon where the farm's main creek spilled. On the other side of the canyon, the ground rose more gently. The mountain trail led that way.

She would sit on her porch—or her balcony—and listen to the music of the creek tumbling down the cleft, gaze at her mountain, and smell the sweetness of the lilac in springtime and the rose in summer. Newt had gone to the Lane County house for her and got starts of the lilac and rose she carried across the plains. She would put them here.

"Yes, this will do just fine."

Smiling, she glanced toward the mountain trail. Selena was watching the little ones. The boys were cutting wood. Maybe it was a good time for a walk. Taking a last twirl to see every direction surrounding her house, she did a little hop skip and started up the hill.

She hadn't gone far when she heard a scamper behind, and turned. Lady, following. The dog usually stayed close to Cap and Tom, but maybe the promise of a good walk made Martha more interesting today. Martha beckoned. "Come on, girl. I'm glad for your company."

Lady responded with a burst of speed until she was trotting alongside Martha, looking up now and then to share her delight. A beautiful day for a walk.

Martha stopped to catch her breath when they reached the overlook to the rapids at the trail's sharp turn. Lady sat beside her, quietly panting, the soft sound mingling with the rush of white water below. The mountains loomed on the far side of the river, rising almost straight up, one of the higher peaks towering above the rapids. Its bold timbered face lay in shadow, the rock cliffs barely visible, while sun gleamed bright on Martha's south slope.

Birds flitted about, singing their spring songs, the smell of new grass and leaves sweet enough to taste. The rapids ended where the river began a wide bend to circle behind her farm before heading on downstream, flowing right past Charlie Henderer's farm on its way to the sea, someplace near Gardiner where men were sawing her lumber.

She smiled, but tears brimmed, and her voice rasped. "You brought me to the edge of the Promised Land, Garrett Maupin, but I had to come into it on my own, didn't I? I didn't want it to be this way."

As her watery eyes turned the colors to daubs of dark and vivid green a soft wet tongue licked her fingers. She wiped her cheeks with the back of her other hand, giving the dog a gentle pat, and turned away from the view to continue up the hill.

The trail turned steeper alongside the gorge. She knew the route well. She had walked over much of her mountain this past year—sometimes with the children, sometimes alone—from the deep gash on the west side the boys called Wildcat Canyon to the grove on the east, and all the ridges in between. She could see the grove now, across the gorge near the eastern end of the wide upper field. The first time she walked into that small woods it had enclosed her in solace. She wouldn't have been surprised to run into God in a place like that.

She often thought of her long journey to this farm. Such a trek, and not just the Oregon Trail. That was hard, but not the hardest. Sometimes she forgot the pain with Garrett and conjured up the happiness in their early years. Most times she set that all aside and focused on the children and friends and the joys of the present.

Just past a clump of trees, she came out onto the open ridge where it flattened out like a saddle. Leaving the trail, she clambered over the hump to that oak at the edge of the downward slope, the place she could look out over the valley and the hills beyond. Her heart leapt at the sight, though she'd been here many times before.

The sun had begun to lower, making the entire distant range a gentle blue, Pleasant Plain gleaming in the sun's slanted light beneath it, a drift of clouds above. What a glorious upheaval of mountains. She never saw anything like them before she left Missouri. They did bar an endless vista, but they made up for it in their grandeur.

One year. She had owned this amazing piece of land for one year. Yet how daunting at the start. She shook her head and murmured in the quiet. "I had to do something. I never wanted my family to live off the charity of friends and relatives. But I think the most terrible thing for me was knowing I had to decide. Not Cap. Not my brothers. Cap was too young, and it wasn't my brothers' responsibility. I had to come to it myself, say, 'Here I will stay. Here I will take my stand.'" She took a sudden sharp breath. "It was the most lonely choice I ever made."

That soft tongue licked her hand again, and Martha glanced down at the animal to fondle its silky ears. "But we're doing all right, aren't we, Lady?"

The dog smiled up at her. That *was* a smile on Lady's face, if Martha had ever seen a smile.

She gently stroked the animal's head and rested her other hand on the oak's trunk. A meadowlark warbled its intricate melody nearby, like a shimmery flute. Another answered. "Listen, Lady," Martha whispered. "Did you ever hear a sweeter song?"

The sun slipped behind the low clouds, grayed the world, then, finding a clear seam, sent sprays of light across the heavens. She voiced a deep sigh. "Look at that, Lady. Isn't it wonderful?"

Martha looked into the warm brown eyes, and back at the glory.

"Oh, Mama, if only you could see. You were right, but if you could only see how it worked out."

EPILOGUE
SPRING 2011

I sat on the couch in my office one drizzly morning reading the first draft of this manuscript. I had just read the final page when something alerted me outside the bay window. Setting down my laptop, I got up while looking out the window.

The double oak with which I'd begun this story trembled wildly, and the larger trunk—already leaning over the slope—tilted farther. Sank. Fell. Crashed against the ground in a fury of flaying branches. Shook the earth. The rumble shook me. I stood staring in horror and disbelief, my hands over my mouth.

Martha.

The offshoot remained standing. I rushed outside to see close-up. The root ball had ripped a huge hole. Desperate to save the offshoot, I grabbed a shovel. While rain sprinkled and a bit of sun shone through, I dug the loosened dirt to push it around the smaller tree's trunk.

I tried to sort out my feelings, my sense of loss. What did this mean? Martha had walked this land before this tree's acorn ever sprouted. Yet in my mind that older, larger part of the double oak had absorbed the energy of her lingering presence. Now its life was over, and my book was written. I still had editing to do. But the story had become an entity in itself.

Gazing at the oak's downed trunk in the next few days, I began to feel an unusual sense of completion. No more scenes pouring into my head. Had Martha moved on?

My daughter Carisa suggested something that resonated. "Maybe she can rest now."

Several weeks later the white hawk came back, or one like it. The graceful bird swooped by my window, hovered over the fallen oak, took a slow circle above it, then flew high and disappeared. I had a feeling I would see the hawk again.

AFTERWORD

Martha lived on her farm for twenty years, rearing the rest of her children to adulthood. Shortly before Cap married in 1888, she sold the property to him and his brother Tom, and the boys built a house for her about a mile away on the next property over. Through various land trades between the brothers, Cap soon gained full ownership of the original farm.

Martha lived in the new house with her youngest son Mike, and sometimes Tom, until she died March 17, 1909, at the age of eighty. Or eighty-one. Sources differ.

All five of her daughters married and had children, but of her four sons only Cap married. Cap's first wife died, along with their first child, one year after the marriage. According to one story, he felt so discouraged he nearly gave up the farm. Then in 1893 he married Adilla Peters. The couple had eight children.

Martha would have to bury two more of her children, Louisa and Garry. In 1893, at the age of thirty, Garry was engaged to marry a local girl, but he contracted some kind of ailment in his leg. The doctor said he would have to amputate, but Garry said he'd rather die than lose the leg. He kept the leg and lost his life. Louisa evidently died sometime between 1880, where I last found her listed on the census, and 1900, when Martha's census listing shows her with eleven children born, seven living. Martha's 1909 obituary shows all the others surviving her.

Martha's daughter Mary, my great-grandmother, was a young widow as her mother predicted. Billy died in 1903 at the age of seventy-seven, a few years before Martha. Mary was fifty-two. Mary and Billy had five children, three boys and two girls, one of the girls dying young. Their second son was my grandfather, Eugene Roy Fisher, known as Roy.

Nora finally divorced David Bunch and later married Ansel Langdon of Kellogg, reportedly not a happy marriage either. Her daughter Mollie moved in with Grandma Martha for a while. Mollie appears on the 1880 census in Martha's household, fourteen years old. Mollie's tombstone, near her grandmother's, shows she died at the age of twenty-five, surely a tragedy for Martha.

Most of Martha's children remained close, except for Selena and Bina, who left the county after marrying, Selena to Benton County, Oregon, and Bina to Washington State. Mary and Billy moved to Gardiner on the coast for a few years around 1880. Perhaps Martha visited them there and finally saw the great Pacific Ocean. Meanwhile, Cap and the girls gave Martha many grandchildren.

Of her five brothers who emigrated to Oregon, only Doc stayed in Lane County, though Ben didn't go far, moving first to nearby Benton County, then to Linn. Doc and Ben died within a month of each other in the summer of 1879, Doc in July, Ben in August, both from injuries in wagon accidents. Elizabeth never remarried, becoming a proud home-owner herself into her late years.

Larry must have remained a staunch Democrat, naming one of his sons Jefferson Davis Poindexter. He joined the Sons of Temperance in Lane County, inspired perhaps by his brother-in-law Garrett. Around 1875 Larry moved to the arid ranching country of northern California and spent the rest of his life in that area. Simpson had a messy divorce from his second Mary in 1874. He accused her of adultery and claimed that the last child during their marriage wasn't his. She accused him of drunkenness and abuse. He took his son Tommy back to Illinois to be cared for by sister Louisa Bronough, later returning west with Tommy, this time to Idaho in about 1885. Larry and Simpson died within days of each other in November 1888, Simpson on the first, Larry on the sixth.

Newt stayed in Lane County long enough to serve two terms as Lane County Sheriff from 1870 to 1874, known there as a jovial, likable man. By 1880 he was blacksmithing in Portland, finally moving in 1895 to eastern Oregon. He died in March 1903. Sometime afterward, his widow, Elvira, visited Martha. Cap's daughters remembered the visit and her delightful, somewhat peppery personality.

In the East, Ambrose died in Missouri in September 1862, having moved there sometime before the 1850 census. Around 1861 as the Civil War revved up, Ambrose and his son John joined the Missouri Home Guard, a local Union militia group in a state fiercely split between North and South. Ambrose died long before the war was over, cause unknown. Brother Stephen apparently served in the war with an Illinois company on the Union side until discharged in 1863, though identification isn't absolute. He disappears from the record after a land sale in 1868. Louisa and John Bronough were leading citizens in Virden, Illinois, where John served as the first mayor. Louisa died there in 1882.

Over the years Martha became a cherished member of the farming community of Kellogg. A neighbor wrote her obituary, printed in the *Eugene Register-Guard*. After giving some of the mundane details of Martha's life, the writer expresses some thoughts in the flowery style of the day.

> *Grandmother Maupin, as she was familiarly known, was a lady of great moral, and physical courage. . . . Foregoing hardships, meeting with reverses, and braving dangers almost unsurmountable, Mrs. Maupin saw in the early '50s the Oregon of today. . . . Truly she was one of the builders of our fair state, and she builded better than she knew.*

Martha rests on a beautiful hill, just up the ridge from her own, in the Dimmick Cemetery, several of her children nearby, overlooking the sweeping bend of the river before it flows past her farm on its snaking journey to the sea. Garrett still rests on the knoll at the Henderer place, a few miles downriver.

AUTHOR'S NOTES
THE PEOPLE AND THE DOCUMENTS

The People

Most of the characters in Martha's story are real, all her family members—parents, siblings, children, cousins, in-laws. Also, historic personages mentioned are real.

In addition to family, another real person mentioned in Martha's Missouri scenes is Isaiah Mansur, whose store ledger of 1839 I had the pleasure of perusing myself.

Nonfamily persons named on the Oregon Trail are fictional, as well as those at the house in Missouri where Martha and her brothers stay overnight. Unnamed persons are fictional.

John Vallerly is real. He settled his Donation Land Claim in Lane County in April 1851, just before Martha and Garrett, who settled theirs in July 1851. Vallerly claimed 320 acres north of them, the second parcel over. Unmarried at the time, he must have been in Oregon prior to December 1, 1850, in order to receive that much land, given the dictates of the new law. He was a naturalized citizen, born in Ireland in 1829. Documents show Vallerly's marriage to Elizabeth Brown in 1853 and her death in 1858, about the time of their first child's birth. The 1860 census shows their child living with grandparents John and Mary Brown of Ray County, Missouri, who traveled west over the plains in 1852. By 1860 he doesn't appear on the census for Lane County or any nearby counties.

The several sheriffs who appear in the story are real and held office at the times shown—James E. McCabe, 1856–1858; Joseph B. Meador, 1860–1862 and 1866–1870; W. H. Haley, 1864–1866. (Meador was defeated in the 1870 election for sheriff by Newt Poindexter and, reportedly upset by the loss, left Lane County soon afterward.)

Mr. S. Ellsworth is the attorney who signed Martha's divorce documents. Census records for 1860 show him as a thirty-three-year-old lawyer, born in New York, with a wife and two small children, an extra twelve-year-old living in his household, plus a servant. His first name was probably Stukely. A Stukely Ellsworth owned several lots in Lane County, according to government land records.

The Cassidas are real. The 1860 Lane County, Oregon, census shows a Martin *Cassaday*, age forty-six, and John *Cassaday*, age seventeen, living in the Maupin household, as well as Irishman John Arthura, twenty-three. I left Arthura out of the story to avoid confusion. John's age varies from one census to another, so I chose an age for him. The Cassidas apparently follow the Maupins to Douglas County, where John marries Louisa, the second daughter of Martha and Garrett, in 1866.

The people Martha meets in Douglas County are real—Ira and Anna Wells, Levi and Mary Kent, Charles and Mrs. Henderer, Lyman Kellogg, the Dimmicks, Howard Martin. A man named Shadrach Hudson did stake first claim on our farm, giving it the historic designation, the Shadrach Hudson Donation Land Claim. Other real persons mentioned include Cyrus Hedden, a well-known personage in Scottsburg, and Mr. Ozauf, who gave Martha a loan to buy the farm.

Joe Roberts of Ireland did build Martha's house.

Documents

The excerpts Martha reads of the 1860 Complaint and Affidavit are direct quotes from microfilm copies of the original documents. Another document shows the court case describing Vallerly's altercation with Garrett in 1856. Godfrey Anchez (sometimes spelled Anchiz) is a real person, shown in court documents in his 1864 case against Garrett.

Other documentation is described in the interludes.

Martha's Age

A question over Martha's birth date appears to come down to sources. Census data consistently show an age indicating an 1829 date, and in the more detailed 1900 census, the February 1829 date itself. Her obituary states she died at eighty in March 1909, confirming the 1829 birth year. But her tombstone and death record give 1828. The source of the census information is no doubt Martha herself. Grieving offspring would have provided the date for the stone and the death record. I take Martha as the better source of her own birthday. Besides, the 1829 date fits better in her mother's spacing between babies.

Names

Family names sometimes vary in the records. Maupin could be Maupine, Maupain, Moppin, even Maussin on the 1850 census, probably a faulty translation from *p* to the elongated *s* often used in those days. The Moppin spelling has continued with a few family lines. Vallerly is often Vallely. The Cassida name is spelled various ways, including Cassaday, Cassidy, and Cassida. In later spellings Cassida seems to hold precedence.

Several people in the story went by nicknames or switched to middle names. I tried to pick names and stay with them to avoid confusion. Martha's brother Stephen sometimes went by Stephen, sometimes by Harrison. Documents might show him as either Stephen Harrison or Harrison Stephen. Simpson was Thomas Simpson, but he seemed to favor Simpson, perhaps to distinguish him from his father, Thomas. Documents often show him as T. S., occasionally Thomas S., but more often Simpson. Ben was Bennett, sometimes mistaken as Benjamin on records. Newt was James Newton, but went by Newt.

Martha and Garrett's Nora was Leonora. Selena often went by her nickname Pony, but I kept her as Selena. Most sources give Baby Girl's name as Martha Ann, while some call her Isabell. I created the indeterminate Baby Girl. The 1860 census lists a five-month-old Isabell in the Maupin family, but that would be Bina. A parent's confusion? Or a researcher's? One source lists Bina as Edwina Isobel. The 1880 census gives her initials as E. C. I do present Bina's given name, Edwina, before going on to call her Bina. Mike's given name was John Lee. I don't know why they called him Mike, but I remembered hearing about him by that name and went with it.

My great-grandfather, nicknamed Billy in the story, was William Henry Fisher. Several sources refer to him as Henry, as if he went by his middle name. However, his obituary says he was "familiarly known" as "Uncle Billy." That led me to call him Billy.

SOURCE MATERIAL

Sources for Family Events

Many events in Martha's story come from various documents and family legend. The trip home to Illinois for the birth of Nora comes from census after census showing Nora's birthplace as Illinois, not Missouri as some family stories suggest. Census records and land records are vital in showing who was where when. So too are marriage locations, military records, voting records. Donation Land Claim records provide details on claimants, including settlement dates on their claims, as well as date of entry into Oregon, verifying the year they crossed the plains if they came to Oregon by that trail.

Other story sources include newspaper articles in the Eugene City *State Journal* and the Portland *Oregonian* about Garrett's death, as well as local histories in Illinois, Missouri, and Oregon, particularly Leona Madison's *The Saga of the Kellogg Crescent* and Harold A. Minter's *Umpqua Valley Oregon and Its Pioneers*. Minter lived with Cap Maupin's family for several years during his youth and knew the family well.

Florence McNabb's Contributions

Martha's granddaughter Florence Maupin McNabb, daughter of Cap Maupin, grew up on her grandmother's farm, where she knew many of the people described in my book and heard the family's stories, often firsthand. She also spoke to old-timers in the area to put together her manuscript, *The Maupin Family*, from which I gleaned many events and details:

1. Garrett's altercation with his father over the care of his horse, and Garrett running off for a few years, his mother not recognizing him because he'd grown a beard. Florence talks about the Maupins and their games and whiskey and gambling, their fine horses and hounds. They were Democrats, she says, "never shy about arguing their beliefs, even if it resulted in a fight." She says they were "crack shots with a rifle," and her father, Cap, remembered seeing Garrett disarm a man with his whip.

2. Garrett losing his horse in the Mexican War and getting another from the Army. She goes on to tell that the Army valued the new horse much higher than the one he lost, and they took that out of his pay, leaving him with five dollars and twenty-five cents for the entire year's service.

3. Garrett's description, from Army records and recall of friends, depicting him as five feet ten inches tall, of slight build, with sandy hair and blue eyes. Florence also describes her Grandma Martha as a small-size woman, all of her daughters short in stature, Selena being the tallest.

4. Garrett getting upset with the Oregon-bound company in 1849 and deciding to wait a year. She tells of Larry going ahead in 1849, and possibly Newt, building a cabin there before returning to lead Garrett and Martha west in 1850.

5. Garrett carrying his grindstone over the plains to Oregon. Florence says, "One remark attributed to him was that no damn Yankee could sharpen his axe at his house." She tells of the uncertainty at Fort Hall over whether to go to Oregon or California, the teasing Garrett received when he claimed land with timber, the statement "Rich, Poindexter, rich, but damn little money." She gives that line to Howard, but she has Howard coming west with Garrett, and documents show he came two years later. I give Garrett the line, as does Gloria Atwater on her website.

6. Neighbors retreating to the loft of Garrett and Martha's house during a Willamette River flood, while bringing animals into the lower floor "to make enough weight to hold it to the ground." An old-timer from the area told Florence's sister the story.

7. The disapproval of Martha's parents. Florence says Martha wrote to her parents during a dark period of her life asking for help, and Cap remembered her getting the draft for one hundred dollars. He remembered thinking they were rich, but recalled his mother crying because there was no letter. The earliest dark period Cap was old enough to remember was probably the 1860 divorce filing when he was five years old. As hard as I tried to find the parents alive then, I did not. My

guess is the story altered over time. Someone probably said Martha wrote the folks back in Illinois. Someone else interpreted the folks as "the parents." I keep the story but choose the most obvious folks to ask for money, the Bronoughs, and I can't believe Louisa would fail ever to write. I don't doubt the parents disapproved for as long as they lived and that Martha carried that disapproval in her heart long after they were gone. It certainly stuck in family lore.

8. Nora losing control of her horse and getting a whipping from her father, never forgiving him for the unjust punishment.

9. Garrett demanding that Nora marry David Bunch when she was fond of someone else who wasn't a Democrat.

10. Martha trying to rescue her young child from the well and yelling so loud a neighbor came to pull them out.

11. The family waiting for Garrett and Cap on that hot August day Garrett was killed, the events of the day told to Florence in considerable detail by her Aunt Bina and the neighbors.

12. Martha and children moving from the Henderer place to the Kent place after Garrett's death.

13. The Wells and Dimmick families being longtime friends of the Maupins.

14. Garrett and Cap visiting the Shadrach Hudson Donation Land Claim before Martha bought it.

15. Roberts drawing the house plans on shingles.

General Sources

Pioneer diary entries provide inspiration for several scenes, including one diarist being surprised at seeing only black slaves in the fields of Missouri,[1]

---

1 From the diary of Abigail Jane Scott, in *Covered Wagon Women: Diaries and Letters from the Western Trails, 1840–1890.* Vol. 5, 1852, *The Oregon Trail,* Kenneth L. Holmes and David C. Duniway, eds. (Glendale, CA: The Arthur H. Clark Co., 1986), pp. 43–44.

and another diarist relating an incident of a Missouri family reluctant to let her Northern family stay in their house.[2] I create similar incidents for Martha's story, believing she would experience the same unfamiliarity with slave workers, given her Illinois upbringing, and believing the reaction of the young Poindexters would be similar if they sought lodging from dubious Southerners. With this I hoped to set the stage for her meeting with staunch Southerner Garrett Maupin.

2 From the diary of Margaret A. Frink, in *Covered Wagon Women: Diaries and Letters from the Western Trails, 1840–1890.* Vol. 2, 1850, Kenneth L. Holmes, ed. (Spokane, WA: The Arthur H. Clark Co., 1990), pp. 69–71.

About the Author

Janet Fisher grew up on the farm her great-great-grandmother Martha bought almost 150 years ago. After earning a master's in journalism with honors from the University of Oregon, she taught college writing and wrote freelance for newspapers. She lived and worked in San Francisco, Kalispell, Montana, and other places, including several cities in Oregon, showing a trace of the Maupin wanderlust. Two of her historical novels were Pacific Northwest Writers Association contest finalists. She recently returned to Martha's farm along the Umpqua River in southern Oregon and became the second woman to own and operate this family treasure.

For more information, visit janetfishernovels.com.

Janet Fisher. PHOTO BY ROBIN LOZNAK